TEIONKWAKHASHION TSI NIIONKWARIHO:TEN

WE SHARE
OUR MATTERS

Two Centuries of Writing and Resistance
at Six Nations of the Grand River

RICK MONTURE

UMP
University of Manitoba Press

In Memory of
CAROLE G. MONTURE (FROHMAN)
1940 – 1983

University of Manitoba Press
Winnipeg, Manitoba
Canada R3T 2M5
uofmpress.ca

Printed in Canada
Text printed on chlorine-free, 100% post-consumer recycled paper

18 17 16   2 3 4 5

Cover and interior design: Marvin Harder
Cover image: Shelley Niro

Library and Archives Canada Cataloguing in Publication

Monture, Rick, 1965–, author
We share our matters = Teionkwakhashion tsi niionkwariho:ten : two
centuries of writing and resistance at Six Nations of the Grand River / Rick
Monture.

Includes bibliographical references and index.
Issued in print and electronic formats.
Text in English.
ISBN 978-0-88755-767-5 (pbk.)
ISBN 978-0-88755-468-1 (pdf)
ISBN 978-0-88755-466-7 (epub)

1. Iroquois Indians–Ontario, Southern–History. 2. Iroquois Indians–
Ontario, Southern–Intellectual life. 3. Iroquois Indians–Ontario, Southern–Ethnic identity.
4. Iroquois Indians–Ontario, Southern–Politics and government.
I. Title. II. Title: Teionkwakhashion tsi niionkwariho:ten.

E99.I7M82 2014   971.3004'9755   C2014-903283-8
                                         C2014-903284-6

This book has been published with the help of a grant from the Federation for the
Humanities and Social Sciences, through the Awards to Scholarly Publications Program,
using funds provided by the Social Sciences and Humanities Research Council of Canada.

The University of Manitoba Press gratefully acknowledges the financial
support for its publication program provided by the Government of Canada
through the Canada Book Fund, the Canada Council for the Arts, the Manitoba
Department of Culture, Heritage, Tourism, the Manitoba Arts Council,
and the Manitoba Book Publishing Tax Credit.

FSC
www.fsc.org
MIX
Paper from
responsible sources
FSC® C016245

CONTENTS

The Haudenosaunee, more commonly known as the Iroquois or Six Nations, have been one of the most widely written-about groups of Indigenous nations in North America. Due to geographic location and political influence from the time of our first contact with Europeans in the sixteenth century to the American Revolution two centuries later, the Haudenosaunee had a significant influence upon the formation of both the United States and Canada. As evidence of the Western world's fascination with the Iroquois, it is widely held that anthropology as an academic field of study began with Lewis Henry Morgan's *League of the Ho-De'-No-Sau-Nee, or Iroquois*, published in 1851.[1] While an overwhelming amount of scholarship has been devoted to the Haudenosaunee since that time in the areas of anthropology, history, political theory, environmentalism, and linguistics, Haudenosaunee people have had very little opportunity to analyze our own history, culture, and traditions.[2] This has begun to change, however, with a small but growing number of Haudenosaunee scholars who have recently taken up the task of re-examining, questioning, and revising the accepted "story" of the Iroquois in a wide range of academic disciplines. As a contribution to this emergent body of work, this book is an examination of the philosophies, intellectual traditions, and assertions of sovereignty that have long been part of the written record of one group of Haudenosaunee people, those from the Six Nations of the Grand River Territory in southern Ontario.

From the time of first arrival at Grand River in the winter of 1785, after being displaced from our original homelands in New York State following the American Revolution, Mohawk Chief Joseph Brant (Thayendanegea) foresaw the important need to produce a text devoted to Native history and traditional knowledge. In a letter written in 1791, he expressed his wish to "visit ... the distant Nations and collect ... matter to proceed upon with my History ... the customs preserv'd by tradition amongst them and also a knowledge of the Medical Plants natural to their Soil & Climate" (in Klinck and Talman 1970, xiv). Unfortunately, Brant was never able to complete such a work, but his desire to do so is highly significant, for it demonstrates an understanding on his part of the need to disrupt the colonialist agendas of England and America at the time. He knew, very early on, that "Indian Nations" would benefit from such a written history because Great Britain and the newly formed United States were eager to inscribe their own history upon this continent. Furthermore, he believed that his own people would suffer politically if the story of the Six Nations' involvement in the Revolution was left entirely to the English to document, especially the significance of their relationship as allies, and not subjects, of the Crown.[3] As it turned out, his assumptions were correct: the last few years of his life, right until his death in 1807, were taken up with attempting to establish Haudenosaunee sovereignty within the Grand River territory. These lands, amounting to nearly a million acres, had been acquired by the Crown from the Mississauga and allotted to the Six Nations under the Haldimand Deed of 1784 in compensation for their New York State homelands that were lost fighting for the British cause.[4] Since Brant's time, this particular issue of autonomy—in terms of land rights, political sovereignty, and cultural independence—has remained at the fore-front of Haudenosaunee assertions of nationhood.

In July 1900, nearly 100 years after Brant's death, the Hereditary Council of Chiefs at Six Nations also felt compelled to translate their most significant oral tradition in order to produce a written version of Haudenosaunee history when they published the story of the founding of the Great Law of Peace, or Kaienerekowa, which is said to have taken place during the twelfth century and which first established the Confederacy Council that still presided over Grand River affairs at that time.[5] Aware that non-Native ethnographers and government officials were increasingly engaged in the process of studying and writing about the Iroquois, always with their own agendas in mind, the committee of Chiefs in charge of this document wisely outlined their reasons for committing their ancient traditions to print: "For several hundred years the Five Nations (since 1715 the Six Nations) have existed without a written history chronicled by themselves, of their ancient customs, rites and ceremonies, and of the formation of the Iroquois League. Books have been written by white men in the past, but these have been found to be too voluminous and inaccurate in some instances" (quoted in Parker [1916] 1968, 61).

What makes this brief passage so interesting is that it demonstrates the level of awareness with which these men were writing their history—from their own perspective—for the first time. As the leaders in a community that still adhered to a traditional form of government, they had certainly felt mounting pressure from Ottawa, and from within their own community as well, to conform to an elected system of government as required by the Indian Act of 1876. But to do so would have been to relinquish the sovereign status that Six Nations had maintained since earliest European contact and that was, albeit begrudgingly, recognized by Canada throughout the nineteenth and early twentieth centuries. Understanding their predicament, the Chiefs recognized the need to codify their own political "constitution," as established in the Kaienerekowa/Great Law, in order to counter the designs of the federal government and the potential imposition of an elected council. The Chiefs then set about to translate and articulate their unique form of government as one that was not dictated by white bureaucrats in Ottawa, but was put forth by a spiritual figure known as the Peacemaker "several hundred years" ago. To them, producing such an account of their social, spiritual, and political history was of great potential benefit, since this culture-bearing story that had been told for centuries among Iroquoian-speaking people had served them remarkably well. But to the colonial, Canadian mind of the time such a history was undoubtedly considered merely legend and folklore due to its narrative of "supernatural" individuals and events. To this way of thinking, such published evidence of this formation of Native government as a "constitution" would have been simply further proof of the need to assimilate Native peoples into a more civilized society and advanced mode of thought. The irony is that this document, produced entirely by Haudenosaunee people, was proof of their ability to function extremely well in the English language.

This clash of worldviews, or the inability to communicate across cultural divides, has been a source of conflict and frustration between Indigenous peoples and colonialist authorities for centuries, and it was no doubt the driving force behind Joseph Brant's desire to write a history of Native people. As a college-educated individual, one of the very few successful Native students at Moor's Charity School run by Reverend Eleazar Wheelock in Connecticut, Brant understood and anticipated European reactions to the basic philosophies of Native traditions. Although he may have appeared as a colonized subject to them, Brant nevertheless saw himself, and his people, quite differently, and he continually resisted early British control over the Six Nations. Over 200 years after his death, Haudenosaunee leaders and scholars alike continue to confront the difficult issue of mediating between Six Nations tradition and Canadian cultural impositions, between colonialism and anti-colonial political struggle, and between generalized, externally imposed views of Indigenous thinking and the need to articulate a distinct Haudenosaunee experience. While we have changed as a people in our daily routines, economic pursuits, and language, our understanding of who we are as a confederacy of nations with a unique history and purpose has remained essentially the same since pre-contact times. Canada, on the other hand, has had a long history of wondering about its identity as a distinct and unified nation—all the while attempting to define our Indigenous identity for us since 1867.

In documenting the literary history of the Six Nations of the Grand River, pivotal events in the relationship between the Haudenosaunee and British and Canadian governments since 1784 will be outlined in order to examine our responses to them. Our people have often been in conflict with colonial authorities—and sometimes with each other—and in the process have created an impressive spoken and written legacy of these engagements. Despite the occasional piece of writing from members of the Six Nations community that conforms to the Western standards of "literature," the best examples of creative expression at Grand River over the past 200 years have often been the works of non-fiction that have arisen from times of social and political crisis. Such texts are potent examples of articulating the authentic experience of Native communities, according to Osage scholar Robert Warrior, who states, "Nonfiction as nonfiction deserves to be regarded as constitutive of the Native written literary tradition" (2005, 117). I contend that it is during the moments of conflict that the Haudenosaunee have drawn from our understanding of the oral traditions that sustained our

ancestors for centuries, thought about them, argued over them, and ultimately given voice to them in diverse yet convergent ways. Throughout it all,
we adhere to a basic belief: *Iawerenhatien oh nahio:ten teiotennionhatie kato:ken
ne ionkwanikonhraien:tas* ("it does not matter what continually changes,
our understanding remains certain"). It is from this foundation of shared
beliefs that this particular study will operate, demonstrating that while
Haudenosaunee thought—in both oral and written form—is an expression of
"intellectual sovereignty" and our unique cultural identity, it is also very much
concerned with developing and sustaining a respectful dialogue with others
in the world. We have a very long history in a particular geographical place to
which we have given a tremendous amount of consideration, and our oral/lit-
erary traditions are therefore a means by which we share our matters so that
all can learn and benefit from our experiential understanding of the natural
world and humankind's place within it.

Whereas His Majesty having been pleased to direct that in Consideration of the early Attachment to His Cause manifested by the Mohawk Indians, & of the Loss of their Settlement they thereby sustained that a Convenient Tract of Land under His Protection should be chosen as a Safe & Comfortable Retreat for them & others of the Six Nations who have either lost their Settlements within the Territory of the American States, or wish to retire from them to the British—I have, at the earnest Desire of many of these His Majesty's faithfull Allies purchased a Tract of Land, from the Indians situated between the Lakes Ontario, Erie, & Huron and I do hereby in His Majesty's name authorize and permit the said Mohawk Nation, and such other of the Six Nation Indians as wish to settle in that Quarter to take Possession of, & Settle upon the Banks of the River commonly called Ours [Ouse] or Grand River, running into Lake Erie, allotting to them for that Purpose Six Miles deep from each Side of the River beginning at Lake Erie, & extending in that Proportion to the Head of the said River, which them & their Posterity are to enjoy for ever.

Given under my Hand & Seal &c &c
25th Octr 1784
(Signed) Fred: Haldimand

Text of the Haldimand Deed of 1784. (Haldimand [1784a] 1964, 50–51)

"We Build the House"   Haudenosaunee Worldview

The community of the Six Nations of the Grand River Territory is the largest
First Nations reservation in Canada, with a current population of approximately 13,000 (out of a total band membership of 25,000). Members primarily
comprise descendants of those who migrated to Upper Canada (now Ontario)
in 1785 following the American Revolution. At that time, some 2,000 people,
led by Joseph Brant, settled along the banks of the Grand River under the terms
of the Haldimand Deed, which promised these lands "as a safe and comfortable retreat ... which them and their posterity are to enjoy for ever" (see
page xvi). The majority of this group was made up of Mohawk and Cayuga,
the two nations whose homelands in New York State were completely taken
away from them at the close of the Revolution. Although the Oneida, Seneca,
Onondaga, and Tuscarora retained small tracts of reservation lands in New
York, some members of these nations also came to Ontario. During this time,
the Great Council Fire of the Iroquois Confederacy was also divided between
those Chiefs remaining in New York and those who travelled to Ontario, where
an identical council was eventually established to govern affairs in the new territory. As a result, there are currently two Confederacy Councils, one based at
Onondaga, New York and the other at Grand River in Ontario.

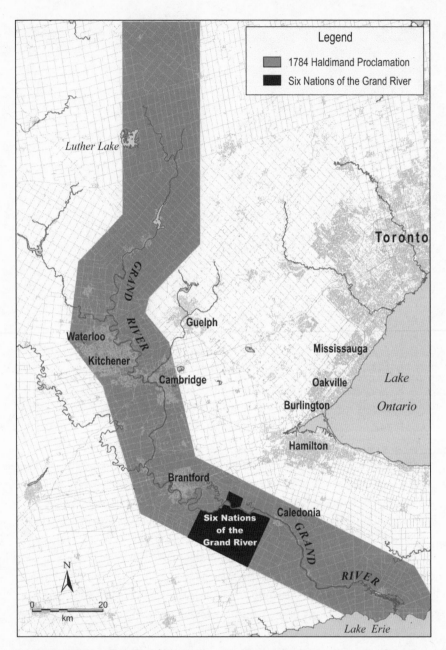

Lands granted by the Haldimand Deed. Map design by Weldon Hiebert. SOURCE: http://www.
sixnations.ca/LandsResources/LCMap.pdf.

Both councils operate more or less independently, but maintain close contact on larger issues of both sacred and secular importance. Although space limitations do not allow for a detailed history of the Iroquois Confederacy, it is important to remember that the ancient form of government first initiated by the Peacemaker continues to meet regularly to discuss social, legal, and political matters on both sides of the border. It is also important to note that some 100,000 Haudenosaunee currently reside at seventeen communities located in New York (eight communities), Ontario (four), Quebec (three), Wisconsin (one), and Oklahoma (one), as well as in urban centres throughout North America. These transnational reserve/reservation communities, like the two Confederacy Councils, exist independently but, despite geographical distance, retain strong connections to each other through intermarriage, ceremonial events, and other social/political occasions. This understood alliance of shared history, languages, and cultural tradition is a unique situation in that it recognizes and reinforces common features of a collective Haudenosaunee experience but also allows for regionally distinct social and cultural flavours. In short, each reserve/reservation community has a sense of itself as a particular place with distinct customs and identity, but each is also aware of its deeper connection to the larger Haudenosaunee world. Although the Six Nations of Grand River has its own unique history shaped largely by its relationship first with the British Crown and then later with the Canadian state, it must be understood in relationship to the larger, ideological foundation of Haudenosaunee thought that serves to define our place in the world, regardless of geographical location.

In all cultures, the story of Creation, of how a particular people came to exist in this world, is a defining narrative. Kimberly Roppolo writes, "Native articulation of philosophy—of who we are and how we see the world, of what our position is in relation to the rest of Creation—has been accomplished by indirect discourse. We are taught by story, and we explain by story, not by exposition" (2001, 268). As Haudenosaunee, we believe that we are descended from Sky Woman, who fell from the Sky World through a hole that was created when a great tree was uprooted. As she fell through this hole, she clutched at the earth around her and in doing so grabbed tobacco and strawberry plants, which are both seen as very sacred to this day. As she was falling toward this world, the animals that existed on the waters below noticed her and several waterfowl flew upward to assist her. After catching her and bringing her gently downward, the animals held a council in which they discussed what could be done for this young woman who, they also noticed, was about to give birth. It was decided that turtle would offer his back for her to rest upon while the other animals—otter, beaver, and muskrat—would attempt to bring up some earth from the bottom of the ocean. After each of the others tried and failed, the task was left up to muskrat, who finally floated to the surface, dead, but holding a tiny piece of earth in his paw. Once this piece of earth was placed upon turtle's back, the young woman began to walk around, and as she did the earth widened and eventually grew to become what we now know today as North America.

Shortly afterward, Sky Woman gave birth to a baby girl, who grew into a young woman and was impregnated by the West Wind. During her pregnancy the twin boys inside of her fought constantly, arguing over who was going to be born first. While the first, "good-minded" twin, known as Sapling or Skyholder, was born the normal way of human beings today, the second, "evil-minded" twin, known as Flint, was impatient and forced his way out of his mother's armpit, killing her. Upon seeing her daughter dead, the grandmother, Sky Woman, asked the boys who was responsible for killing their mother. Flint blamed his brother, who would be treated with contempt by his grandmother ever after, despite his more kindly nature. After the young woman was buried, corn, beans, and squash grew from her grave, the plants which the Haudenosaunee refer to as tionhenkweh ("our life sustainers"), also known as the Three Sisters and considered highly significant to our cultural and ceremonial life.

As the boys grew into young men they remained in constant conflict. One day, Skyholder began to form small images of himself out of the earth, and when these figures were complete he took a small portion of his own brain, blood, and spirit and placed them inside these beings. He breathed into their mouths and thus brought them to life. These beings then became known as the onkwehonwe, or "real human beings." The good-minded twin, or Creator, then set about making animals and plants that would be of benefit to the onkwehonwe and make their existence on the earth a healthy and happy one. It is said that during this same time Flint tried to imitate his brother's creations, but his animals were a threat to those that were to help humankind, and his plants could be harmful to humans and make them ill. Eventually, the two brothers waged a great battle to determine who would hold influence over the world. After days of epic struggle, Skyholder prevailed, but by doing so he came to understand the powers that his brother possessed. As a compromise, he allowed his brother to retain influence over the nighttime, while the influence of the good-minded twin would prevail during the daylight hours. In this way, the Haudenosaunee believe that there exist good and bad elements upon the earth that perpetually balance themselves out between the daytime and nighttime worlds, as well as within the seasonal cycles of decay and renewal.

While various versions of these stories exist in much longer form, adding and subtracting details depending on the teller and the context of the telling, the basic elements are virtually identical throughout Haudenosaunee territory.[1] One of the most significant features in the Creation story is the idea of transition or movement from a familiar to an unknown place; meaningful objects from the former environment are carried with an individual into the new place to become of central importance to those who come afterward. With this theme of change, adaptation, and development at the foundation of their Creation story, the Haudenosaunee are instructed to view life and society as in a state of constant movement and transition. While landscape and social relations may change dramatically due to unforeseen circumstances, the people must remember to honour that which was important from their earliest beginnings. This includes, for example, reverence for tobacco and strawberries as plants that came directly from the Sky World, as well as respect for the animals that assisted their earliest ancestor, and the corn, beans, and squash that continue to give us nourishment. Such a connection to a collective past reinforces identity while the stories serve to sustain the onkwehonwe in most any situation in which they may find themselves, so long as the stories are used to translate cultural beliefs into proper behaviour and action.

The belief in honouring our origins by maintaining connections to the natural world is also reinforced through the ceremonies that were given to the Haudenosaunee from the very earliest of times. It is said that the first onkwehonwe were instructed to give thanks every day for that which the Creator had provided for them. This speech, known in the Cayuga language as the *Ganonhonyonk* (Thanksgiving Address) or as *Ohenton Karihwetenhkwen* (the "words that come before all else") in Mohawk, reflects the Haudenosaunee worldview that human beings are dependent upon the natural world around them, and that it is their responsibility to remember to give thanks daily. Because it acknowledges and gives thanks to all elements of creation, from insects and plants to the thunder, winds, sun, moon, and beyond, it is a speech that can take hours to recite in its entirety, or just a few minutes, depending on the circumstance at hand. Like the Creation story and the Great Law, there are a few key elements that must be addressed, while others can be omitted without affecting the basic structure and intent. The Thanksgiving Address remains a very important part of any Haudenosaunee ceremonial or social function to this day, more evidence of the significance of the spoken word as a persistent expression of culture and thought in which human beings are regularly called upon to remember their relationship of dependence within this world.

After the first human beings lived upon this earth for a long while, they began to forget their responsibility of giving thanks and needed to be reminded of it by being shown four additional ceremonies that once again reinforced their spiritual relationship to the world around them. These ceremonies—the Great Feather Dance, the Drum Dance, the Personal Chant, and the Bowl Game—were introduced by a figure known as the Fatherless Boy. This individual was said to have instructed young boys his own age to teach these rituals to the older generations so that the people would once again remember their duty to give thanks to the Creator and all that was provided on Mother Earth.[2] It is said that these ceremonies sustained the people for another long period of time, until they once again fell into a period of social and spiritual decay.

By this time in Haudenosaunee history five distinct groups had been established across what is now New York State. The Mohawk, who lived on the Mohawk River near present-day Albany; the Oneida, who lived west of the Mohawk; the Onondaga, who resided at Onondaga Lake by Syracuse; the Cayuga, in the Finger Lakes region; and the Seneca, who inhabited the largest area, south of Rochester and west to the Niagara River. Although all nations had a shared system of clan relationships, over time they had become engaged in a violent cycle of blood feuds and revenge killings that left all people living in a state of chaos and fear. As a result, people no longer trusted one another, and strangers were treated with suspicion and contempt. While the people were living in this dark time, a young Huron woman gave birth to a son in a village north of Lake Ontario near present-day Deseronto, Ontario. It is said that this boy grew remarkably quickly and was different than others his age, often going into the woods by himself for long periods. One day, his mother and grandmother decided to follow him and eventually came across him in the forest, where he was constructing a canoe of white stone. It was then that he told them there were people across the lake who needed his help and he would be leaving shortly to teach them a new way to live in the world. Although they were reluctant to see him go, and doubtful that his vessel would carry him over the water, the mother and grandmother helped to launch his canoe. When it did indeed float, as the story tells us, it was apparent that this was no ordinary young man, but one who had great spiritual power and purpose. To the Haudenosaunee, he is known as the Peacemaker.

After crossing the lake, the Peacemaker came upon a group of Mohawk hunters on the south shore of Lake Ontario, near the present vicinity of Oswego, New York. Although they were suspicious of this man, the hunters could not help but notice that he was someone of special importance, as indicated by his mode of travel. Therefore, when the Peacemaker asked these young men to return to their village and notify the people that he requested a meeting with them, they complied. When the people from the village gathered to hear him speak, the Peacemaker proceeded to outline his message of peace, telling the people that the Creator did not intend human beings to be living in fear and committing violent acts upon one another. He also told them of his plan to unite the nations into a Confederacy built upon the social, spiritual, and political structures of peace, power, and righteousness. But, having grown accustomed to living in fear, the people were still skeptical. The village Chief told the visitor that they would accept his message only if he were able to survive a challenge. The Peacemaker was led to a tall tree next to a great waterfall. He was then told that he was to climb to the top of the tree, which would then be chopped down, fall into the river, and be carried over the waterfall. If he survived this ordeal, the people would gladly accept his message. The Peacemaker agreed. Once the tree was toppled and he was swept out of sight, the people thought that surely he was dead. But when they returned to the village, the Peacemaker was already there, patiently awaiting them. Having witnessed this, the people had little choice but to accept the Peacemaker's word that he was indeed someone sent by the Creator to help them.

With a group of these Mohawk people accompanying him, the Peacemaker began travelling westward to the land of the Oneida, where they too accepted his message. With this growing support, a larger group continued west until they came to the Onondaga village, but here they were met with refusal, for the people there were living in tremendous fear of a Chief so wicked that it was said that there were snakes growing in his hair and that he had the power to kill people from afar simply by casting a spell on them. Sensing the futility of this situation for now, the Peacemaker and his party chose to bypass the Onondaga and travelled further west until they arrived in the territory of the Cayuga nation, near present-day Auburn, New York. The Cayuga also accepted the Peacemaker's ideas and they too joined with his group, who were now headed west to the land of the Senecas, the largest of the Haudenosaunee nations. Although the Seneca people were also willing to accept the Peacemaker's message, there were two leaders who could not be convinced that such a Confederacy built simply upon peace was realistic. Because these men lived in the westernmost regions of the Seneca territory they were aware of several other nations to the west of them that could not be trusted due to differences in culture, language, and spiritual beliefs. For despite the violence that was permeating the Five Nations during this time, there were marked similarities among their languages, as well as almost identical cultural practices. At this point, the Peacemaker made concessions to the situation and told the two Seneca leaders that they would, in effect, be "war Chiefs" who would be utilized if and when the Confederacy was ever threatened by an enemy. Satisfied with this arrangement, the two Chiefs complied, and the Seneca formally accepted the Peacemaker's *Kaienerekowa*, also known as the Great Law of Peace.

Now, with four nations united, the Peacemaker and his followers travelled back to the Onondaga village in order to convince them also to accept the Great Peace. Knowing that Atortaho, the wicked Chief, would be expecting them and would take action to counter them, the Peacemaker stopped the procession some distance from the village and instructed the people to assemble behind him. Then he began to sing a song as he continued on toward Atortaho's lodge. Soon, the leaders of the four nations joined in this song, which was so powerful that as the procession marched toward Atortaho, the snakes that were entwined in his hair began to disappear, evidence that his mind was being "straightened" and opened to the idea of peace. Upon reaching Atortaho's lodge, the Peacemaker was able to address him with words that continued to strengthen and clear his mind. Once this was accomplished, the old Chief also agreed to accept the Great Law of Peace. And, in recognition of his power, the Peacemaker appointed the Onondaga as the Firekeepers of the Confederacy, while Atortaho was given a special title within the Confederacy Council of fifty Chiefs, making him the Grand Chief with the responsibility of convening Council meetings. Significantly, the song that the Peacemaker sang that day is still heard today at the installation of new Chiefs in Haudenosaunee territories.

Following Atortaho's consent to join the League, the Peacemaker gathered the Chiefs and Clanmothers together in order to outline further their duties and responsibilities to the people under the Kaienerekowa. He instructed them on the importance of using a good mind in order to persuade the people to be kind and helpful to one another, and to use kind words, rather than violence, to accomplish things together for the benefit of society. The Chiefs, especially, were told to be role models for the people and to lead unselfishly, making sure that no one was in need. In fact, the word for "Chief" in Mohawk is royaner, or "men who are of the good."As a means to further illustrate to the people how they should conduct themselves, the Peacemaker told them that from now on they were to call themselves Haudenosaunee, or "we build the house (together)." This was a reference to the longhouse dwellings in which all of the original Five Nations lived, and it was understood that all nations now existed under this metaphoric "roof" known as the Great Law, with each nation symbolized by a rafter. As such, each nation was to treat each other as family, with respect and goodwill. Also significant is the fact that these longhouses were considered the property of the matrilineal household; that the Clanmothers hold such great power within the structure of the Great Law, as the ones who select the Chiefs, is evidence that women were, and are, highly regarded within Haudenosaunee society.[3]

Another symbol that the Peacemaker used upon establishing the Kaienerekowa among the Haudenosaunee was that of the Great Tree of Peace, which was to stand as a symbolic beacon among all nations as the place where others could seek refuge and an alternative to violence and war. This is an important concept, for it was always maintained from the earliest of times that the *Kaienerekowa* did not belong to the original Five Nations exclusively, but that its message of peace, power, and righteousness was available to any who would choose to accept its principles.

Lastly, the Peacemaker instructed the people on how to care for each other after the loss of one of their leaders by setting out the procedure of the Condolence Ceremony, or Requickening Address, that is to be conducted after the death of a Confederacy Chief. Space does not permit a discussion and analysis of this elaborate public ceremony that is itself a narrative of the founding of the Great Law; but, to summarize briefly, it involves the lifting of (or condoling) the collective grief of the "bereaved" nation and clan by other "clear-minded" nations and clans as the way to strengthen the resolve of the people to uphold the Great Peace. It reminds them of their responsibility to care for one another, and by "raising up" a new Chief to replace the deceased, it also illustrates that human society, like the natural world, has the ability to renew itself. Significantly, as each new Chief receives his title through this ceremony, he gives up his former name and takes on the name of the Chief who was the leader of his particular clan and nation at the time when the Peacemaker established the Great Law. In this way, the Haudenosaunee are constantly reminded of their ancestors who took part in the formation of the *Kaienerekowa* and are therefore always conscious of the deep connection to the past. When a Chief is installed through this ceremonial process, he is said to be a "condoled" Chief, spiritually mandated with upholding the principles of the Great Law.[4]

To the Haudenosaunee, the story of the Peacemaker and his message is evidence of the power that is created when human beings set their minds to achieve something beneficial and good for all. It was this message of goodness that the Peacemaker shared with the Five Nations long ago and it is the guiding principle that continues to influence decision making among the Confederacy Chiefs and Clanmothers to this day. Furthermore, the power of the human voice to communicate and to persuade through dialogue or song is significant, not only in the story of the Peacemaker and the formation of the Great Law, but also throughout Haudenosaunee traditions. In an oral society, a speaker's ability to enlighten and convince people was, and remains, a very important talent.

Following the formation of the Great Law, the next significant event within Haudenosaunee culture was the introduction of the Gaihwi'yo in the early nineteenth century. Also known as the Code of Handsome Lake, it is often referred to as the modern "longhouse religion," a term that followers have difficulty with due to the narrow, Western definition of religious belief. What is most significant about the Gaihwi'yo is that it once again demonstrates a pattern that is familiar to Haudenosaunee thought and experience: that of adapting to a new situation while bringing forth the best of the old social order. It is also built around a story that resonates with all Haudenosaunee, for it recalls another dark time in our collective history, one that is well documented by written and oral accounts alike.

Sganyadai:yo', or Handsome Lake, was a Seneca Chief who was born in western New York around 1735. He was a veteran of the American Revolution and, like the rest of his people, greatly affected by the war and its political and social aftermath, a situation that had caused the Haudenosaunee to become virtual exiles within their traditional homelands. Not only were Americans angry with the Iroquois nations that had sided with the British, but the U.S. Army's infamous Sullivan Campaign that had swept through central and western New York in 1779 had wiped out entire villages, crops, and food stores that were intended to supply Haudenosaunee villages for years.[5] In addition, the human costs of war, disease, and famine during this time had greatly decreased the population of the Haudenosaunee, taking elders, warriors, and children alike. It was said that this period in Haudenosaunee history was once again marked by social and spiritual decay brought on by intense hardship and demoralization over the loss of land and the only way of life that the Haudenosaunee had ever known. The hopelessness of the people was exacerbated through heavy drinking and violence that frequently occurred in the villages, creating a situation where all felt threatened and afraid. For a people who had been told of the bad times that existed prior to the Peacemaker's arrival among them, this must have seemed eerily familiar. And, as at that time, a figure—this time known as Skanyadai:yo'—once again emerged that would inspire the Haudenosaunee to live a better life through his teachings of the Gaihwi'yo, or "Good Message."

Unlike those important figures who had the greatest influence on the Haudenosaunee in pre-contact times, Skanyadai:yo' is a person about whom much is known, although the substantial story of his life and teachings is almost entirely reliant on oral traditions that were resurrected some twenty years after his death in 1815. It is this oral narrative, so important to modern Haudenosaunee culture, that survives to this day.

Gravely ill due to complications brought on by alcoholism and old age, Handsome Lake is said to have begun to have a series of visions beginning in 1799 while living in his village in western New York. During these moments he was visited by four beings from the Sky World who took him on a journey and showed him the future of the Haudenosaunee if they continued to practise inappropriate and self-destructive behaviour. Handsome Lake was then instructed by these beings to tell his people many things about how they could begin to live in a good way again. While they were to retain their ancient ceremonial cycles of Thanksgiving as outlined above, they were to turn away from the things that the white man had brought and that caused social disruption among them. Foremost among these things were the Bible, gambling, the fiddle, and alcohol. In addition, Handsome Lake told the people that they were to concentrate on farming and to realign their family structure around the single-family household, which had by then replaced the larger longhouse-style dwelling which housed multiple families based upon clan affiliation.

Western education was strongly discouraged and intermarriage with whites was forbidden, as these things would lead to a further loss of cultural knowledge and identity. The *Gaihwi'yo* also contains warnings about environmental catastrophes that would result from the selfish activities of humans on the earth. This is significant, for it is a strong reflection of Haudenosaunee beliefs surrounding humankind's proper relationship to the natural world, which goes back to the first instructions given to the *onkwehonwe* by the Creator, and best exemplified by the Thanksgiving Address. As such, it demonstrates how particular modes of thought are reinforced through "updated" spiritual messages and practice. What is alarming to Haudenosaunee today, however, is the fact that several of these prophetic warnings set down by Handsome Lake are now evident in the world around us, including air and water pollution, new forms of disease and sickness, and especially the increased intensity of storms brought on by changes in global climates.[6]

The stories of these five historical and cultural epochs—Creation, Thanksgiving Address, Four Ceremonies, Great Law, and the Code of Handsome Lake—are all spiritual traditions that are common to the Haudenosaunee. While they are more prominent within some contemporary communities than they are within others, one cannot overestimate their significance upon Haudenosaunee expressions of thought through the centuries. Many books have been written about the role of the Iroquois Confederacy in colonial history, the influence of the Haudenosaunee on the U.S. Constitution, and the previously mentioned connection to anthropology, but a work that incorporates the influence of spiritual traditions alongside these complex political and social forces has yet to be written.[7] What follows this brief history of spiritually derived systems of thought will be an equally brief social and political history of Haudenosaunee responses to European presence within their territories, actions that were heavily influenced by traditional beliefs that had existed for centuries before contact.

"WE SHALL EACH TRAVEL THE RIVER TOGETHER"

Because the Great Peace was already well established among the Five Nations in pre-contact times, their initial interaction with the Dutch, French, and British was mostly amicable during the seventeenth and eighteenth centuries. Recognizing that these newcomers seemed content to live within their own small villages along the Hudson River while conducting a mutually beneficial trade and exchange with them, the Haudenosaunee sought to define a formal, peaceful relationship with the Dutch in 1613. This first agreement was known as the *Tekeni Teiohatatie Kahswentha*, or Two Row Wampum belt, and is the philosophical foundation of how the Haudenosaunee have conducted themselves politically in relation to Europeans ever since. It was eventually followed with the Silver Covenant Chain agreement (also known in Mohawk as *Tehontatenents awa:kon*—"the thing that binds us together") that reiterated and confirmed the nature of this relationship. Wampum, the beads made from freshwater quahog shells, has been considered sacred within Haudenosaunee culture since the time of the Peacemaker. If arranged in various configurations on strings or woven into large and sometimes very elaborate belts, wampum are said to come alive when humans speak words into them. For years, anthropologists have classified wampum strings and belts as mnemonic devices, or memory aids, but for traditional Haudenosaunee they are much more than that. When a wampum belt is constructed to symbolize a treaty relationship between nations of people, it is considered a sacred and binding agreement. This is why the Haudenosaunee continue to place significant emphasis on the importance of belts such as the Two Row Wampum and Silver Covenant Chain as the guiding principle between European and Haudenosaunee nations.

The Two Row belt itself is rather simple in design, with two parallel lines of purple beads on a bed of white wampum. It is said that the parallel lines represent two vessels, the Haudenosaunee and the European, travelling side by side down a river. The onkwehonwe are in their canoe with their language, culture, history, and traditions, while the Dutch are in their sailing vessels with all of their own customs that also make them a distinct people. As these two vessels coexist, they are to be considered separate but equal in status, never interfering in each other's social or political affairs. To the Haudenosaunee of the seventeenth century, this was a declaration of sovereignty as well as recognition of the rights of outsiders within their territory. Arising from a tradition that respected the well-being of others, the Two Row was a reflection of basic Haudenosaunee principles of sharing and cooperation. As the decades went by, this same agreement was negotiated with the French and later the British as these nations entered into closer trading and military relationships with the Haudenosaunee. In both cases, an identical belt was exchanged.[8] Four hundred years later, this same straightforward ideology of autonomy and political independence exists among the Haudenosaunee today—but is largely forgotten and ignored by those who entered into this agreement with us.

At various times throughout the historical relationship between Haudenosaunee and colonial governments this agreement has been tested, and these moments have revealed the force with which the Iroquois have sought to articulate their independent, sovereign status. One of the earliest recorded examples of the Haudenosaunee asserting their resolve to maintain their traditional ways took place in 1744 after the governments of Maryland and Virginia offered to educate some of their youth. The Haudenosaunee leaders replied:

We know that you highly esteem the kind of learning taught in those Colleges, and that the Maintenance of our young Men, while with you, would be very expensive to you. We are convinced, that you mean to do us Good by your Proposal; and we thank you heartily. But you, who are wise must know that different Nations have different Conceptions of things and you will therefore not take it amiss, if our Ideas of this kind of Education happen not to be the same as yours. We have had some Experience of it. Several of our young People were formerly brought up at the Colleges of the Northern Provinces: they were instructed in all your Sciences; but, when they came back to us, they were bad Runners, ignorant of every means of living in the woods ... neither fit for Hunters, Warriors, nor Counsellors, they were totally good for nothing. (quoted in McLuhan 1971, 57)

Aware that those who were educated among the whites returned to life among their own people "totally good for nothing," these Chiefs were later echoed by Handsome Lake half a century later in his condemnation of Western education. It is also a refrain that certainly applies to the residential school experience, and is sometimes heard among Indigenous communities even today. Regardless of the time period, the issue of assimilation has been a constant threat to the survival of First Nations, Inuit, and Métis cultures. While education and the acquiring of knowledge is a highly esteemed, almost sacred, pursuit among traditional thinkers, the pervasive influence of Western society has continuously challenged the concept of what is actually useful for Indigenous youth to learn. This is a dilemma that has been present within First Nations communities for 300 years.

As a figure that best embodied this controversy during his own time, Joseph Brant was a product of a white man's education system that did indeed influence him to adopt certain qualities that befitted an English gentleman and military officer. At the same time, however, it also made him a literate individual who understood the colonial mind far better than the colonist understood the Native worldview. In the end, this made Brant a unique and well-positioned negotiator when it came to securing lands for the Six Nations in the wake of the American Revolution. Using his Western education and applying the philosophies contained within the Two Row Wampum, Brant pressured the Crown into acquiring lands for the Haudenosaunee in

Canada after they had been forgotten following the Revolution and ignored in the terms of the Treaty of Paris in 1783. These lands, in Brant's mind, would become the sole domain of the Haudenosaunee to do with as they saw fit. In a letter dated 1798, however, Brant was moved to question the motives of the Crown some fourteen years after the Haldimand Deed had promised that the "Mohawk Nation, and such others of the Six Nation Indians as wish to settle in that Quarter to take Possession of, & Settle upon the Banks of the [Grand] River ... allotting to them for that Purpose Six Miles deep from each Side of the River beginning at Lake Erie, & extending ... to the Head of the said River" (Haldimand [1784a] 1964, 51). Raising the issue of the Six Nations' service to the King during the Revolution, Brant argued that they had entered into agreements in good faith before and after the war, only to realize later that the Crown no longer considered the Haudenosaunee as sovereign nations once they had relocated to Upper Canada:

> Had it not been for this confidence and affection we bore the King we still had opportunities left after the war, in providing for ourselves in the free and independent manner natural to Indians, unhappily for us we have been made acquainted too late with the first real intentions of Ministry; that is, that they never intended us to have it in our power to alienate any part of the lands ... they seemingly intending to forbid us any other use of the lands than that of sitting down or walking on them. It plainly appears by this that their motives can be no other than to tie us down in such a manner, as to have us entirely at their disposal for whatever services they may in future want from us. ([1798] 1998, 14)

Brant is writing in response to being reprimanded for attempting to sell off parcels of the Grand River territory in order to create "an income, the hunting being entirely destroyed" (15). While this is the kind of activity for which he was later criticized by both historians and other Haudenosaunee, at this point in Six Nations history he was simply exercising sovereign rights, with the consent of the Confederacy Chiefs, who had given him the Power of Attorney in 1796, to sell their lands as they deemed necessary. With the intervention of the Crown in these transactions, however, Brant understood that the colonial authorities were intent on suppressing any notions of Haudenosaunee independence in Upper Canada. This debate is still an ongoing feature of political life at Six Nations, and the articulation of this unique relationship to Canada has been a central theme in much of the writing produced by the Grand River Haudenosaunee for over 200 years. Most recently, this very issue has been asserted again during the land reclamation at Douglas Creek Estates near Caledonia, Ontario.

In spite of the Crown's desire to subjugate the Haudenosaunee in their new lands, the Confederacy Council remained in place until 1924, albeit under the ever-watchful eye of the local Indian Agent on the reserve. Up to that time, the traditional leadership had endured Canadian Confederation in 1867, the introduction of the Indian Act in 1876, and an ever- increasing population of Canadian citizens in the most heavily populated region of the country. Obviously, the Six Nations at Grand River had been able to maintain a substantial portion of their traditional culture despite mounting pressures to assimilate into mainstream Canadian society. How was this possible? Or, more precisely, what made the Haudenosaunee so resistant to assimilation-ist policies over the past two centuries, and what continues to do so? Part of the answer to these questions, I believe, lies in the sustained power of the stories that are at the foundation of Haudenosaunee philosophical thought. Once part of a vast network of oral traditions that integrated ancient thought with contemporary experience, these stories have now been written, passed down, and shared in myriad ways that empower, enlighten, and educate Haudenosaunee communities today.

THE PAST AS PRESENT: CARRYING CULTURE FORWARD

Like every culture, the Haudenosaunee have identified certain moments in their history that define their experience and from which they have come to understand themselves and their place in the world. According to Seneca scholar John Mohawk, these oral narratives have become the "grand mythol-ogies" of the Haudenosaunee that "construct visions of the past which address the question about how the world became the way it is and, equally important, how we, as cultural beings in a certain culture, came to be the way we are. Such stories also urge upon us the expectation that things have been known to happen in a certain way, and are likely to happen in that way again"

(2005, ix). One of the most significant images in Haudenosaunee cosmology is that of Sky Woman's fall from the Sky World to this one. It is important to understand that the idea of the "fall" does not have the same implication as that which is familiar to either a Jewish or Christian worldview. As mentioned previously, it is a story that is concerned with movement and the transformation from a familiar environment to a new and unknown one. It is a story of survival, adaptation, resilience, and growth. What is also crucial to this story is the fact that Sky Woman managed to bring some very important things along with her to this world that have enabled her descendants to sustain themselves since that time long ago.

Since then, this story has resonated among the Haudenosaunee at various times in their history, and perhaps no more powerfully than when Joseph Brant led 2,000 of them into Ontario for the first time in the winter of 1785. Like Sky Woman, these people were also undergoing a transformation from a place that they and their ancestors had known for thousands of years to a place where most had never been. And like Sky Woman, they too brought with them important items of cultural significance, including their ceremonies, government, language, agricultural practices, and traditional customs. Fortunately for the Haudenosaunee, the ceremonies that they practise are not reliant on place or a specific geographical location, as they are in some Indigenous cultures, in order to be performed properly. Therefore, these ceremonies are transportable to a degree, and can be adapted to a specific situation and context so long as the proper words are spoken, dances performed, and protocol observed. Such cultural flexibility is a useful characteristic when a people are displaced from their traditional homeland, but it is also a feature of Haudenosaunee language and thought, which are reflective of a world in constant motion. In such an environment, change is a necessary feature that permeates the natural world. Addressing this feature of Iroquoian thought, Mohawk scholar Deborah Doxtator describes how the past affects the present within such a worldview: "In the creation stories, the Rotinonhsyonni [Haudenosaunee] world has no real beginning or end, only certain repeated patterns about a particular place or centre ... [T]hings continue in their patterns until they end, by very virtue of repeating their patterns, to grow outward and to incorporate their previous forms. Repetition is creative of change. Change is accumulative and the basis of continuity. Since nothing in the world is ever 'finished' and is continually becoming, change is an inherent and expected element of social life, not a disruption. Nothing ends since emerging forms subsume the past" (1996, 51). Because social, spiritual, and political thought among the Haudenosaunee is so deeply embedded with symbols found in the natural world, they view many elements of human society as organic and, like objects within nature, subject to cycles of growth, death, and renewal.

Drawing upon this already established cultural belief system when he first travelled among the Haudenosaunee, the Peacemaker utilized symbols that were familiar and therefore meaningful to the people. He talked of the Great Tree of Peace with its four white roots extending in all four directions so that people from around the world could seek shelter beneath it. He then spoke of how this tree is watched over by the eagle that is to warn the Haudenosaunee if any threat to the Peace is approaching. He also made deer antlers the emblem of a Chief, since the deer are a peaceful and gentle animal that does not disrupt its environment. All of these things "were the symbols of his time," according to John Mohawk, and they "were offered in a way that people who lived then could understand" (1986, xxii).

Mohawk argues that the very practical images and symbols used by the Peacemaker to illustrate his philosophy of peace, power, and righteousness among the Haudenosaunee is a clear example of the difference between Indigenous thought on this continent and that which was imported from Europe: "Nature is depicted as a threatening and irrational aspect of existence in the West's cosmologies. The Haudenosaunee cosmology is quite different. It depicts the natural world as a rational existence while admitting that human beings possess an imperfect understanding of it. ... Conversely, the idea the natural world is disorganized and irrational has served as something of a permission in the West [to subjugate it] and may be the single cultural aspect which best explains the differences between these two societies' relationships to Nature" (1986, xix). Given these contrasting ideologies, it is no surprise that traditional Indigenous societal structures were, and are, often considered "primitive" by modern mainstream sensibilities. While the use of medicinal plants and other aspects of Indigenous knowledge has grown to become an increasingly accepted form of Western healing in recent times, it is highly doubtful that the dominant society would be equally receptive to the idea of belonging to an animal clan, having only women select leaders, or visualizing an eagle atop a tree as the protector of a people (although the United States continues to see the eagle as a national symbol with militaristic overtones). Yet, these are some of the very fundamental practices and ideologies that contribute to the idea of cultural and political autonomy among the Haudenosaunee in contemporary times. It is now the responsibility of our people to make these images and symbols become relevant again within the world around us, employing the tools and technologies of the present. Aware of the importance of conveying these ideas in the modern context of land claims and the issues that surround sovereignty and identity, Haudenosaunee scholar Theresa McCarthy states: "The reclamation activities and ongoing negotiations involving Six Nations and the Grand River tract lands have reaffirmed educational priorities about Haudenosaunee traditions, languages, history and culture" (McCarthy 2008, 135). Importantly, the dissemination of this knowledge is relevant to all people, according to McCarthy, who asserts "whether to enable government officials to negotiate competently, to curb the confusion and anger reflected in public and media responses... to impress upon municipalities Six Nations interests in the future development of Grand River tract lands, or to enhance community members' articulation of their land rights, these complex educational needs remain an urgent and demanding task" (44).

The challenge at hand then is to convey these concepts through symbology or language that is effective, accessible, and respected by a mainstream consciousness. For example, a "great tree of peace" is a significant symbol and metaphor to the Haudenosaunee, but it is also an "ordinary" white pine found throughout the northeastern United States. As such, anyone can observe it and understand that it is tall and strong and that humans can find shelter underneath it while its roots grow deep in the earth in all directions. This is the potential effectiveness of using images found within nature to enlighten, since they are visible objects that people can understand regardless of what language they speak. But too often, the European mind will stop at these associations and will be unable to see the white pine tree as anything but an inanimate object that, while perhaps beautiful and awe-inspiring, has no meaning as a metaphor of political structure or of anything useful in their everyday lives.

Echoing Mohawk, Sioux scholar Vine Deloria, Jr. suggests that such inability to conceptualize an Indigenous North American ideology based upon relationships to the natural world is due to the fact that "[i]n the Western European context human experience is separated from the environment" (*Spirit and Reason* 223). This mindset was to later become a dominant feature of colonialism, according to Deloria, and it is also an illustration of the fact that Western society is a relative newcomer to this continent. Consequently, the Euro-American is "lost" within this environment that is familiar to Indigenous cultures that have had thousands of years of experience interacting and developing relationships within it.[9] Deloria writes that in "Indian [sic] tradition we find continuous generations of people living in specific lands, or migrating to new lands, and having an extremely intimate relationship with lands, animals, vegetables, and all of life. As Indians look out at the environment and as Indians experience a living universe, relationships become the dominating theme of life and the dominating motif for whatever technological or quasi-scientific approach Indian people have to the land" (*Spirit and Reason* 226). Therefore, when the Peacemaker arrived among the Haudenosaunee, he was able to build upon ideas that were already familiar within their culture, but he called upon the people to begin to understand them in different ways that recalled their spiritual relationship to the earth. These teachings then allowed them to see that relationships found in the natural world could become activated in the human world as means of social and political thought. Deloria places great importance in this kind of collective experience and believes that these intimate connections to place and space are what lie at the foundation of Indigenous philosophies, and create an understanding of "a relationship of specific responsibilities, specific insights, specific knowledge, and a specific task in the world" (*Spirit and Reason* 228). This creation of a cultural philosophy based upon a close relationship to the land is certainly true in the case of the Six Nations of the Grand River, who were able to successfully "transplant" social and political structures after being displaced from their traditional territories.

While Native scholars such as Mohawk and Deloria address the idea of difference between European and Native thought, Mohawk political scientist Taiaiake Alfred cautions that such an emphasis on conflict and dichotomy can also be counterproductive in attempts to negotiate sovereignty and human rights for Indigenous peoples. Citing the example of how the Peacemaker sought to unify a people violently at odds with each other, Alfred argues that to equate difference with incompatibility can only lead to dismissive attitudes and exclusivity that prevent dialogue between peoples. For if the basic premise of the Great Law assumes a "universal rationality" among human beings, Alfred argues, the dichotomization of "Indian and European values" does not allow for others outside of Indigenous communities to understand the concepts of "attaining the level of moral development that indigenous societies promote" (1999, 20). He writes, "Challenging mainstream society to question its own structure, its acquisitive individualistic value system, and the false premises of colonialism is essential if we are to move beyond the problems plaguing all our societies" (21). For the Haudenosaunee to understand that people's minds can be changed for the better, and that they can give up their past behaviours of injustice and cruelty, they only need to look to the story of how Atortaho's mind was straightened by the power of the collective goodwill of people who proposed a societal change based on justice, cooperation, and peace.

Alfred is one of many Indigenous scholars and thinkers who believe that it is therefore vital to return to the intellectual traditions contained in cultural philosophies and to introduce these ideas back into Indigenous communities. These scholars contend that the social structures that have been imported from Western society have largely failed in making this country a better place for First Nations, Inuit, and Métis peoples (let alone for Euro-Canadians and "new" Canadians), and that Indigenous intellectual thought holds great potential for solutions to current problems. Through the process of reactivating traditional thinking, Indigenous intellectuals (and leaders) feel that other areas of critical inquiry could possibly benefit from some of the social and political ideas that emerge from a scholarly discourse centred on Indigenous philosophy. As John Mohawk states, "the political thought of the Haudenosaunee deserves to be judged on its own merits, not as an artifact of the past. We should investigate it today, question it, expand on it, learn from it just as we would from any doctrine of political thought. It will stand against that kind of scrutiny" (1986, xv).

For Alfred, this type of questioning and analysis of traditional thought should go even further and become the foundation of the decolonization movement within Indigenous communities: "The traditions are powerful, real, and relevant. As intellectuals we have a responsibility to generate and sustain a social and political discourse that is respectful of the wisdom embedded within our traditions; we must find answers from within those traditions, and present them in ways that preserve the integrity of our languages and communicative styles. Most importantly, as writers and thinkers, we should be answerable to our nations and communities" (1999, 144). Although I agree with what Alfred is arguing here, I am also aware of some potential problems within this statement. Most notably, depending on what definition of "traditional knowledge" we use, we must be highly attentive to what role language plays within it. I have often been told by fluent Haudenosaunee speakers that many of the concepts that are used when we talk about the Great Law, the Code of Handsome Lake, and the Two Row Wampum, for example, are imperfect translations of what these philosophies "really mean" in our languages. In fact, there have been several very heated debates at Six Nations over the years in which many people have argued that public presentations of the Great Law should not be conducted using English in any form. And when the Gaihwi'yo is recited once a year at Grand River and other Haudenosaunee communities, it is always done in the language, never in English. Acknowledging the endangered state of Indigenous languages and their role within traditional cultures, Seminole historian Susan Miller writes, "The loss of a language is the loss of a unique worldview that cannot be transferred to English or any other language. When they lose their worldview, a people lose knowledge gained over millennia about how to relate to the sacred as well as government, diplomacy, science, technology, diet, education, philosophy, ethics, art, ecology, and more" (2011, 15). We must remain mindful of what Alfred proposes, then, when he calls for assertions of Indigenous sovereignty and nationhood that are somewhat weakened when we come to rely too heavily on translation, the use of English language, and especially academic discourse.

Such a dilemma brings us back to the very issue raised by those Haudenosaunee leaders who responded to the "kind Offer" of colonial officials to educate their youth in 1744. It reflects the problems that Joseph Brant faced in his lifetime and also serves as an example of what Handsome Lake warned the Haudenosaunee would happen if they followed a "white man's" education system: individual and collective conflict will arise when contrasting ideologies are brought together, no matter how good the intentions are. This is a situation that seems to have occurred time and again among the Haudenosaunee, and one that has often been played out in the literary history peopled by the figures that will be discussed in this book.

Beginning in Chapter 1 with Joseph Brant, I will outline how his unique position as a Mohawk "Pine Tree" Chief, a British officer, and a literate Christian led to the establishment of the Six Nations of the Grand River Territory. In addition, I will discuss the struggles he faced in attempting to maintain Haudenosaunee sovereignty in Upper Canada. The second chapter will focus on two significant figures from the late nineteenth century, Pauline Johnson and Seth Newhouse, who were engaged in making Six Nations history and culture accessible to a non-Native audience as a means to promote awareness of the continued presence of the Haudenosaunee in Canada. Chapter 3 will examine the significance of Deskaheh's embassy to King George V in London and to the League of Nations in Geneva in 1923. I focus especially on his famous 1925 radio address, showing how he called upon cultural tradition in the wake of World War I to bring attention to the unjust treatment of the Six Nations by the Canadian government after the forcible removal of the Confederacy Council at Grand River in 1924. The post–World War II era saw significant changes in the relationship between First Nations and the Canadian state, particularly during the Red Power Movement of the 1960s and 1970s. In Chapter 4, I discuss the works of songwriter Robbie Robertson, Methodist minister Enos Montour, traditional healer Alma Greene, and poet/playwright Daniel David Moses to demonstrate the diversity of voices emerging from Grand River during this time. After the events at Oka, Quebec in July 1990, the social and political landscape within Native communities was altered yet again, and this change has been marked by an outpouring of culturally influenced works by several writers, artists, and academics from Six Nations who continue to express the same principles argued by Joseph Brant over 200 years ago. In the final chapter, I demonstrate how Brian Maracle, Chief Jake Thomas, Richard Green, Shelley Niro, and others continue the long tradition of articulating Haudenosaunee concepts in a language that is accessible to settler societies in the hopes that awareness and understanding can be reached. It is not surprising that the tradition of the Two Row Wampum serves as the best metaphor for these occasions when differences need to be accounted for, acknowledged, and respected. Therefore, it is important to recognize that the three rows of white wampum beads that represent the concepts of peace, power, and righteousness between the two vessels can also serve as the words and ideas that bind us together within the borders of the belt, or the "river" that we all travel together.

Assiniboine scholar Kathryn Shanley suggests that such boundaries existed and were recognized between First Nations in pre-contact times, and that settler societies in North America are merely the most recent nations that Indigenous people have had to develop relationships with. Throughout their history, then, First Nations have had to engage in various forms of "boundary-crossings" in order to maintain a peaceful existence between nations. Although our common struggle to deal with threats to our lands and our self-determination has led to "pan-Indian" alliances and resistance movements in contemporary times, there is an increased understanding among Indigenous peoples that creative cultural expression and historical perspective must exist closely together when First Nations assert their individual, cultural autonomy. Ultimately, such connections circle back to the issue of sovereignty for First Nations in this country, who must also contend with the dangers of being seen only in terms of their "ethnicity." Sioux author and critic Elizabeth Cook-Lynn points out the dangerous relationship between academic work and this very important distinction: "Indian Nations are dispossessed of sovereignty in much of the intellectual discourse in literary studies, and there as elsewhere their natural and legal autonomy is described as simply another [North] American cultural or ethnic minority" (1998, 127). Ironically then, while literature in both the United States and Canada has largely been responsible for many of the stereotypes and attitudes pertaining to Indigenous peoples, more recently, it is in literary studies that these same stereotypes and false perceptions of First Nations people and their historical narratives are being confronted and challenged by Indigenous writers and critics.

Regarding this current academic and political climate Shanley asserts that "as the body of [Native] writing grows and older works are rediscovered, that literature spins out theories of its reason for being—fuller versions of the

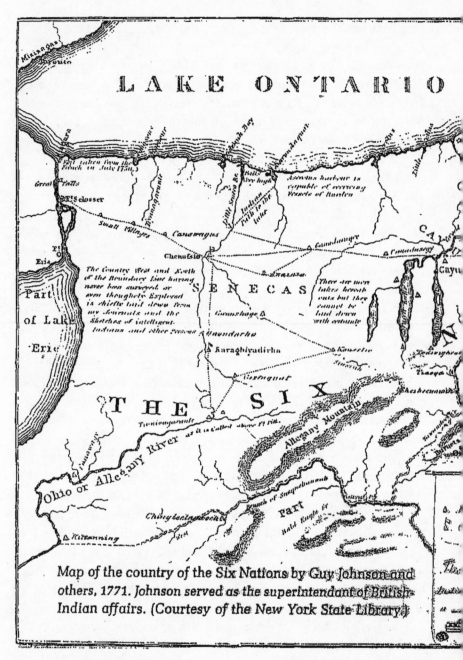

LAKE ONTARIO

Map of the country of the Six Nations by Guy Johnson and others, 1771. Johnson served as the superintendant of British Indian affairs. (Courtesy of the New York State Library.)

1771 map showing traditional Haudenosaunee territories in New York State. (New York State Library)

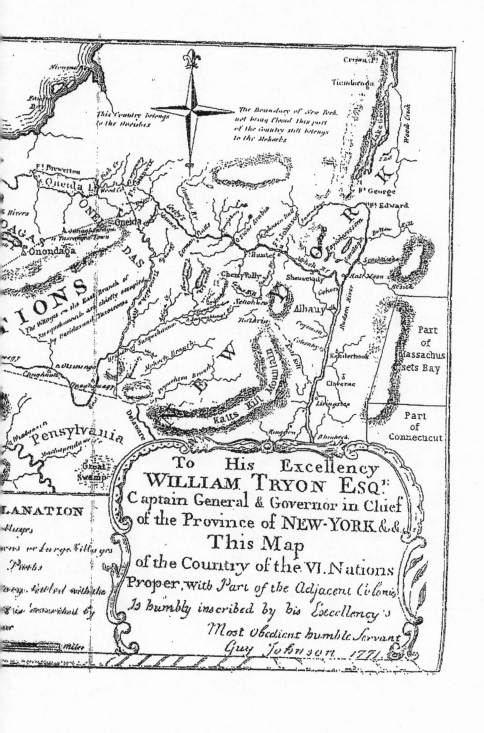

To His Excellency
WILLIAM TRYON ESQ.
Captain General & Governor in Chief
of the Province of NEW-YORK &c.
This Map
of the Country of the VI. Nations
Proper, with Part of the Adjacent Colonies
Is humbly inscribed by his Excellency's
Most Obedient humble Servant
Guy Johnson 1771

how, the what, the why. Native North American literatures and the attendant literary criticism movement are at such a juncture" (2001, 4). She argues "that [Native] criticism must also be historically grounded, just as the literature itself often must explain its cultural terms if it hopes to be published and understood by a non-indigenous readership.... More importantly, grounding the literature in history matters to the integrity of the art as well as to the politics it reflects and furthers. At every turn in the growth process, an emergent literature's critical arm must take account of its continued connection to the peoples whose struggles gave it life to begin with" (5–6). Shanley's assertion that literature, criticism, and history remain interconnected within Indigenous societies is an important feature of the work that First Nations, Inuit and Métis scholars have taken up in recent years. Maintaining these important connections to tradition and with those who have gone before empowers those who have now chosen to take up the struggle for Indigenous nationhood within the university and beyond.

Taiaiake Alfred sees this responsibility as one of the fundamental ways to combat colonialism and to renew tradition: "We must add our voices to the narrative that is history, translate our understandings of history and justice, and bring the power of our wisdom to bear on the relationships we have with others. We cannot do this from a position of intellectual weakness" (1999, 142). Like Sky Woman in her journey from one world to another, First Nations, Inuit and Métis communities are also now moving from one political era into another; and like her transition from one time and place to another, these communities need to make adjustments to their world by employing those traditions that will sustain them in the future creation of their new environments, whether they be physical, social, or political. Through an analysis of the oral traditions, letters, poetry, speeches, short stories, non-fiction, and film produced by its members, what follows will examine how the Six Nations of the Grand River have taken up this very formidable task for more than 200 years.

1

"Sovereigns of the Soil" Joseph Brant and the Grand River Settlement

Several decades before names such as Sitting Bull, Geronimo, and Crazy Horse entered into the North American consciousness, Joseph Brant was one of the best-known Native leaders of the eighteenth century and the subject of much literary interest. In 1838, William Stone published *Life of Joseph Brant—Thayendanegea*, a two-volume biography of the famous Mohawk Chief, and in 1872 a book entitled *A Memoir of the Distinguished Mohawk Indian Chief, Sachem and Warrior, Capt. Joseph Brant* appeared, "compiled from the most Reliable and Authentic Records" by William E. Palmer (Brant 1872). As the nineteenth century wore on, however, and Canada and the United States engaged in the process of building their respective nations, Brant and the Grand River Haudenosaunee were increasingly forgotten after their usefulness as military allies declined following the War of 1812. After more than 500 years of Native/Euro-American contact, the colourful images of the above-mentioned American Indian leaders have become prominent symbols of Indigenous resistance and a fierce independence that most do not associate with Brant and his own attempts at negotiating with colonial authorities.

In fact, there remains today considerable debate among the Grand River community itself as to how Brant's legacy should be assessed with regard to his political dealings with the Crown. According to historian James W. Paxton, the popular historical accounts of Brant, describing him as a "Loyalist," have resulted in an "Anglo-Canadian society [that] has embraced Brant more completely and warmly than have the Haudenosaunee" (2008,85). What Paxton rightly points out is that Canadians have forgotten "Brant's intense battles with colonial administrators, his ultimate desire to limit and control the [non-Haudenosaunee] people who settled at Grand River, and his many flirtations with the United States" (85). They tend to ignore these elements and instead "subsume him within the smothering traditions of the United Empire Loyalists" (86). While it is perhaps tempting, and all too convenient, for the Haudenosaunee to look upon Brant's legacy from our own post-Oka perspective and label him as far too complacent in his response to colonial authority, I suggest that he often drew upon a traditional understanding of Six Nations sovereignty to promote a peaceful nation-to-nation relationship with the British, and that his beliefs were strongly opposed to English authority. As Paxton argues, Brant's convictions are evident in his numerous letters to government authorities that consistently reminded them of the Haudenosaunee's role in the Revolution and the political autonomy that they were promised in its aftermath. While Brant was at once an officer in the British army, a Freemason, and an Anglican, he was also Thayendanegea, a Mohawk "Pine Tree" Chief who never abandoned his people and their struggle to secure and maintain an independent homeland in Upper Canada. This chapter will examine how his speeches and letters indicate a strong Haudenosaunee position on our sovereign identity that has largely been overlooked by Haudenosaunee and non-Haudenosaunee alike for the past 200 years. Importantly, Brant's words have continued to echo throughout much of the literary production that has emanated from Grand River ever since.

Thayendanegea, or Joseph Brant, was born in present-day Ohio, on what was then the westernmost edge of Haudenosaunee territory, in March 1743. When he was around eight years old, his family moved back to Canajoharieke, his mother's Wolf Clan village in the traditional Mohawk territory of eastern New York State (Brant-Monture 1960, 6). Although the Iroquois Confederacy had been somewhat weakened by a series of epidemics that had spread through their villages, they still held tremendous political and military influence in the mid-eighteenth century and were constantly sought out as allies by the French and British, who were intent on claiming control over these territories. By the time young Thayendanegea arrived among his people, the British were the favoured trading partner and military ally among the Mohawk and most other nations of the Confederacy. This was an alliance that became permanent after the conclusion of what was known as the "French-Indian Wars" in 1759.[1]

Growing up in this period, Brant would have witnessed first-hand the decision-making process of the Confederacy Chiefs and been exposed to the final years of what was traditional Haudenosaunee culture before the American Revolution completely altered it forever. The Superintendent of Indian Affairs in New York at the time, Sir William Johnson, recognized that Brant was an intelligent youth and arranged for him and two other young Mohawk men to be sent to the newly established Moor's Charity School in Lebanon, Connecticut, to become educated in the ways of the colonist (Paxton 2008, 28). Twenty-five years after Six Nations leaders declined the offer of such an education for their young men, it was now viewed as a beneficial opportunity; for they realized that their people would have to become knowledgeable about European ways in order to effectively negotiate the ever-changing social and political relationship with them. According to one early account of Brant's life,

> He soon made such proficiency as to be able not only to read and write English surprisingly well but soon undertook to translate English into the Iroquois or Mohawk Language... so well that the late Sir Wm. Johnson found him very serviceable in translating Indian Speeches of moment [sic] to be made to the 6 Nations in Council and translate them in writing into the Iroquois Language in order to convey to the Indians the full meaning and substance of such Speeches [which] Indian interpreters who in general are a dull illiterate kind of white people never were capable of doing. (Bryant 1873, 13)

As he matured, Brant also took up the Anglican faith, and as with his education, it appears that he was able to reconcile and adapt what he learned of European ways with his Mohawk identity and Haudenosaunee traditions. These cross-cultural belief systems were to be the guiding principles that influenced not only his own life, but that also had considerable impact upon the rest of the Six Nations throughout the late eighteenth century. Undoubtedly, it was Brant's ability to negotiate these two cultures that has made him such a compelling figure over the years, inspiring historians and biographers to use such phrases as a "man of two worlds" and "divided loyalties" to describe his life and legacy.

What these historians have failed to realize, however, is that from a Haudenosaunee perspective, particularly during Brant's lifetime, such negotiations of identity and personal choice were acceptable and necessary attributes when dealing with the unfamiliar circumstances that were shaping their world in the late eighteenth century. Scholars have only recently recognized such agency on the part of Native people as a very deliberate and pragmatic attempt to maintain control of their lands in the face of ever-increasing colonial pressures. Historian Alan Taylor argues that by embracing English education and religious beliefs, "Brant hoped to appropriate elements of British culture to serve Indian ends: to build a syncretic cultural fire wall against colonial domination" (2007, 49). By becoming "literate Christians," Taylor continues, "the Mohawks could better fend off cunning and conniving land speculators and could better conduct diplomacy with colonial officials" (49). In other words, becoming Christian allowed them to preserve their lands as well as their political importance. Positioned this way, between cultural tradition and Western religion, Taylor concludes that "the Mohawks could prolong their distinct identity as a native people" (49). Brant also realized that the same would be true for all the Haudenosaunee nations negotiating with the British and Americans at this time, but he never appeared to advocate for a widespread conversion to Christianity, nor a complete turn to British education, as a means to retain traditional lands. He therefore understood the importance of culture and tradition, and more importantly, of the respect for personal choice that had permeated Haudenosaunee society since its earliest beginnings.

It is significant, then, that because of his education and ability to communicate with the British, Brant was made a "Pine Tree" Chief within the Confederacy Council in the time immediately preceding the American Revolution. A "Pine Tree" Chief is an honorary title that is earned, rather than passed down through matrilineal lines as is the usual custom among the Haudenosaunee, and it is reserved for those who prove themselves worthy through their oratorical skills or abilities as a warrior. Recognizing that Brant was already a proven warrior, also a fluent English speaker who got along well with the powerful colonial Administrator (and later, his brother-in-law), Sir William Johnson, the traditional Chiefs understood that they needed a mediator who could understand the language and rhetoric of the colonial officials who were attempting to win their favour. Significantly, the Great Law, or Kaienerekowa, provides for the recognition, or "raising up," of such individuals who would benefit the people in turbulent times, and further demonstrates the foresight and flexibility of traditional political philosophy. The following is from a recent translation of the Kaienerekowa by the late Cayuga traditionalist Reg Henry, which was originally dictated in the Onondaga language by Chief John A. Gibson at Grand River in 1912:

> If ever a disruptive idea were to enter where the Great Fire [of the Confederacy] is located, where the power is situated, if the Chiefs are unable to agree, thereupon someone among the warriors or the people—just whoever in the crowd is able—that one shall help, assisting them at the Council, the League Chiefs ... [H]e will place in front of them his own opinion, he having observed where they can escape in order for the entire group to survive, so that the day will dawn for generations of our grandchildren.... After the Chiefs accept it, the suggestion of the one not holding office, they will confirm it, and if it turns out well ... then the Chiefs will think carefully about the man, the warrior holding no office, thinking about his ability.... Thereupon they will decide to include him where they are seated to counsel together, the Chiefs of the five nations. And they will stand him up, in front of the Chiefs who will then give him a title which they will call Pine Tree Chief, the self-made Chief, and this is because he helped the Chiefs and also the entire group. (Gibson [1912] 1992, 464–68)

Therefore, the traditional Hereditary Council was not breaking any rules of protocol and decorum in appointing Brant as a Chief, even though such a title was not his by matrilineal lines. They simply relied on an ancient system of government that allowed for such individuals to assume a position of authority when particular situations arose. This tradition also makes it clear that the Pine Tree Chief "has as much power as the antlered Chiefs of our various nations, all of the trees being of equal height" (Gibson [1912] 1992, 468–69), meaning that no Chief has more power than any other; but warns that the "self-made" Chief can also be stripped of his title "if ever he spoils matters between the Chiefs and the people ... [and if] he is not truthful in his dealings" (469–70).

While the majority of Six Nations members today understand that Joseph Brant was not a hereditary Chief who had attained his title through the ancient "condolence ceremony" used to elevate leaders, his popular image as the "supreme" leader of the Six Nations during this time has remained quite entrenched in mainstream society's image of him. This misrepresentation is one of many examples of how our history has often been interpreted for us, with no real understanding or discussion of how traditional political structure is designed to accommodate individuals like Brant and, more importantly, how we as a community have viewed his place within our history. As a result, Brant has often been singled out as an historical icon characterized by his Loyalist sympathies and attraction to European manners (which are a prominent feature of his contemporary portraits), rather than as but one Chief operating within a much larger social and political structure to which he was accountable. Too often, Brant is credited with leading the Six Nations in the period after the Revolution, when in reality he was given these powers of authority by the traditional body of leadership, with the understanding that if he acted in opposition to their wishes, his title would be revoked. In other words, while Brant may be the acculturated figure most closely associated with Six Nations history in Canada, his ideologies emerged from an ancient philosophical tradition that he and the hereditary Chiefs and Clanmothers adapted to the changing circumstances around them. He was the individual who was able to provide the means of "escape in order for the entire group to survive," as spoken of in the Great Law.

During the Revolution, Brant's military abilities were considerable enough to earn him the rank of captain, and it was at this time that a large part of his reputation was also established, one which fit well with the image of the noble warrior savage, made all the more attractive so long as he fought for the British cause. Understandably, his historical reputation in the United States is often in direct contrast to how he is perceived in Canada, and Revolutionary battles such as those at Cherry Valley and Wyoming are best remembered by Americans for how cruelly Brant treated "helpless" revolutionary settlers, earning him such nicknames as "the Monster Brant" and "Scourge of the Mohawks." Since then, many of these accounts have been proven false and, in fact, further research has revealed how humane Brant was in comparison to both British and American military leaders during this conflict.[2] Undoubtedly, Brant was able to use his knowledge of the upstate New York landscape to great strategic effect during the war, and the sense of urgency felt by the Haudenosaunee during the Revolution could not have been lost on him, since many significant battles were fought within Haudenosaunee territory or in close proximity to it. Furthermore, the promises that the British had made prior to the war led the Six Nations to believe that they would be well taken care of, win or lose. In a speech at Niagara, Brant later reminded the British of their words.

> In the year 1775 ... Lord Dorchester, then Sir Guy Carlton, at a numerous council, gave us every encouragement, and requested us to assist in defending their country, and to take an active part in defending His Majesty's possessions, stating that when the happy day of peace should arrive, and should we not prove successful in the contest, that he would put us on the same footing in which we stood previous to joining him. This flattering promise was pleasing to us, and gave us spirit to embark heartily in his Majesty's cause. We took it for granted that the word of so great a man, or any promise of a public nature, would ever be held sacred. (1872, 60–61)

It is significant here that Brant points out that these promises were made to the Haudenosaunee at a "numerous council," meaning that a large group of people were present, including, most likely, the traditional body of leadership. To the Haudenosaunee, words that were passed at such a gathering carried tremendous weight and power, and were to be honoured. For the British, such words were apparently not as important, especially as they were neither written down nor carried out.

We will never know the exact discussions that went on in Council meetings regarding the American Revolution and Haudenosaunee sentiments toward it, but the Clanmothers and Chiefs of the time would have had to consider carefully the consequences of victory or defeat and the subsequent impact upon their lives in the only homeland they had ever known. In other words, the ferocity with which Brant and the other Six Nations warriors fought had less to do with their belief in the rightfulness of the British cause and more to do with the fact that they were, in large part, defending their homeland as the conflict wore on. Many historians seem to have overlooked this particular issue, choosing instead to portray Brant as a devout Loyalist who looked poorly upon the American patriots as insubordinate troublemakers in their uprising against the King. Notably, recent scholarship in Canada has focussed on dismantling the "Loyalist myth," and I would argue that Brant's role within the Revolution would give further evidence for such a deconstruction, as his personal motives were primarily driven by a collective response from the Six Nations to a situation that was not of their making. They were simply making choices dictated by forces around them, using conventional responses to times of conflict that had served them in the past. Although Brant was a pivotal figure during this period, he, too, was exploited by the British before, during, and after the Revolution, especially as it served their purposes to construct a narrative of noble Loyalist subjects seeking a new home far from the uncivilized American rebels.

Following the British defeat, Joseph Brant's service to the Crown did serve eventually to procure a new land base in Upper Canada, but only after much intense lobbying on his part. Previous to his requests, however, it is apparent that the British held little regard for "her Majesties faithful Allies," since the peace treaty of 1783 did not include any mention of the Haudenosaunee despite the fact that they were the people most directly affected by the British defeat. Such neglect of the Six Nations caused Brant's early biographer, William L. Stone, to write in 1838, "In the treaty with the United States, ... Great Britain had made no stipulation in behalf of her Indian allies. Notwithstanding the alacrity with which the aboriginals, especially the Mohawks, had entered the service of the crown—notwithstanding their constancy, their valor, the readiness with which they had spilt their blood, and the distinguished services of their Great Captain Thayendanegea [Brant], the loyal red man was not even named in the treaty" ([1838] 1969, 1:237–38). Stone may have been an early commentator on the injustice of such treatment in the aftermath of the Revolution, but he made no real criticism of the British and their policies of the time. Unfortunately, this disregard for the well-being of the Native people of this continent was to become an all-too-familiar pattern as the nineteenth century progressed.

Brant, in his attempts to secure a land base for the Mohawks whose "whole country had been ravaged with fire and sword; and ... [who] had sacrificed the entire of their own rich and beautiful ... native valley" (Stone [1838] 1969, 238), did not forget the other nations of the Confederacy and the responsibility they had toward each other, a relationship that had endured for centuries previous to contact. Therefore, Brant was intent on gaining lands in Upper Canada that were in close proximity to the other nations of the Confederacy who chose to remain in New York State, particularly the Seneca. After some negotiation, Brant was able to secure a tract of land six miles wide on each side of the Grand River, which flowed into Lake Erie approximately 40 miles from Niagara Falls. Such a location would allow relatively easy access and communication between the Haudenosaunee nations in the event of further troubles with the Americans. This was also a location that the British approved of, and on October 25, 1784, Sir Frederick Haldimand signed the document that became known as the Haldimand Deed, ensuring "that a Convenient Tract of Land under [His Majesty's] Protection should be chosen as a Safe & Comfortable Retreat for ... [the] Mohawk Nation and such others of the Six Nation Indians as wish to settle ... upon the Banks of the [Grand] River, ... which them & their posterity are to enjoy for ever" (Haldimand [1784a] 1964, 50–51). Although the 975,000 acres of land promised in the Deed was but a fraction of traditional Haudenosaunee territory lost to the Revolution, Brant was satisfied with these conditions, and in November 1784 wrote in a letter "I shall winter here [near Kingston], myself and family; early in the Spring I shall leave ... and go to my new country at Grand River" (quoted in Stone [1838] 1969, 247).

This letter is also significant, for in it Brant expresses his frustration at trying to make himself understood in written English. Despite his education and experience in dealing with colonial officials over the years, he was still aware of his inability to completely express himself in an effective manner, a situation that he must have understood to be a precarious one: "It would relieve me many points if you would be so kind as to answer me this letter, as far as you will understand my English, and please to explain me at once of your sentiments concerning this kind of complaint of mine, let it be what it will, because whatever must be done its not help for it, it must be so. If I could see you, and talk with you, I could explain myself better than a letter half English half Indian" (quoted in Stone [1838] 1969, 247). With virtually no one else to rely upon to accurately translate correspondence, much less the meaning behind certain terms and phrases of English common law and propriety, the responsibility that Brant faced cannot be underestimated—he was the one and only line of defence between the Six Nations and the fate that awaited them in the highly unstable period following the war. As Stone comments in a footnote, "Captain Brant improved in his English composition very much and very rapidly in after years" (247). What is left out of this kind of observation, of course, is the question: how well was Brant able to translate concepts from English into the Iroquoian languages? This is of fundamental importance; Brant was constantly engaged in cross-cultural dialogue, and necessity dictated that he describe colonial concepts in terms that would be understandable to the Haudenosaunee who were reliant on his ability to accurately translate and analyze their significance. Brant's need to translate concepts back and forth across cultural divides was an enormous task made more complex by the situation that the Six Nations found themselves in at the end of the American Revolution. With their traditional territories decimated by years of warfare and the settler population hostile toward them, they were now refugees in the "ancient country" that had been "the residence of their ancestors from the time far beyond their earliest traditions" (Stone [1838] 1969, 238). Aware that it was his influence that had persuaded the Mohawk, Onondaga, Cayuga, and Seneca to ally with the British in the first place, Brant undoubtedly felt extreme pressure to provide for the future well-being of these nations.

Not only had the Six Nations been dispossessed of their homelands, they also faced the difficult task of rebuilding the Confederacy Council of Chiefs and Clanmothers that had been fragmented during the Revolution. In addition, they had to relocate themselves physically and adjust to a life vastly different than it was in the years prior to the war. Brant, as an advocate of adopting certain qualities of a "progressive" late-seventeenth-century lifestyle, would have had to impress upon his own people the benefits of such change. As mentioned earlier, change is a prominent feature of Haudenosaunee worldview, but the wide-scale adoption of a foreign culture's way of life is a completely different matter. Haudenosaunee suspicion toward this kind of cultural adoption was compounded by the fact that those who had promised to assist them in the past were those who were also responsible for the great upheaval in their lives. While the colonists saw religion and education as the avenues through which all Native people could improve themselves, Brant recognized that the British and the Haudenosaunee viewed happiness in very different ways. Apparently aware of the irony of the situation, Brant also believed that becoming educated in the ways of the whites could have the opposite of the intended effect among Native people. If anything, Brant warned in a letter written on 8 March 1791, "the more knowledge the Indians acquire, the clearer they will see the impositions which has been practic'd upon them by the White people, and consequently they will be the more averse to adopting the Manners of such people in place of the customs of their Forefathers who liv'd happy, & free from strife before they became acquainted with them..." ([1791b] 1964, 270).

While Brant promoted both Christianity and education at Grand River, there is no record or account of his ever attempting to aggressively convert people to the Anglican faith. It is of considerable significance, however, that he oversaw the construction of a church, now known as the Mohawk Chapel, almost immediately upon settling on the Grand River near present-day Brantford, Ontario in 1785, and constantly urged British officials to supply a full-time pastor for the village. In addition, he set about the task of translating the Gospel of Mark into the Mohawk language, along with a variety of other biblical materials. He also actively sought a schoolteacher to instruct Haudenosaunee youth shortly after the early villages were established. This last effort was quite successful, it seems, and in 1792 one visitor reported that the schoolmaster at Grand River "had sixty-six [students] on his list, some of whom had excellent capacities for learning, and read distinctly and fluently" (Campbell [1792] 1964, 60). These two initiatives are evidence that Brant, and others in the community, were tolerant of changes to their traditional approaches to religion, education, and knowledge in their new environment. It also demonstrates that education and literacy were valued early on and have been in place at Grand River for over two centuries.[3]

But what of traditional Haudenosaunee culture at Grand River at this time? From most available accounts, it appears that many people simply

The Mohawk Village at Grand River, with the Mohawk Chapel in the foreground, c. 1805. The Chapel is the burial place of Joseph Brant, and still stands today in the city of Brantford, Ontario. (Library and Archives Canada, No. 1990-113-1)

continued to practise the seasonal cycle of ceremonies and thanksgiving in much the same way they had done previous to their relocation. Since the majority of these ceremonies are still practised today at Grand River, we can assume that most did indeed survive the relocation to the new territory. Brant, for his part, seems to have tolerated, if not supported, these traditions, and would have understood the importance of their function for the mental and spiritual well-being of the people. Living in the late eighteenth century, his sentiments were most likely aligned with those of his contemporary Red Jacket, the famous Seneca orator, who summed up Haudenosaunee views on religious tolerance in 1805: "We are told that your religion was given to your forefathers, and has been handed down from father to son. We also have a religion which was given to our forefathers, and has been handed down to us their children. We worship that way. It teaches us to be thankful for all the favors we receive, and to love each other, and to be united. We never quarrel about religion" (2006, 142). Furthermore, all people would have been aware of the need to be accepting and supportive of each other, particularly during this time of great social upheaval, and there are no records to indicate that members of the Grand River community discriminated against each other when it came to religious views. At least, there are no indications that conflict arose around the issue of religious practice, and in fact it appears that a large number of people engaged in both traditional and Christian events, each practice being given due respect and reverence.

One important element of tradition that did provide a certain familiar quality to life in the new territory was the practice of agriculture, a highly significant component of Haudenosaunee culture. Because the soil in the Grand River Valley is nearly as fertile as the land that they had been removed from, it was possible to continue growing the crops that had sustained the Six Nations for centuries—namely, corn, beans, and squash. The most notable difference between the new land and the old was that large village fields were replaced with much smaller, single-family plots. This altered the old system of collective labour in which everyone contributed to the cultivation of fields that would provide food for the village, and signalled a move toward a more Western individualism. Subsequently, Brant invited his Loyalist friends to live among the Grand River Haudenosaunee, not as an example of how to become acculturated but to serve as instructors in the new methods of farming and raising livestock that would be appropriate to their new surroundings. In keeping with Haudenosaunee patterns of transformative change and the pragmatic need to adapt to the environment, the people appeared to make the adjustment with little difficulty. This transition from landless refugees to successful farmers and landholders was witnessed by one visitor to Grand River in 1792, Patrick Campbell, who wrote: "I visited several houses in the village, and found the inhabitants had abundance of the necessaries of life to supply their wants, and are better and more comfortably lodged than the generality of the poor farmers in my country ... [the Indians] have a deal of crop, and excellent cattle, inferior to none I have seen in the province" ([1792] 1964, 60).

As the people adjusted to life in their new lands, Joseph Brant remained in constant conflict with British officials as to the extent of Six Nations sovereignty over the Haldimand tract. Although the terms of the deed itself state that these lands are for the Six Nations, "which them and their posterity to enjoy forever," it was obvious that the colonial administrators of Upper Canada understood the Haudenosaunee to be settlers, and not owners, of the new territory. For Brant and the rest of the Six Nations, accustomed as they were to centuries of political autonomy, such a change in status must have seemed absurd and insulting. The Haudenosaunee understood their nation-hood as an inherent right that was non-negotiable, given to them by their ancestors and recounted in their oral traditions. Therefore, their service to the British during the Revolution was not as subjects but as allies. For that reason, they viewed the lands that were provided for them in Upper Canada as compensation for those that they had lost fighting alongside the British. What was even more insulting was that colonial officials in Upper Canada were constantly plotting ways in which to retain the military service of the Six Nations at Grand River, while at the same time encroaching upon the meagre land base that the Six Nations had just recently established.

Writing on 24 March 1791 to Baron Dorchester, the Governor-in-Chief of British North America, Brant shows willingness to compromise and negotiate land dealings, but is also quick to call attention to the unreasonable nature of the request that Six Nations relinquish parcels of their land:

> About the Lands at the Mouth of the Grand River you seem much to Wish that we should Spare you at least Six Miles up the River in order to have your New Settlement to be in one String along the Lake ... the Sentiments of the Indians here on this head seems to thought rather hard that they should give it back after its given to them. However they have agreed to give it up five Miles & a half up the River, because six Miles, it would take in a Seneca Settlement who we could not think to remove them as they are fond of the Place and half a Mile cannot make any odds with You:
>
> The Deed or Grant for the Lands here which you are going to give us, we hope You will make the Deed or grant near the same sort which General Haldimand first promised to us, we hope the Council would not restrict us too much—other ways we shall look upon it not much better than a Yankee deed or grant to their Indian friends. ([1791a] 1964, 57–58)

At this point, Brant is still aware that the final terms of the land survey have yet to be determined, but appears to recognize that the British are perhaps little better than the Americans he has just fought against and given up his homeland to. This must have been a difficult realization for Brant, made more so by the understanding that he was largely responsible for the fate of the Grand River Haudenosaunee.

"We are at a loss what to think of our Great men here changing their Minds so often," Brant declared of the British in November 1796. "We cannot from their Conduct towards us by any means learn what their Intentions are; nor what we are to expect from them.... From their Treatment it appears that they are trifling with us. — It is not what we expected nor what we deserved" ([1796a] 1964, 82–83). As the 1790s progressed, the correspondence between Brant and authorities in Upper Canada grew even more heated as both sides fought to gain control over the Grand River, which was becoming increasingly important as a transportation route into southern Ontario. Frustrated with the ongoing dispute over land title, Brant even considered returning to the United States on more than one occasion in order to possibly negotiate a land deal there. Writing to the Superintendent of Indian Affairs in New York State on 19 January 1796, Brant declared his dissatisfaction with the British: "Gov. Simcoe still continuing to interfere with our lands on the Grand River, makes me much more desirous of having some tract of land within the limits of the United States, that we may call our own, and I hope the Congress will take into consideration, the natural right we have to the land on the Kaikhake [in Ohio, south of Lake Erie], and to the Eastward of it" ([1796b] 1964, 78).

Recognizing the monetary value of their new territory, Brant began to sell and to lease blocks of land in the northern part of the tract in the early 1790s to generate income for the fledgling community. Almost immediately, he was reprimanded by British officials for overstepping what they viewed as his legal jurisdiction. In response, Brant reminded them of the rights that the Haudenosaunee had enjoyed prior to the Revolution, rights that they maintained were brought with them to Upper Canada. In a speech at Niagara, Brant declared:

We were promised our lands for our services, and these lands we were to hold on the same footing with those we fled from at the commencement of the American war; when we joined, fought and bled in your cause. Now is published a proclamation forbidding us leasing those very lands, that were positively given us in lieu of those of which we were the sovereigns of the soil, of those lands we have forsaken, we sold, we leased, and we gave away, when, and as often as we saw fit, without hindrance on the part of your Gov't, for your Gov't well knew we were the lawful sovereigns of the soil, and they had no right to interfere with us as independent nations. (1872, 61–62)

Once again, Brant is forced to remind the British of Iroquois military service to the King and the assurances that were made to the Six Nations less than twenty years before, facts that the British continually appeared to overlook. He also points out that the British did not question the sovereign status of the Six Nations when they made land deals with them prior to the Revolution, and that they had no problem when the Six Nations negotiated land sales and surrenders with the Americans after the war. By stressing the fact that the Crown "well knew" the sovereign power of the Haudenosaunee to make decisions regarding their land, Brant indicates his dissatisfaction with the colonial officials who were now the new representatives of authority in Upper Canada. This development signalled a distinct shift in the relationship between the Haudenosaunee and the Crown, and it was the beginning of a contentious history of colonialism in this country—an experience that First Nations, Inuit, and Métis people have come to know and understand all too well.

Because so much attention has long been focussed upon Brant's decision making and high-profile leadership role at Grand River, almost no mention is made of the Confederacy Council that existed at this time. This is another example of how historians have chosen to disregard the persistence of Haudenosaunee tradition at Grand River. From most history texts, one would be led to believe that any semblance of traditional governmental structure among the Iroquois was all but eliminated following the Revolution, and that Brant was the most important—if not the only—leader at this time. This was certainly not the case, and although he was the most well-documented individual at Grand River because of his proficiency in English, he was still a "Pine Tree" Chief in the settlement and not the sole voice of authority. One incident that illustrates this fact, and that also demonstrates what happened when he tried to alter tradition among his people, was recorded in 1792, after the death of a well-liked and influential Mohawk Chief, Captain David Hill, when Brant attempted to make Hill's son Aaron the new Chief. Fully aware that the women assign the title of Chief through the matrilineal line as set forth in oral tradition, it appears that Brant nevertheless tried to use his influence and convince the Council to make an exception. This was turned down, however, as Patrick Campbell reports, "Captain Brant did all he could to get the son ... to enjoy the titles, but it would not do; the ancient laws, customs, and manners of the nation could not be departed from" ([1792] 1964, 61). While it is evident that Brant was held in high regard among the Grand River community, it is also very obvious that his influence had limits, particularly when it came to modifying the structure of government and overriding the role of women in Haudenosaunee society.

As proof of their continued trust in him, however, Brant was given the power of attorney in 1796 to negotiate land deals along the Grand River on behalf of the Six Nations("Brant's Power" [1796] 1964, 79–81). Although thirty-five Chiefs signed this document, it was hardly an indication that he had ascended to absolute authority in the eyes of the people. It was merely another example of how the traditional leadership of the time understood Brant's capacity to communicate with the British when it came to legal protocol. Again, we have no account of what took place at meetings between Brant and the hereditary Chiefs and Clanmothers around the issues of land negotiations, but it is highly unlikely that he could have made decisions without their input and consent. He was also a tireless administrator who was relentless in his demands on colonial officials to provide the Six Nations with answers regarding their lands along the river, and employed various rhetorical devices in the process. One address, to William Claus, is both apologetic and forceful: "I have taken up much of your time in listening to any long Grievances. Our situation demands our being Candid. You will therefore excuse me, As it is in a Business no ways interesting to you, but truly to us Indians and our Posterity, we must request that you will use every Endeavour to bring the Business to an Issue, so that we may no longer remain in that state of Suspense, in which we have been for now some years, and which has caused us all great uneasiness of Mind"([1796a] 1964, 83–84).

While the difficulties of translating English terms and concepts into Haudenosaunee thought remained an issue, Brant also faced the challenge of conveying Haudenosaunee sentiments to English-speaking people, as the brief passage above demonstrates. In Haudenosaunee society, it is vital that all people, not just Chiefs, make decisions based upon how their actions will affect people seven generations in the future. Furthermore, for a people to make sound decisions, they need to have a clear mind, free of doubt and negativity. Therefore, when Brant is commenting on the fact that the people at Grand River have been held in a "state of suspense" regarding their position on their lands, he is also saying that they are unable to make the best decisions regarding their future, or "posterity," thereby endangering the well-being of succeeding generations. While all of this would be clearly implied to a Haudenosaunee person, it is highly unlikely that a European reader of the time would have fully understood the urgency of such a situation, nor the pervasive anxiety felt by all Grand River Haudenosaunee at this moment in their history.

British officials, meanwhile, continued to strategize over ways in which to appease Brant and the claims of the Six Nations while also maintaining their authority in Upper Canada. While they admitted that "the land in question was given to the Six Nations, ... [and] it belongs to them solely and exclusively," they also stressed "they are positively restricted from alienating or disposing of it to any other Persons whatsoever" (Portland [1797] 1964,84). This measure was to be undertaken in order to guard against "the most remote possibility of such an important Tract of ground ever becoming the Property of any other Persons, without His Majesty's special assent" (84). Furthermore, officials were instructed to make the Six Nations "duly sensible of the Parental regard which His Majesty feels for them" (84). This use of paternalistic language would have greatly angered the Haudenosaunee, for it misrepresented their long relationship as political allies of the Crown in very serious ways, and served as evidence that their claims of autonomy in Upper Canada were not being taken seriously. Such language violated the principles of both the Two Row Wampum and the Silver Covenant Chain agreements.

In a letter written 10 December 1798, Brant seems to realize the extent of colonial attitudes that were now encroaching upon Six Nations sovereignty, and in which direction the relationship with the Crown appeared to be heading: "we have even been prohibited from taking tenants on [our lands], it having been represented as inconsistent for us, being but King's allies, to have King's subjects as tenants, consequently I suppose their real meaning was, we should in a manner be but tenants ourselves, as for me I see no difference in it any further than that we are as yet rent free" ([1798] 1998, 14). Sounding rather ominous, Brant indicates his growing distrust of colonial officials who were placing increased restrictions on the freedom of the Six Nations in Upper Canada to do as they saw fit in their new territory. Furthermore, Brant is highly aware of his own position as a military officer within the British hierarchy, and uses this fact to both include *and* distance himself from Crown authority:

> I hope I shall not tire your patience, in making a few remarks on what I suppose may naturally be the thoughts of Government on our conduct—With respect to myself they might say he has half pay and yet talks so much on these matters, it is very true I enjoy that bounty of his Majesty, so many worthless fellows like me do, that have never risked their property or any thing else in his causes but am I for this entirely to forsake the interests of my people? that put their dependence on me besides my family which is very numerous cannot be benefitted by my half pay when I am no more; which at my time of life I have reason to look on as a period not so very distant. I think it therefore incumbent on me to secure what they must look to for a future support. ([1798] 1998, 14–15)

By employing such "us" and "them" language, Brant clearly aligns himself with the collective interests of the Haudenosaunee at Grand River, and once again points out the sacrifices that they made as allies of the British. Their losses in the war, he suggests, were much greater than those Loyalist neighbours who had now begun to exploit the weakened state of the Six Nations immediately after their relocation by demanding the best portions of their land. As a result, he recognizes that the future well-being of the Haudenosaunee was threatened in ways that other settlers in the area would not have to contend with.

Another important issue to contemplate is Brant's understanding of what the Haldimand Deed entailed—surely he saw the Six Nations as autonomous peoples, but the British obviously had their own understanding of land ownership and the suitability of Native control over territory in Upper Canada. Despite Brant's military record, his education and religious beliefs, it was quite apparent that the British still regarded him merely as an Indian. Therefore, his assertions of Six Nations sovereignty and independence were grudgingly tolerated so long as the Haudenosaunee remained potentially useful as military resources to the British in the unstable period between the Revolution and the War of 1812. What the British failed to realize, I would argue, is Brant's own understanding of his identity and how much he retained a belief in the ways and customs of the Haudenosaunee, despite his outward speech and appearance. This would include an intimate knowledge of how the political and social structure was intertwined in Haudenosaunee tradition, and how closely these belief systems were tied to the land and people's relationship with it.

While he may have been an Anglican and a British officer, Brant also understood that he was the descendant of a centuries-old Confederacy of nations that had survived many dark periods by turning to ancient oral traditions that had proven useful in solving contemporary problems. In this way, Brant would have been able to see their new situation, not as surrender to the "Fate of War" (Haldimand [1784b] 1964, 52–53) that had befallen them, but as another epoch of their history. Using his European education alongside Haudenosaunee intellectual tradition, Brant saw the Six Nations' situation differently than did the British administrators he was dealing with. They saw themselves as assisting an unfortunate people (whose lands could be exploited in the process), while Brant and the rest of the Haudenosaunee— not just at Grand River—undoubtedly saw their new reality as the most recent pattern of upheaval, change, and renewal that was so embedded in their oral traditions, both sacred and secular. It was therefore up to them to determine how well they could adapt their already existing traditions to the situation in which they now found themselves.

A letter written in November 1806 provides evidence of this attempt to reassert political custom and marks the emergence of a strong, united Confederacy at Grand River. This letter requests further clarification regarding land rights and inquires about the monies received for Grand River lands that had been sold. Although Brant was in constant communication with British officials on these issues, this is one of the earliest pieces of writing that identifies a collective position of leadership and alludes to traditional approaches to government among the Haudenosaunee: "We have already expressed in a preceding Speech at Niagara that the Council Fire of the Five Nations had been again re-established at the Onondaga's on the Grand River, & that in conformity to the customs of our ancestors, at this general Council Fire every affair of importance, relating to the whole confederacy,

Portrait of Joseph Brant in his later years. (Courtesy of Deyohahá:ge: Indigenous Knowledge Centre, Six Nations)

should be deliberated on, & agreed to by the Chiefs of the different tribes, before it should be passed as the unanimous voice of the Five Nations" (Six Nations' Council [1806] 1964, 136). Whether the impetus behind this letter was to assert a stronger collective voice by reference to traditional procedure rather than rely on Brant as the sole communicator or as a means by which to decrease his power is difficult to ascertain. His is one of three signatures on the letter, however, so it is apparent that he was included and aware of its contents. Whatever the case, the Confederacy Council of Chiefs appeared to be officially announcing that they were "back in business" along the Grand River. Such a declaration on their part was a timely and strategic step, for it was this same governing body with which the Europeans had been negotiating for over 200 years. Therefore, the assertions of sovereignty that Brant had been making as an individual were now coming from the very council that had first established this nation-to-nation relationship with the Crown.

The emphasis on more traditional structures of government indicated a renewed reliance upon the political philosophies of the Haudenosaunee. As mentioned earlier, Brant was acculturated to a degree, and despite his strong advocacy of the sovereign rights of the Six Nations, he seems to have avoided any outright mention of the Great Law as a guiding spiritual and political doctrine in his correspondence; neither did he refer to the agreements with the British as encoded into the many dozen wampum belts that existed. Surely, he was aware of these philosophies and their significance but chose instead to enter into the legal discourse familiar to the British. Whether he believed that the British would not understand such Indigenous philosophies or that the Six Nations situation could in fact be articulated convincingly through the English language and legal system is difficult, if not impossible, to determine. When Brant did attempt to reconcile the two kinds of language, he appears very self-conscious. An example of this occurs in a speech delivered at Fort George in February 1801. Following traditional protocol, he delivers a short "condolence" speech to Captain Claus, one of the British negotiators, whose mother had recently passed away. The purpose of this speech, part of a much longer ceremony among the Haudenosaunee, is to clear the mind of someone who has suffered the loss of a loved one and to prepare him or her for the business at hand so that they can continue to negotiate in a positive manner: "Brother! We are here now met in the presence of the Spirit above, with the intent to keep up the ancient custom of condolement. ... Brother! We therefore with this string of Wampum wipe away the tears from your eyes and would take away all sorrow from your heart. But that is impossible, still it is the customary way of making the speech. We, therefore, mention it and with the said Wampum we wipe away all stains of whatever should remain on your seat so that you may sit down in comfort" ([1801] 1998,16). This short passage is interesting, for Brant's brief aside suggests that he is not entirely comfortable with the substance of the speech. He seems almost embarrassed that the words he speaks cannot have their desired effect, that to ease one's suffering at times of mourning is "impossible."

Brant's words in this instance betray the inner conflict that he may have felt when referring to the ancient customs and procedures of his people. Perhaps to him, as an educated Christian, they were of little use in the new social reality in which the Haudenosaunee now found themselves. This symptom of cultural unease would then have presented a much larger problem for Brant as he carried on discussions with the British, for in establishing the independence of the Haudenosaunee he would have been forced to articulate a distinct Haudenosaunee belief system in which spirituality, metaphor, and political dialogue are often linked closely together. These philosophies and oral traditions consist of myriad doctrines that would have seemed peculiar to the European mind, both then and now. They are, however, essential philosophies to convey in order to provide an accurate account of how the Haudenosaunee view their place in the world and their ongoing relationships among themselves and with other peoples. Such ideology is the foundation of our belief in our sovereign identity; as Creek writer Craig Womack has argued, "A key component of nationhood is a people's idea of themselves, their imaginings of who they are" (14).

Vine Deloria Jr. argues that Western philosophy has long regarded American Indians and other tribal peoples "as the last remnants of a hypothetical earlier stage of cultural evolution, and this so-called 'primitive stage' of human development is a necessary preamble to any discussion of human beings and the meaning of their lives" (2004, 3). He suggests that the West "needs" the stereotype of the primitive in order to "anchor the whole edifice of Western social thought" so that it can "congratulate" itself on how far it has come. As a result, "the attitude of many philosophers is that American Indians must represent the stage of human development in which superstition and ignorance reigned supreme" (3). Given this contemporary belief among Western intellectuals, Deloria asks if there was ever a time "when tribal peoples and Western peoples could have discussed abstract concepts in a philosophical setting?" (4). He believes that this time existed in the first centuries of contact between the two groups, when most Indigenous peoples were isolated from the industrial world. This, of course, is the precise setting in which Brant was openly engaged in discourse with the British and had the most opportunity to exchange intellectual ideas with them. While he and other Haudenosaunee leaders certainly attempted to explain and demonstrate their traditions and beliefs to the British, they were merely tolerated or, at worst, largely ignored. Significantly, but not surprisingly, the protocol and other forms of social propriety required by Six Nation councils were closely followed by the British in the decades prior to the American Revolution—when the Haudenosaunee retained real power in New York State—but these customs appeared to fall off considerably immediately following the conflict and soon gave way to more paternalistic attitudes as the British began to control the political agenda.

Other than the occasional mention of such things as condolence speeches taking place at meetings (as outlined above) it would seem that the Haudenosaunee also refrained from invoking traditional philosophies while in discussions with the British, at least according to the written documents that exist. Although the Two Row Wampum was the first and most important treaty agreement that was made between the Haudenosaunee and the British during the seventeenth century, it appears to have played no direct role in Brant's negotiations over the land issue at Grand River. As described in the introduction, the Two Row Wampum symbolizes the "separate but equal" relationship that is to exist between the Haudenosaunee and the European nations. Although this agreement was a fundamental point in the debate over land title in Upper Canada, for some reason Brant chose not to employ this historical understanding of nationhood. Given the time and energy that he devoted to this cause, one would assume that this particular wampum belt, that spoke to the issue so well, should have been the centre of the negotiation process. Why, then, did Brant not call upon the philosophical content of the

Two Row, or its mutually agreed-upon principles, when asserting sovereignty at Grand River? Once again, his failure to do so would suggest Brant's somewhat uncomfortable relationship with oral tradition and, perhaps, his experience of how British officials perceived such things. While he firmly believed that the Haudenosaunee were autonomous people, based upon their history and traditions, he seems to have been reluctant to discuss how the spiritual philosophies of the Great Law created the very government that he represented. In addition, it would have been difficult to express the unique identity of his people when Brant himself was an acculturated person in many ways. In other words, if one were to apply the ideology of the Two Row, that the vessel carrying the onkwehnonwe contained their language, dress, and religion, Brant would have probably looked more at home in the European "boat." Such appearances could not have been lost on those colonial officials who were negotiating with him.

Although the political philosophy contained in the Two Row Wampum may have been absent in the early discussions concerning sovereignty and political boundaries at Grand River, the fact that the Confederacy Council gained increasing presence in the early 1800s signalled a return to a more traditional governmental and social structure within the community. At this time, documents began to appear that emphasize the presence and authority of a restored Hereditary Council at Grand River. Not surprisingly, these documents also address traditional concepts and protocol and, ironically enough, are written in English, evidence of a community that is becoming more comfortable with writing as a means to communicate for political purpose.

A letter written at "Onondaga, Grand River" on 19 February 1807 and signed by thirty-seven men (many of them Chiefs), begins with a lengthy evocation that reflects the words traditionally spoken when greeting those who have gathered to meet in council: "The Master of life whose seat is in the Heavens, the arbitrator of all events, has been pleased to permit, that this should be the day of our meeting. Him, from whom we derive our existence I salute in gratitude for his many favors, & for having preserved you who yet remain of the Chiefs & Warriors whom I now view in the enjoyment of health listening for the narrative they are now expecting to hear" ("Letter" 1807). This document is unique in that it reads like a transcript of a meeting among the Confederacy Council, who are assembled to make a request for yet another clarification on the status of their lands along the Grand River. There are also several important clues within it as to how the council was operating at that time, and how it viewed itself as an independent entity removed from the Confederacy Council that existed at Onondaga, New York during the same period. While the two councils were aware of each other, and remain in close communication to this day, it is obvious from the following that the council at Grand River was conscious of its status as a renewed form of government in a new territory. After describing the difficulties that prevailed in establishing the council at Grand River, the author(s) of this letter declare,

> Let us repair the house & securely shut it against that intruding evil which has so much involved us as nearly to extinguish our Council Fire so much revered by our ancestors who left it for us—such was its truthe that while the system of our confederacy was in its vigour—as the ascending smoke mixed with the clouds it was viewed by all the surrounding people with reverential awe.... Let us without delay raise again the house now falling into decay, rekindle the Fire which our Ancestors gave us from the yet remaining embers, that our brethren & mutual children may have a secure dwelling, & that the Fire may shine clearly so as to be distinguishable by all our brethren & that it may be looked on with respect by those of the West as it was when the glory of our Confederacy remained. ("Letter" 1807)

While it is unclear exactly what the "intruding evil" was that is spoken of here, it may possibly be the rhetorical language used to describe the general chaos of the Revolution that fractured the Confederacy three decades earlier. This disruption, and the resulting need to strengthen the "longhouse" of the Six Nations, is also in keeping with the pattern of renewal that follows such catastrophic events, as well as employing the metaphor of the nations of the Confederacy comprising a single household.

Mohawk scholar Michael Doxtater describes the image of "sheltering the sources of our happiness" (2001, 10) as a significant concept within Haudenosaunee philosophical thought. He suggests that within the agricultural worldview that predominates Haudenosaunee ways of thinking, knowledge is also seen as something that should be sheltered from disruptive forces and nurtured in much the same way that seeds need to be protected in order for them to germinate, grow, and provide sustenance for the people. Consequently, the metaphor of constructing a house is also of tremendous importance within the Great Law tradition and is symbolic of the completed longhouse in which the original Five Nations were to dwell as relatives after accepting peace among themselves. According to Doxtater, this too is an important concept, for people also need to be protected and healed during times of sickness and distress; such was the situation following the relocation to Grand River in 1785. He believes that the Haudenosaunee longhouse is a "sign-and-symbol-of-culture," and that the physical, and metaphorical, building of this structure "teaches us that interdependency has the potential to heal conflict, restore peace, and mediate change" (19). Thus, the "house" referred to in this letter from 1807, with its brightly burning fire, is significant because it represents the renewed life of the Confederacy Council and its ability to protect the people. This is also characterized by the image of the "embers" of the original Council Fire that was lit by "our Ancestors," a symbolic connection to the past and reaffirmation of upholding tradition with all of its attendant responsibilities. In other words, as bad as things may be, it is important to remember that there are still remnants of the past that can be brought forward and made useful in the present.

The letter above is also interesting because Brant's name does not appear on it, nor is there any mention of him or his activities. It is possible that he was either ill or at the home he had recently built on Burlington Bay, the plot of land that was provided him by the Crown in payment for his military duties. At this point, he was approximately sixty-five years old and no longer in the best of health. While there is evidence of his attendance at meetings during this time, sources indicate that he was often weakened from travel and unable to oversee negotiations in the manner that he had previously (Taylor 2007, 364). During this time, however, Brant gave his close friend John Norton (Teyoninhokarawen) the responsibility to continue this work. It is quite possible that the highly literate Norton authored the letter above, as his name appears on it, along with several other pieces of correspondence from this period. Although he was not a hereditary Chief within the Confederacy Council, and was in fact a Cherokee/Scotch adopted into the Mohawk nation, Norton rose to prominence at Grand River in the early

1800s and appears to have been a well-trusted individual who lobbied for Six Nations rights with almost as much enthusiasm as Brant himself.

Because Brant had great difficulty in travelling by this point, Norton was sent as his emissary to England in order to inquire directly about the Six Nations land title in 1804. According to a source at the time, he was "commissioned by a grand Councel [sic] of the 5 nation's [sic] to undertake this important Embassy; and for this purpose procured credentials from Capt. Brant & from the concel [sic] of the 5 nations; to this was affixed a seal representing a turtle, a wolf, & a Bear" ("An Account" [1804?] 1964, 271). From this evidence, we can assume that Norton had the full backing of the Grand River Confederacy Council, who entrusted him with their wishes. However, he was still an "outsider," and his requests that British officials take action on the Six Nations' behalf were, as the passage below suggests, less aggressive than Brant's assertions of sovereignty over the lands at Grand River: "It is therefore humbly hoped that His Majesty's Ministers will consider their case, and either of themselves give redress or send instructions to the Governors of Canada, for that purpose, so as the brave and loyal Six Nations may enjoy that security and comfort which Government originally intended for them, as well as that these tribes may be preserved entire and confirmed in their attachment to the British cause, which they have always been forward to support" (Norton [1804] 1964, 272–73). Despite the fact that Norton was not one of their own people, the Council at Grand River trusted that he would not misrepresent them. This too can be interpreted as faith in their cultural belief system, since the Haudenosaunee have many oral traditions that speak to the beneficial influence that outsiders can have on their society. Therefore, Norton's position within the Grand River community would have been seen not as their dependent need to have others speak for them, but as the employment of a useful ally who had the potential to effect positive change. While they no doubt also looked upon this situation pragmatically, the more traditionally minded Chiefs of the time may have also understood individuals like Norton in this more philosophical way.

Norton's reminder that the Six Nations are "brave and loyal" allies to the Crown also meant that to ignore their requests could result in their reluctance to join with the British the next time the need arose. While the War of 1812 was still a few years away, it was obvious to the British that further conflict with the Americans was quite possible. Furthermore, the fact that Brant was now aged and losing influence at Grand River must have been a concern for the British, since for decades they had relied heavily on his ability to maintain support for the Crown among the Haudenosaunee, despite his frustrations over the land question. With the Confederacy Council of Chiefs asserting more authority in Upper Canada, colonial officials could not be confident that the more traditional contingent of the Six Nations would once again engage in a conflict after they had paid such a price in the previous one. Settling the land issue would have certainly promoted good relations with the Haudenosaunee, as Norton suggests, but the Crown did little to address the problem and the issue remained unresolved at the time of Brant's death in November 1807.

Nevertheless, the Six Nations of Grand River did participate as allies of the Crown in the War of 1812, although somewhat reluctantly and only after much intense lobbying on the part of British military officials, who urged their service in one speech at the beginning of the conflict by asserting that "they were bound by every tie of gratitude and interest to take up Arms during the present contest with the United States in defence of their King, their Country and their personal safety" (Willcocks [1812]1964, 196). While the Six Nations' responses to these pleas were not generally recorded, their slow reaction in getting substantial numbers of men to volunteer is evidence that they were not especially sympathetic to the British cause. It was not until the Battle of Beaver Dams in May 1813 that a large contingent of warriors, approximately 250, from Grand River took part. Pleased with the Six Nations' participation in this successful battle—one that is so significant to Canadian history—it is apparent that the British expected further support and were angered when it did not occur. In a speech to the Six Nations in October 1813, General John Vincent expressed the following: "Brothers I will not conceal from you my surprise and disappointment, in having failed when making an appeal to your friendship—Having requested ... a party consisting of only thirty or forty of the Six Nations to join the Troops ... at Stoney Creek, I had much reason to feel mortified on being informed that the Chiefs could not persuade that number to go out" (Vincent [1813]1964, 207). Once again, the Haudenosaunee were being asked to fight a war that was not of their making but that directly affected their lives due to the close proximity of the conflict to their homes. From their reluctance to join the British, it is obvious that their attachment to the Crown was rather tenuous, particularly without Joseph Brant to influence their decision. Moreover, the fact that the "fire" of their Confederacy Council had recently been "rekindled" among them after years of social turbulence, and that this renewed tradition was a spiritual and political structure founded on peace and unity, the people of Grand River must have looked upon another war with grave misgivings.[4] Significantly, the influence of John Norton, known primarily as a Mohawk "war Chief," also dissolved during this period, and he removed himself from Grand River shortly after the war.

Although Joseph Brant's son, John (1794–1832), inherited much of his father's status among the Six Nations, including that of able warrior in the War of 1812 and local politician, he was not the charismatic figure that Brant had been. While he did continue to actively promote Christianity and education, two initiatives begun by his father, the Grand River community was reluctant to fully embrace such practices. According to several sources, the presence of European religion and training appeared to have little effect on the overall "habits and dispositions of the Indians [who] are ... opposed to civilization." John Howison, after visiting Grand River in 1821, went so far as to conclude that "various attempts have been made to civilize the Indians; but the failure of most of these, with the very partial success of others, convincingly proves, that they are a people whose habits and characters are incapable of improvement, & not susceptible of amelioration" ([1821]1964, 291). This resistance to adopting the ways of the "whites" is easily understood given the treatment that the Haudenosaunee had received from the colonial population; they simply had little respect for the culture of a people who had repeatedly betrayed their trust for several decades. In addition, as one government report stated in 1842, "the glaring inconsistency ... between the profession and practice of many of the nominal Christians among the white people who have settled around them, and who are generally of very bad character, has furnished them with a plausible objection to the Christian Religion" ("Past and Present"[1842] 1964, 310).

Another significant event in Haudenosaunee society that would lead to an even further distancing from settler culture was occurring in New York State during this period and would eventually find its way to Grand River in the 1830s. As discussed in the Introduction, this movement, known as the Gaihwi'yo, or Code of Handsome Lake, was a revitalist doctrine that called upon the Haudenosaunee to isolate themselves from outside influences that would cause them to lose their identities as *onkwehonwe*, or Native people. Contained within these teachings was a strict forbidding of Christian beliefs as well as a strong warning against the "white man's education." Clearly, such a movement was directed at maintaining a strong core of Haudenosaunee values in the face of an ever-encroaching European population, and it countered the very values that Joseph Brant had promoted just a few years earlier.

Despite a strong presence of Handsome Lake's teachings at Grand River throughout the mid-nineteenth century, a considerable number of the people there were Christians who allowed their children to be educated either at the boarding school established by the New England Company in Brantford or in one of the five day schools that were established in the community. One report described the status of education at Grand River in 1842:

> A few years ago there was difficulty in procuring 14 Scholars for this [boarding] School. There are now fifty applications in addition to the 50 already there ... The total number of Children under instruction, including those at the Boarding School is 160. The mode of teaching is the same as that among Common Schools for the Whites, and the Books in use are those recommended by the Board of Education—Viz—the Bible, Mavor's spelling book, English Reader, Daboll's Arithmetic, Murray's English Grammar and Geography— The Instruction is carried on altogether in English. The children shew as much aptitude in acquiring Knowledge as the Whites. ("Past and Present" [1842]1964, 310)

By this point, the legacy of Joseph Brant's influence at Grand River was quite evident. The Haudenosaunee were successful farmers, many of them were Christian, and the children were being encouraged to become educated in the ways of the European. Traditional beliefs and practice were still widespread, however, and the existence of the two religious faiths alongside each other did not appear to interfere with people's daily routines or marriage practices. Iroquoian languages were strong, and most people spoke a number of them, along with English. The question of Six Nations ownership of the Grand River tract was an ongoing issue that was not resolved until a heated internal debate over a "general surrender" of lands in 1841 resulted in the present-day reserve boundaries that were permanently established in 1851. Ultimately, Joseph Brant never did receive his wish—that the Haudenosaunee would be "sovereigns of the soil" in their territory—since all reserve lands in Canada were ruled as belonging to the Crown in 1868. This remains the situation to this day.

What, then, to make of Brant and his attempts at negotiating Haudenosaunee independence in the face of an overwhelming imposition of colonial authority? Was he assertive enough in his claims of Six Nations sovereignty? Did he compromise traditional Haudenosaunee customs and beliefs in order to appease British officials? Or was he also a victim of colonial paternalism that refused to allow any form of First Nations autonomy in Upper Canada, or elsewhere? While recent scholarship leans toward a more nuanced assessment of his Haudenosaunee identity, the following words, written by William E. Palmer in 1872, still speak quite well to the enigma that is Joseph Brant/Thayendanegea, even as we continue to engage with his story in the present: "Much has been written about the distinguished Chief of the Mohawks, who, perhaps, in all the phases of his character, was the most celebrated of all the Aborigines who have distinguished themselves in the eyes of Europeans on this continent since the work of civilization began. But in general his history has been so mixed up with that of contemporaneous events, that without access to extensive libraries of books, and an intelligent and careful study and comparison of impartial authorities, a true index to the character and acts of Cpt. Joseph Brant was impossible" (1872). More recently, historian James W. Paxton asserts that "Brant excites strong feelings among scholars and modern Haudenosaunee alike. Viewed from the vantage point of the present day, [Brant] appears to be a cultural chameleon, shifting effortlessly back and forth between Mohawk and English cultures." As a result, Paxton concludes that "it is easy to be disappointed with him," but then goes on to make an important observation that could only emerge from our early-twenty-first century perspective: "Secretly, perhaps, we would prefer that he acted more like Pontiac or Tecumseh, that he had led warriors in a brave but futile attempt to preserve his people's land and culture.

Such desires say more about us than about Brant, more about the pervasive and pernicious idea that First Nations cultures are static and unchanging, and more about an imagined past than about the hard realities and limited choices of living under colonialism" (2008, 78). Despite the wealth of historical records that are now available to us regarding Brant's motives in negotiating Grand River lands, Paxton is correct in stating that, living in the present, none of us, Haudenosaunee and non-Haudenosaunee alike, could ever accurately assess the complexities of navigating late-eighteenth-century colonialism and its designs for all First Nations. Late in his life, Brant himself appears to have recognized how he underestimated the deceitful nature of British officials when he lamented that "my sincere attachment [to England] has ruined the Interests of my Nation" (quoted in Paxton 2008, 77).

Two hundred years after his death, Brant therefore remains something of a controversial figure at Grand River. It is quite fitting, then, that another compelling individual from Six Nations first gained attention at an event honouring his life in 1886. At that time, a statue of Brant was unveiled in Brantford, Ontario in order to commemorate his life and to celebrate the centennial of the town's settlement. In attendance was a twenty-five-year-old woman from Six Nations named Emily Pauline Johnson, who had been commissioned by the city of Brantford to write a poem for the occasion, entitled "Brant: A Memorial Ode." Like Brant, she was an acculturated, educated Mohawk who advocated for a reconciliation of British and Iroquoian differences, and like the famous Thayendanegea, she has been looked upon with a mixture of celebration and criticism in her own community. Her story, and her literary vision for Native people, will be the focus of the following chapter.

2

The Challenge to Haudenosaunee Nationhood *Performing Politics, Translating Culture*

In 1895, Emily Pauline Johnson published a short newspaper piece in *The Brantford Expositor* entitled "The Iroquois Women of Canada." Addressing the popular misconception that "an Indian is an Indian, an inadequate sort of person possessing a red brown skin, nomadic habits, and an inability for public affairs," Johnson argued that "the great Red population of America, differ as much one from another, as do the white races of Europe" (2002, 203). She outlines quickly the political and military history of the Iroquois, before describing the Iroquois woman of the day:

> That the women of this Iroquois race are superior in many ways to their less
> fortunate sisters throughout Canada, is hardly necessary to state. Women who
> have had in the yesterdays a noble and pure-blooded ancestry, who look out on
> the to-morrows with minds open to educational acquirements; women whose
> grandmothers were the mothers of fighting men, whose daughters will be the
> mothers of men elbowing their way to the front ranks in the great professional
> and political arena in Canada; women whose thrift and care and morality
> will count for their nation, when that nation is just at its turn of tide toward
> civilization and advancement, are not the women to sit with idle hands and

brains, caring not for the glories of yesterday, nor the conquests of to-morrow. (203–204)

Johnson's direct statement regarding the "superiority" of Iroquois women over, presumably, the women of other First Nations is troubling and problematic, as is her implication that the reason for this hierarchy is that Iroquois women are more like other "white" Canadian women. Perhaps this is the reason why this piece, written at the height of her popularity, does not appear under her own name, but rather as "By One of Them," as if she were anxious to self-identify, albeit anonymously, as one of those acculturated Iroquois women who had more in common with her non-Native counterparts than other First Nations women.

Certainly, Johnson's romantic descriptions are designed to educate mainstream readers as to the strengths of Iroquois women and the cultural differences among Native people generally, but they also reveal something more: a strong desire to place the Iroquois as an "almost" assimilated people, elevating them to a better social status than other Indigenous groups:

> The Iroquois woman of to-day is one who recognizes the responsibilities of her position, and who makes serious and earnest efforts to possess and master whatever advantages may drift her way. She has already acquired the arts of cookery, of needlework, and of house-wifeliness, and one has but to attend the annual Industrial Exhibition on the Indian reserve, an Institution that is open to all Indians in Canada, who desire to compete for prizes, to convince themselves by very material arguments that the Iroquois woman is behind her white sister in nothing pertaining to the larder, the dairy or the linen press. (2002, 204)

While it is clear that Johnson attempts to champion the rights of Native women within this piece and uses her own celebrity status as a means to gain access to publication in order to express these sentiments, the tension that so often surfaces in her writing—the pull between her Iroquois identity and the desire to make herself, and all Iroquois, more acculturated Canadians— are also apparent here. As Haudenosaunee literary scholar Mishuana Goeman argues, "At a time when instituted European government policies were attempting to construct Native women in the image of European contemporaries or exile and expunge them from the nations "proper" territory, Johnson advocated for what was commonly understood as women's rights or women's autonomy and sovereignty and often invoked sentimental discourses to rationalize the inclusion of Native women as part of the nation" (Goeman 2013, 44). Given these multiple and often competing agendas, what was Johnson's vision of Iroquois/Haudenosaunee nationhood? How did she view her work as contributing to this vision? Did she believe the Iroquois to be a sovereign nation that should resist assimilation, or were they simply a group of people who were meant to accept the circumstances that "may drift [their] way"? A century after her death, Pauline Johnson remains an enigmatic figure who continues to capture our attention, since her life and work are so remarkable in the context of the time in which she lived. Although she has been the subject of no fewer than three major publications in recent years, these texts have not studied her as a community member or an Indigenous figure who voiced political views during a very turbulent time for First Nations, Métis, and Inuit peoples. Engaging with her work in relation to the political climate that spanned the decades between the creation of the Indian Act in 1876 and the time of her death in 1913, it is evident that her conflicted opinions were both useful and damaging to Indigenous peoples in Canada. Although she was not the only member of the Grand River community who was writing at this time, she is certainly the best known, and for this reason her work will be the predominant focus of this chapter.

At the time of Johnson's birth in March 1861 the boundaries of the Six Nations reserve had only recently been set, after decades of dispute over land title that had persisted since the time of Joseph Brant. The traditional Confederacy Council was still the official governing body of the reserve and effectively managed the day-to-day affairs of the approximately 3,000 people who lived there. Although roughly half of the Confederacy Chiefs were Christian, there seems to have been little conflict between longhouse adherents and those who attended church on the reserve, with many people observing various forms of both traditions. Families were aware of their matrilineal clan affiliation, and hereditary Chiefs were appointed in the traditional way, through the ancient Condolence Ceremony that was prescribed by the Peacemaker hundreds of years before. Although the movement that later became known as the "Dehorner" campaign was still some years away,

The Six Nations Council House built by the Confederacy Chiefs in 1863, four years before the Confederation of Canada. The Council House still stands in the main village of Ohsweken. (Courtesy of Deyohahá:ge: Indigenous Knowledge Centre, Six Nations)

there were "progressive" individuals on the reserve who were beginning to be critical of the Confederacy Council,[1] since they felt that their interests were being overlooked by leaders who did not subscribe to the same assimilative philosophies they did.

Pauline's father, George Johnson, was one of those men considered a progressive by the standards of the day, and her grandfather, John "Smoke" Johnson, was a respected veteran of the War of 1812 as well as a noted orator on the reserve. Although George was not in line to become a hereditary Chief, his mother, Nellie Martin, was an influential Mohawk Clanmother who used her status to ensure that her well-educated son would have some form of power within the Council. Consequently, he was made a Mohawk Wolf Clan Chief and eventually became the official translator of Council business and the mediator between the Chiefs at Grand River and the authorities of Upper Canada, a post often held by his father. This was a very important and lucrative position, one that he took great pride in and which was reflected in the house he constructed along the Grand River in 1855. Chiefswood, as he called it, was the largest home on the reservation, with two identical "front" entrances. One faced south to the river and greeted visitors from the reserve, and the other faced north and greeted non-Native visitors from all over North America. Pauline was born in this home on 10 March 1861, and its influence never seemed to leave her, as her work always had the sense of speaking from a double perspective.

While George Johnson was an outgoing and well-liked individual, Pauline's non-Native mother, Emily Howells, was much more reserved and withdrawn, never quite being accepted into the social life of the reserve. Although mixed marriages were not uncommon at this time, the overwhelming majority of them were between Native women and white men. Therefore, many people at the time, both Native and non-Native, had some difficulty accepting George and Emily's marriage, including their own families. Despite these social difficulties, Emily was a doting mother who instilled a love of literature and music in all of her children from an early age. Since she was a direct relation to the noted American author William Dean Howells, Emily provided Pauline with a literary pedigree that, along with her father's position on the reserve, gave the young woman a sense of privilege and opportunity.

Her most significant connection to Mohawk identity and cultural life on the reserve was her grandfather, John "Smoke" Johnson (1792–1886). As a young girl, Pauline would listen as he told stories of Iroquois history and their prowess on the battlefield, as well as their great skills at diplomacy. These stories would have a lifelong effect on her and her work. They served as the basis for such writings as "Brant: A Memorial Ode," "Ojistoh," "Wehhro's Sacrifice," and the piece mentioned above, "The Iroquois Women of Canada." Because he was a Pine Tree Chief who knew Joseph Brant and a veteran of the War of 1812, Smoke Johnson was an important witness to events on the Six Nations reserve through much of the nineteenth century.

Unfortunately, he left behind very little written record of his knowledge of Six Nations history. Some material was published on his collaboration with noted anthropologist Horatio Hale, and his granddaughter was one of the few individuals who transformed his oral narratives into writing, albeit in poetic and fictional form. She clearly regretted the further opportunities she had missed, however, and upon his death in 1886 wrote, "I shall never forgive myself for letting grandfather die, with his wealth of knowledge, and I did not find out more of what he knew" (Gray 2002, 86). This sentiment is a common one within communities that are largely based upon oral cultures, particularly during periods of substantial change, such as those that the people at Grand River were experiencing in the nineteenth and early twentieth century, when Pauline was at the peak of her popularity. While her grandfather certainly excited her interest in Iroquois legend and history, there can be no doubt that Pauline employed creative licence in her later approaches to Six Nations subject matter, as she often relied on literary and fictionalized accounts rather than historical or traditional representations of important cultural information. Furthermore, her views on Iroquois nationalism and its place within Canada were predominantly her own, since it appears that she was rather isolated from the political environment at Grand River, especially after her father's death in February 1884 and the family's subsequent move to Brantford later that year. Without the support of her father's government salary, Pauline, then twenty-three years old, began to look seriously toward writing as a career.

SETH NEWHOUSE AND THE GREAT LAW AT GRAND RIVER

1884 was also the year that the federal government began to devise more aggressive policies toward the elimination of traditional governments through the creation of the Indian Advancement Act, with the aim of installing elected band councils on every reservation. Since the passing of the Gradual Civilization Act in 1869, later to become known as The Indian Act in 1876, Canada had been actively engaged in the process of assimilating the Native population into the "body politic" of the country, and the new Advancement policy directly targeted First Nation leadership. At around the same time that Pauline Johnson began to develop her literary voice, others at Grand River also began to employ the written word as a means of resistance to Canada's political agenda of assimilation and acculturation.

One of the most interesting individuals to emerge during this time was Seth Newhouse (1842–1921), a "self-appointed historian" who some consider to be "the most productive Iroquoian scribe of the nineteenth century" (Weaver 1984, 166). Raised in a predominantly Christian family and educated at the Mohawk Institute in Brantford, Newhouse was an Onondaga/Mohawk who began gathering material on oral traditions around Grand River and at other Haudenosaunee communities in the early 1870s, with the intention of translating the Great Law and other cultural narratives into English. Although not a hereditary Chief through matrilineal lines, he was raised up as an Onondaga Pine Tree Chief around 1875 and was a vocal member of the Confederacy Council, being both politically minded and fluent in Mohawk, Onondaga, and English. There is some debate as to whether Newhouse was commissioned by the Council to embark upon his translation work or was acting on his own accord, but all sources agree that he did so as a response to the mounting pressure felt at Grand River to comply with the Indian Act of 1876. This infamous document outlined a series of restrictive policies for all Native people in Canada, including the dissolution of all existing traditional councils and the establishment of a federally approved elected-council system, all as a means of controlling activity on reserves. Although they grew increasingly concerned over such federal legislation, the hereditary Chiefs at Grand River believed that they were exempt from Canadian law regarding Native people since the Confederacy had successfully governed the Six Nations community for at least seven decades prior to the creation of the Indian Act. Furthermore, the Confederacy had long maintained their nationhood and a close political relationship with the British Crown, which included the Haldimand Deed and other treaties, and which they intended to uphold rather than begin a new relationship with Canada. Some members of Council, including Newhouse, felt that if the federal government required documented proof that the Haudenosaunee had an established political structure, they merely needed to put their traditions down on paper to verify that they too had a "constitution" that clearly defined their unique political identity as a sovereign nation within Canada. As early as 1880, Newhouse had completed a short draft of the Great Law in English, but it is the 312-page handwritten document that he completed five years later, titled "Cosmogony of De-ka-na-wi-da's Government of the Iroquois Confederacy," that has captured the most attention, and which has yet to be published in its entirety.

During this turbulent period, the Confederacy Council at Grand River had to contend not only with pressures from Ottawa but also with the small but increasingly vocal "Dehorner movement" in the community, which was also advocating for an elected system to replace the hereditary Chiefs. Charging that the Confederacy Council was outmoded, slow, and ineffective in making decisions that addressed current conditions, these reform-minded individuals at Grand River tended to be educated Christians who had no access to local government since they were not in line for a hereditary title. As a result, they believed that their interests were not being met by the traditional leaders who tended to be conservative-minded men the progressives felt were not educated enough to understand and negotiate with the Canadian government.

Because Newhouse was positioned between these two camps, being a Pine Tree Chief from a predominantly Christian background, it is not surprising that the written version of the Great Law that he brought forward for the Council to consider in 1885 was an attempt to reconcile the oral tradition with modern policies and procedures that were more conducive to expediting the traditional decision-making process and the selection of Chiefs, two of the major complaints brought against the hereditary system. Although he begins his text with a narrative retelling of the birth of the Peacemaker and his subsequent travels, he presents the Great Law itself in three sections: "The Tree of the Long Leaves," "The Emblematic Union Compact," and "Skanawatih's Law of Peace and War." These divisions were entirely constructed by Newhouse, as they had no apparent relationship to the Great Law in its original oral form. In addition, the story of the Peacemaker and his instructions are largely presented as a series of protocols that appear with Roman numerals and subsection Arabic numbers, presumably as a way to better represent lawmaking procedure. Also included in his manuscript is a strong emphasis on the importance of the Mohawk nation, seemingly as a means to placate the more progressive Mohawks who were constantly lobbying for a stronger voice within local government at Grand River. For example, he writes, "6 ... the Mohawk Lords [are] the heads and the leaders

of the Five Nations Confederacy. The Mohawk Lords are the foundation of the
Great Peace and it shall, therefore, be against the Great Binding Law to pass
measures in the Confederate Council after the Mohawk Lords have protested
against them" (6-VI, TLL; see Parker 31–32); "No council of the Confederate
Lords shall be legal unless all the Mohawk Lords are present" (13-XIII, TLL).

Clearly, Newhouse chose to structure this document in a format
that would appear familiar to government officials in Ottawa. But for the
Confederacy Council at Grand River, who understood the Great Law as a
sacred, oral narrative that prescribed ancient customs and procedure, such
a text was quite foreign in structure and therefore unacceptable for a variety
of reasons. This included the elevated status of the Mohawk Chiefs and the
appearance of numbered laws as "articles" that did not exist as part of the
original philosophical content that was told in a much more metaphorical form. Obviously, the task of translating Haudenosaunee concepts into
English was a formidable one that had rarely been attempted at that time
(other than by a handful of anthropologists). In addition, because Newhouse
had done extensive research among other Haudenosaunee communities in
the U.S. and Canada, his varying sources resulted in an interpretation of the
Great Law that did not sit well with those Chiefs at Six Nations who understood their traditions a little differently. Whatever the reasons, historian
Sally Weaver states that this first-ever attempt at codifying the Great Law was
"bluntly rejected" by the Grand River Confederacy and served as proof that
"the council ... was not interested in recording its traditions" (1972, 178). Or
not, at least, in the manner in which Newhouse had chosen to present them.

William Fenton, noted "Iroquoianist," was the first to do a scholarly
study of Newhouse's work in an article entitled "Seth Newhouse's Traditional
History and Constitution of the Iroquois Confederacy" (1949). Until that
time, Newhouse was something of a mystery to those ethnologists who
devoted their study to Iroquois culture and tradition at Grand River, and
Fenton was the first to identify Newhouse as the actual author of the 1885
version that appeared only under Newhouse's Onondaga name, Dayodekane.
Fenton was quick to dismiss Newhouse's manuscript, however, since it did
not "fit" with what he and other non-Iroquois scholars of the time expected
of their Iroquois "informants." Rather than engage with Newhouse's work as
a valuable piece of writing by a Native intellectual, Fenton regards it largely as

a curiosity: "As literature, it is scarcely acceptable as English, but it is a large sample of reservation English spoken on the Grand River before 1900. ... It is not entirely satisfactory as folklore ... [because] it is not a consistent narrative of one piece, but it is a composite work of native scholarship, which folklorists will want to consult. ... As ethnology, the Newhouse manuscript holds greatest store for the student of primitive political organization, for it carries the League from the myth of its beginning down to its failure to serve the needs of local government on the Six Nations Reserve" (1949, 158). In addition to this dismissal of the relevance of traditional philosophies to sustain Iroquois people in the present, Fenton makes the damaging assessment that "the preceding analysis does not lead us to the conclusion that the entire document should be published" (158). Such a statement asserts that one does not need to read the words of real Haudenosaunee people, but only to listen to the "experts" on their culture, namely non-Haudenosaunee scholars.

Significantly, Fenton also argues in this same article that Newhouse's work was rejected by the Council due to its Mohawk bias and reform-driven content, an assessment that has been regarded as fact ever since, and also strongly supported in the work of Sally Weaver. More recently, however, this thesis has been challenged by historian William Campbell, who believes that "the Council's decision had little to do with the internal intricacies of the manuscript. Rather, during an era of great upheaval on the Grand River Reservation, the independent methods employed by Newhouse, as well as his apparent displeasure with the financial compensation offered by the Council for his manuscript, resulted in the collapse of negotiations with the Council, and the subsequent rejection of the manuscript" (2004, 184–85). Campbell suggests that Newhouse did not demonstrate a complete Mohawk bias since he was himself an Onondaga Pine Tree Chief who stood to gain nothing by favouring Mohawk preeminence in Council. He also points out that a number of Mohawk Chiefs actually voted to have Newhouse removed as an official member of Council in 1875 and again in 1884 when the Council went through one of its periodic "downsizing" movements. Clearly, then, there was not a great deal of Mohawk support for Newhouse as a Pine Tree Chief, nor for the work he was undertaking. While I agree with Campbell's assessment to a degree, I am troubled by his suggestion that this was a situation also complicated by Newhouse's "independent methods" and demand for financial reward, as if Newhouse was driven by an individual desire for money and fame rather than making a very important contribution to the political and intellectual life of his community.

Although it is true that Newhouse sought monetary support from the Confederacy Council for his endeavours, it is significant to note that he also requested funding from another, highly placed source. In a letter to Prime Minister John A. Macdonald in August 1886, he wrote: "I wish to inform you I have now about completed of 'The Original Historical Narratives of the Five Nations Indians Confederation' ... [and] I want to have it printed ... I ask your aid of whatever sum you would subscribe towards it" (in Campbell 2004, 185). This letter demonstrates that Newhouse understood his work as an important political document, and not merely as a quaint piece of mythology that could have easily been made available, and sold, to the ethnologists who were then beginning to comb the reserve in search of such cultural material. If it was his intention to make money from his work, then why did he continue to work on his translation for nearly two decades when no compensation appeared to be forthcoming? In a letter written in September 1898 to prominent Tuscarora anthropologist J.N.B. Hewitt, Newhouse is clearly hesitant to assess the value of his work even when asked about it directly:

> It seems to me a little difficult to set my price ... when I look at [the] long stretch of 13 years time, gathering the materials [on] the composition of the League. Not only on our Reserve, but I have looked & obtain[ed] some, in Muncy Town, & the Bay of Quinte Reserves & as you know we can't go any distance without an expense.... [And] of all the experance [sic] I have found with the whites. "Indian's time & his properity [sic] is of no value." [And] the white's time & his properity [sic] is Millions and Millions. So the Policy of the whites is, they will get the Indian's property or his time for nothing, if possible. (in Fenton 1949, 154)

What this letter demonstrates is that Newhouse remained committed to his project despite the lack of financial backing, and was holding off "selling" his manuscript for fear that the publisher, or worse, the government, would somehow obtain control of the text. Furthermore, if Newhouse was seeking a degree of fame for his work, why choose to use only his Onondaga name in the two versions that he produced? I would also argue that Newhouse understood his work as belonging to the Haudenosaunee as a collective group of nations, and was therefore rather conflicted by his individual endeavour of committing it to writing, so much so that he was unable to put a price on something that he knew didn't really "belong" to him as his intellectual property. In this way, Seth Newhouse's motivation to write about the political situation of the Haudenosaunee in the late nineteenth century is vastly different than that of Pauline Johnson, who was largely driven by her financial need to meet the expectations of an audience unconcerned about the issue of Haudenosaunee sovereignty.

While Newhouse never did receive financial reward, and was only recognized for his work nearly thirty years after his death, his translation of the Great Law did provoke extensive discussion among the Council at Grand River that resulted in another version being produced a few years later. In July 1900 appeared the "Chiefs version," so-called because it was "prepared by the committee of Chiefs appointed by the Six Nations' Council of Grand River, Canada" (Parker [1916] 1968, 61), a group of ten men that included John A. Gibson, a Seneca Chief well known for his extensive knowledge of Haudenosaunee tradition. This version is also notable for its "Introductory" section, which addresses an audience beyond both the Grand River community and government officials: "The student of ethnology may find something which may be of interest to him in this record, compiled as it is by the elder ceremonial Chiefs who are now among those who are ruling the people of the Six Nations as Chiefs ... in perpetuation of that system of government ... as it was constituted by [the Peacemaker]" (62). Calling attention to the scholars and ethnographers who had been writing about Haudenosaunee history and cultural traditions demonstrates that these traditional Chiefs were not oblivious to the outside world, as sometimes conveyed by the reformers on the reserve (and in some of Pauline Johnson's writings), but very much attuned to it. Their objective as put forth here is not unlike Joseph Brant's desire over a century earlier to write a Native history from a Native perspective, but they make it clear that theirs is more concerned with the political nature of Haudenosaunee tradition. In addition, they acknowledge that although certain cultural practices

Seth Newhouse with Two Row Wampum belt, c. 1895. (Courtesy of Deyohahá:ge: Indigneous Knowledge Centre, Six Nations)

may have changed, the consistent presence of the "hereditary succession" of the Confederacy Council of Chiefs indicates the effectiveness of ancient culture and a strong unity of belief among the people:

> There is no doubt in the minds of the writers of this preface that many of the ancient traditions of the Six Nations have become much modified, and some have been long relegated to oblivion.... [But] it is a noteworthy fact that the League of the Five Nations (now known as the Six Nations) as constituted centuries ago by [the Peacemaker] and his associates, has been followed in accordance with the rules of the confederacy as laid down by this founder of the league, and that the installations of the lords (Chiefs) as rulers of the people as laid down in these unwritten rules hundreds of years ago is still strictly observed and adhered to by the Chiefs of the Six Nations and their people. (62)

By stating that their culture has the ability to change and grow, these men are simply reiterating that the need to adapt to changing circumstances is built into Haudenosaunee philosophical thought. What they argue, then, is that despite these social transformations, their government has remained largely unchanged and is the one feature that they will not compromise, as it has served the Haudenosaunee well for hundreds, if not thousands, of years. Moreover, the people continue to have faith in this system and abide by it. This confidence in their unique and independent political structure is what they intended to make Canada aware of.

As a strategy to strengthen their claims of nationhood, the writers of this preface also allude to the history of other European nations who have since laid claim to Native lands in North America. In doing so, they seek to remind the colonial authorities of Canada that they too have an oral history not unlike that of the Haudenosaunee and other Indigenous peoples:

> It was in recognition of the fact that all nations have a traditional history similar to this one (and some of them have long since become enlightened and educated to better things) which originated with these people while they were still in a crude state (notably, for example, may be cited the English, Irish and Scotch legends and traditions) that this small fragment of Iroquois traditional history was written by the Chiefs, so that they might preserve it as other nations have done.

It is only natural for a people undergoing a transition from a state of
barbarism to that of civilization and christianity to evince a desire to have their
past mythological legends and crude history preserved. (quoted in Parker [1916]
1968, 63)

The sarcasm and wit is obvious in these words, as these men were educated
and literate enough to understand that their legends and stories were no
more "primitive" than those of the colonizer. Therefore, they saw themselves
as equal to those who sought to control their history, lands, and government.
While this is the kind of terrain that Pauline Johnson often trod upon in her
work, it is important to remember that these arguments were emerging from
a political struggle that was much more serious than Johnson's world of
poetry and performance as entertainment, and one that was occurring at the
very height of her popularity.

It is significant, then, that the traditional leadership at Grand River
agreed to put forth, in writing, their ancient basis of government at this
particular time. Although Newhouse had certainly initiated this movement
and motivated the Chiefs to consider thinking about codifying their belief
system, the political climate had grown even more urgent at the turn of the
century. Because the pressure that was being applied to them on all sides
was tremendous—from within the community as well as from Ottawa—they
understood that they were faced with a critical moment in their history unlike
any that had ever faced their predecessors. This was the question of whether
to compromise one of their most important traditions, the *Kaienerekowa*/Great
Law, by translating it into another language, and another form, for the first
time. It must have been a very difficult decision, but it was one for which they
took full responsibility:

It was therefore at the request of, and by the authority of the Six Nations
Council, that that portion of the traditional history of this people relating to
the formation of the League of the Five Nations, together with the condolence
ceremonies, now used in the creation and induction into office of new Chiefs
as successors to deceased members of the council, was written from dictation
by the ceremonial Chiefs ... with the express purpose of having it published by
the Department of Indian Affairs, so that the future generations of the people of

the Six Nations may have preserved to them these traditions of their forefathers which otherwise in time would become lost. (quoted in Parker [1916] 1968, 63)

Since no records exist of the discussions that occurred during this process, it is all but impossible to ascertain what kind of debate took place before these traditional leaders agreed to commit their oral traditions to the page. I suspect that they were not so much concerned about our survival as Haudenosaunee at that time as they were that Canada would eventually attempt to gain control of our government through federal legislation such as the Indian Act. Therefore, by publishing a written document in English, which was produced by the Confederacy Council while it was still in power, they may have felt that the Grand River Haudenosaunee might one day rely on such proof to confirm our independence. This feature of Haudenosaunee thought—bringing forward something from the past and adapting it to empower the people in the present and in the future—was no doubt on the minds of that group of ten Chiefs who contributed to the work that was eventually produced. Remarkably, this has proven to be the case, since the Confederacy Council was indeed forcefully removed by the federal government in 1924, and the Haudenosaunee of today often refer back to these early written versions of the Great Law to develop contemporary political strategy based upon our traditional systems. Ironically, as people's grasp of our original languages fade, the written word persists and gives us a significant portion of the information we need to assert our nationhood.

"IN MANY A DANGEROUS POOL AWHIRL": E. PAULINE JOHNSON/TEKAHIONWAKE

Pauline Johnson's earliest works consisted mainly of poems dealing with the themes of friendship ("My Little Jean"), nature, and dogs ("Rover"). However, when she and her sister Evelyn were invited to Buffalo, New York in October 1884 to be present at the reinterment of the remains of the famous Seneca leader Red Jacket (1752–1830), she was compelled to write what is most likely her first major work dealing with Native subject matter. Red Jacket, a contemporary of Brant, was not a hereditary Chief, but was a spokesman for the people of the Seneca Nation who remained in New York State following the Revolution. He was present at several important meetings between the Six Nations and the United States in the early nineteenth century and spoke out against the selling of any territory that the Haudenosaunee still maintained control of, as well as the influx of missionaries into Haudenosaunee communities that often preceded land "negotiations." "When we sold our lands in the East to the white people, we determined never to sell those we kept, which are as small as we can comfortably live on," Red Jacket stated in 1811 to an assembly of eager land speculators. "We like them—they are fruitful and produce us corn in abundance for the support of our women and children" (Collected Speeches [2006] 165). Because the Seneca had backed the British in the Revolution, they were also engaged in negotiations with them to seek compensation in its aftermath. But Red Jacket saw little difference between treaty-making with the Americans and the British when it came to dealing with Iroquois claims to the land:

> The white man with sweet voices and smiling faces told us they loved us, and that they would not cheat us, but that the king's children on the other side of the lake would cheat us. When we go on the other side of the lake the king's children tell us your people will cheat us, but the sweet voices and smiling faces assure us of their love and they will not cheat us. These things puzzle our heads, and we believe that the Indians must take care of themselves, and not trust in your people or the king's children. (144)

Like Joseph Brant at Grand River, Red Jacket was ultimately unable to halt the encroachment on what remained of Seneca land in New York, and, upon his death in 1830, he was buried on what was then the Buffalo Creek Reservation. When this was lost to the Seneca and became the city of Buffalo in 1845, his bones were removed and taken to the nearby Cattaraugus Reservation until they were reinterred, ironically, at Forest Lawn Cemetery in Buffalo as part of the public ceremony to which Pauline Johnson and other dignitaries from Grand River were invited.

It is highly probable that thoughts of her own recently deceased father found their way into "The Re-Internment of Red Jacket," the poem she wrote to commemorate the fiery Seneca who so strongly resisted New York State

settlement on Iroquois lands. This loss, coupled with the stories her grandfather told, merged together to form a theme of past glories, displacement,
and what seems to be the resignation of the Iroquois, despite Red Jacket's
strengths as a spokesman for his people:

> Through war's o'er-clouded skies
> His higher flush of oratory 'woke,
> And factious schemes succumbed whene'er he spoke
> To bid his people rise.
> ....
> The world has often seen
> A master mind pulse with the waning day
> That sends his waning nation to decay
> Where none can intervene.
>
> And few to-day remain;
> But copper-tinted face and smoldering fire
> Of wilder life, were left me by my sire
> To be my proudest claim.
> (2002, 11)

This piece is significant, for it is the first example of the conciliatory theme
that is to be found in most of Johnson's "Iroquois poems" for the next thirty
years. While she certainly went on to produce writing that directly attacked
the injustice of stolen lands, such as "The Cattle Thief" and "Cry from an
Indian Wife," she rarely applied such strong sentiments when it came to
addressing Haudenosaunee displacement. Rather, the tone that she repeatedly evoked was one of reconciliation and forgiveness between the Six
Nations and those who now inhabited their traditional territories, as evident
in the following lines from the ode to Red Jacket:

> O, free, unfettered people that have come
> To make America your rightful home,

Forgive the wrongs my children did to you,
And we, the red skins will forgive you too.
(12)

The unfortunate fact of this piece is that Red Jacket himself would never have
stood for such a sentiment, though it is one that the white audiences of the
day would have certainly accepted and applauded.

Johnson's first substantial literary break came in 1886, when the city
of Brantford celebrated its centennial and commissioned a statue to honour
Joseph Brant, for whom the city was named. Certainly, it was her popular
piece on Red Jacket that prompted city officials to ask Johnson to write a
poem for the occasion, and she responded with "Brant: A Memorial Ode."
This particular work, with its celebration of Six Nations nobility and allegiance to the Crown, as well as its recognition of Canadian progress and
patriotism, is notable because it serves as an ideological foundation for much
of the material that Johnson would produce to great success throughout her
career:

Young Canada with mighty force sweeps on
To gain in power and strength, before the dawn
That brings another era; when the sun
Shall rise again, but only shine upon
Her Indian graves, and Indian memories.

Reflecting popular belief of the time, that Native peoples were a vanish-
ing race in the face of civilization, Johnson confirms the notion that a new
beginning is at hand, one in which Native people play little part other than to
furnish the new nation with memories of past greatness. She then goes one
step further to suggest that such an erasure of a people is an inevitable and
tragic consequence of the imperialist mission:

so fades the race
That unto Might and therefore Right gives place.

Despite her subtle sarcasm and accusatory tone, what must have been the reaction of those members of the Six Nations who sat listening in the audience that day in October 1886? While Joseph Brant has always been a controversial figure at Grand River, most members recognized his attempts at securing an independent territory, and few were ready to give up the struggle in the way that Johnson seems to have done here. Rather than use the opportunity to call attention to the sovereignty of the Haudenosaunee, she chose to espouse the Loyalist relationship between the Six Nations and the British and to remind people of the shared struggle to build the nation that became known as Canada:

> Then meet we as one common Brotherhood,
> In peace and love, with purpose understood—
> To lift a lasting tribute to the name
> Of Brant—who linked his own, with Britain's fame,
> ....
> To-day
> The Six Red Nations have their Canada,
> And rest we here, no cause for us to rise
> To seek protection under other skies ...
> (2002, 21)

Like Brant, Johnson was also an acculturated, educated Mohawk who advocated for a reconciliation of British and Six Nations interests, but her ideas of nationhood were more complicated and problematic than Brant's when viewed from a Haudenosaunee perspective. Therefore, the last two lines of the poem are particularly interesting, since they dismiss the notion of Six Nations autonomy and replace it with a reliance on the protective "hand on which all British subjects lean— /The loving hand of England's noble Queen" (22). In merging the Haudenosaunee together with "all British subjects," Johnson completely ignores the relationship of military and political alliance that Brant himself had fought so hard to maintain. Johnson's misinterpretation (or repudiation) of Six Nations nationhood could not have been lost on many of her fellow Haudenosaunee in attendance that day, and may have been one of the reasons why she received so little community support during her career.

But such reconstructions of history were not uncommon in the late nineteenth century, as Canada was attempting to create a literature that defined the new country in a way that set it apart not only from England but also from the United States. The timing could not have been more beneficial for an individual like Pauline Johnson. Conscious of her unique identity as a Mohawk/English poetess involved in the process of literary nation building, she once wrote that "There are those who think they pay me a compliment in saying that I am just like a white woman. My aim, my joy, my pride is to sing the glories of my own people" (quoted in Keller 1981, 5). Although Johnson clearly aligned herself with her Six Nations heritage and often reminded people of her Mohawk name, Tekahionwake, she nevertheless advocated the benefits of living within the Canadian nation. This placed her at odds with a large majority of Six Nations people such as Newhouse and the heredi- tary Chiefs and Clanmothers at the time, who were opposed to a Canadian identity and sought to maintain Haudenosaunee autonomy and nationhood. Despite the political ideology of independence that was present at Grand River, Johnson clearly attempted to promote a new kind of relationship with Canada in her work, and once remarked in a stage presentation that if there were "unpatriotic citizens in Canada ... they are certainly not the Iroquois Indians" (quoted in Strong-Boag and Gerson 2000, 212–13). Obviously, her views differed from those of the large majority of people at Grand River, who did not consider themselves as being under the authority of the Canadian government; however, such political commentary remained a constant fea- ture of her career as both writer and performer. Her non-Native audience may have accepted and applauded much of what she spoke about, but "Johnson roused mixed feelings among the people she publicly celebrated as her own" (Strong-Boag and Gerson 2000, 37). Johnson's relative isolation from the reserve during her most prolific period cannot be ignored when we assess and engage with her work, aware of the sentiments of the Grand River com- munity and political environment of the day. Her career made her a highly visible figure, most likely the first, and perhaps the only, Native person that many in her audience had ever seen or heard. This gave her an overwhelm- ing responsibility—and a tremendous opportunity. "The power of her direct appeal in the days before radio and television can never be recovered," write literary scholars Veronica Strong-Boag and Carole Gerson, but they wonder what the ultimate effect actually was. "How much her charismatic presentation of the First Nations perspective furthered greater understanding in Canada is, unfortunately, unmeasurable" (11). While I would agree with these statements to an extent, I believe that at Grand River, at least, we can gauge reaction, measure the effect, and assess how we have been represented by our best-known literary figure.

Despite the influence of her grandfather and father in creating a sense of pride in her Mohawk identity and Iroquois ancestry, Johnson obviously served as an advocate for the benefits of Native assimilation; but she also punctuated this overarching view with the occasional harsh criticism of Canadian society's treatment of the Indigenous population. While this chapter does not allow for a prolonged discussion of identity politics and theories of hybridity in her writing, it is obvious that Johnson's literary approach and technique lend themselves to such analysis. I'm more interested, however, in what effect her writing and performance had on those who were and are the people most closely associated with her name, as well as how her body of work is a reflection of the attitudes that existed within mainstream society during her lifetime. Certainly, terms such as *race*, *blood*, *nation*, and even *assimilation* carried different meanings in her day, and we must be mindful of how such nineteenth-century vocabulary operated when applied to Native people in Canada. Add to this the dominant society's strong predisposition to view "Indian" culture as inferior to European ways without really trying to understand it, and we quickly see how Johnson wrote within a highly volatile political environment—one in which Native people had extremely little input on policies that affected their daily lives.

Consequently, I would argue that she was often considered a barometer of Native sentiment since, as stated above, she was the most well-known and articulate Native person most white Canadians encountered. Therefore, when she espoused and promoted the idea that Native people should "turn to civilization" as a way to improve their lives, her audience would have seen her as a credible source and found it easy to embrace both her and her social views on the "Indian problem." Questions then arise regarding the methods of approach to her subject matter. Did she feel pressure to pander to popular opinion of the day regarding Native people in order to maintain her predominantly white audience and the financial benefits that they presented?

Or, was she an outspoken activist who was willing to take risks and provoke her audience as a way to create awareness and promote the political agenda of Indigenous nations? This latter approach figures predominantly in poems such as "The Cattle Thief," yet this poem's accusatory tone did not appear in any of her pieces that focussed specifically on the Six Nations, which most often described them as loyal subjects rather than as an autonomous nation(s) of allies. In short, did Pauline Johnson help or hinder the Grand River Haudenosaunee in the attempt to establish themselves as a sovereign nation of people living within Canada?

Consider one of her more popular poems, "Canadian Born," written and performed in 1897.

> We first saw light in Canada, the land beloved of God;
> We are the pulse of Canada, its marrow and its blood:
> And we, the men of Canada, can face the world and brag
> That we were born in Canada beneath the British flag.
> ....
> We've yet to make our money, we've yet to make our fame,
> But we have gold and glory in our clean colonial name;
> And every man's a millionaire if only he can brag
> That he was born in Canada beneath the British flag.
> (2002, 125)

Although this piece should probably not be mistaken for a completely sincere and impassioned call for unity and Six Nations inclusion in the new Dominion, it does demonstrate the ease with which her Canadian sensibilities superseded her Haudenosaunee identity. While Johnson was obviously comfortable in celebrating her mixed ancestry, an audience ignorant of the historical alliance between the Iroquois and the Crown would undoubtedly interpret such a poem as confirmation of Iroquoian submission not only to Britain but also to Canada. And since she was a public figure who made her allegiances obvious, most readers and audience members would have been assured that this learned, patriotic figure supported Canadian paternalism over the Indigenous population, despite her occasional criticism of the country's treatment of First Nations and Métis people. After all, who could question the rightfulness of the "clean colonial" intent of such a country, particularly when compared to the brutally violent actions taken by the United States Army during the massacre at Wounded Knee, South Dakota only seven years before? Of course, most Canadians likely would have suppressed their memories of the similar course of action taken by their own country in dealing with the Riel Rebellion just a few years before that.

Another factor that played out in Johnson's favour during her most creative period was the general attitude that the Iroquois at Grand River were the most educated and acculturated Native people in Canada at the time. She therefore functioned as an embodiment of how intermarriage and the instilling of British values led to a refined and cultivated "Canadianness." The potential to become civilized or absorbed into the cultural fabric of Canada was furthered by the fact that the Six Nations had a shared history of loyalty to the King before, during, and after the American Revolution. By the late nineteenth century, Canadian authorities believed that their policies pertaining to the advancement of Native people had shown the best results at Grand River, primarily in the area of agriculture. What most authorities in Canada chose not to recognize, however, was that the Haudenosaunee had been an agricultural people for hundreds of years, cultivating crops such as corn, beans, and squash. Their successful harvests were not an indication of their successful "transition" to Euro-Canadian ways, but merely the persistence of cultural practice in their new surroundings at Grand River.

This is a theme that Johnson manipulates and plays upon to great effect in "The Corn Husker." By employing the image of an old woman with "age in her fingers, hunger in her face," who has come to harvest the corn fields for yet another year, Johnson evokes a sense of the timeless, cyclical nature of the seasons and traditional cultural practice. Furthering this motif is the indefinite time period of the poem, since the setting is described as

Hard by the Indian lodges, where the bush
Breaks in a clearing, through ill-fashioned fields.

This is not the more contemporary setting at Grand River that Johnson knew, but a past time before the Haudenosaunee lived in single-family dwellings with clearly defined properties. We do know, however, that this is not the distant past either, since we are told:

> And all her thoughts are with the days gone by,
> Ere might's injustice banished from their lands
> Her people, that to-day unheeded lie,
> Like the dead husks that rustle through her hands. (2002, 121)

This sense of undefined time would not have been wholly apparent to the majority of her non-Native audience since most would have assumed that Native people continued to live in "Indian lodges" in the 1890s. The theme of protest is subtle, but apparent, yet it can be quickly lost in the direct image of the "dead husks" at the end. I suggest that this is one of Johnson's better crafted poems in that it operates in a concise, clever, and culturally subversive way that serves to draw attention to the displacement of Native peoples while signalling the ability of the people to endure by maintaining traditional customs and consciousness of the ancient teachings that remain a part of those practices. By using the metaphor of corn and the harvest, Johnson has invoked one of the foundational themes of Haudenosaunee cosmology. Not only do the Haudenosaunee view corn as a spiritual gift that sustains life, but it is also recognized as representative of the reproductive power of women, as one kernel of corn planted as seed can create endlessly more in the future. In this way, the old woman is not the tragic figure that most readers would understand her to be. Instead she is a symbol of strength, resilience, and wisdom, both physically and spiritually. The cornhusks that protect the ears of corn as they grow and mature are also representative of the nurturing power of the people to guard and protect others, and knowledge as well. Therefore, it is significant to note that at the end of this poem, the old woman "remembers" the past and equates the people with the husks that she has stripped, since they, like the corn, are responsible for her continued survival. Read this way, I suggest that this poem is not simply one of loss or lament—although it certainly has that tone and feel—but that it can also be read as one of empowerment and endurance, testament to the idea that elements of culture continue to exist, and that we need to be aware of their larger implications and philosophical importance in everyday practice. Moments like these are what keep Pauline Johnson interesting as a Haudenosaunee writer, since they provide a tension against the stereotypical representations that recur in her writing and subject matter.

We also see such tension in the poem "Ojistoh," in which the narrator is a Mohawk woman captured by the Huron in their attempt to destroy her powerful husband "who had flung their warriors into graves." As a means of escape, she seduces and kills her captor in a pseudo-sexual fashion that would have undoubtedly raised a few eyebrows when the poem was performed in the 1890s:

> I wound my arms about his tawny waist;
> My hand crept up the buckskin of his belt;
> His knife hilt in my burning palm I felt;
> One hand caressed his cheek, the other drew
> The weapon softly—"I love you, love you,"
> I whispered, "love you as my life."
> And—buried in his back his scalping knife.
> (2002, 116)

This scene poses a dilemma. Although it can be considered a moment of empowerment since it depicts a courageous and strong Indigenous female figure at a time when few such images circulated, it can also be interpreted as perpetuating the sensationalized image of a highly sexual and violent Native woman. In an article published in the *Toronto Sunday Globe* in 1892, "A Strong Race Opinion on the Indian Girl in Modern Fiction," Johnson condemned the depiction of Native women in literature up to that point, claiming that "the term 'Indian' signifies about as much as the term 'European' but I cannot recall ever having read a story where the heroine was described as 'a European.' The Indian girl we meet in cold type, however, is rarely distressed by having to belong to any tribe, or to reflect any tribal characteristics" (2002, 178).

In her own poetic portrayal of a Native woman, then, Johnson made sure to identify the tribal affiliation of the heroine in "Ojistoh"; however, according to her argument in "A Strong Race Opinion," Mohawk people, and women in particular, typically embody cunning, seductive, and murderous characteristics. The mixed possibilities in this poem serve to illustrate the slippery terrain that Johnson constantly entered into when representing Native characters to her white audience, and because these images came directly from a Native writer, audiences would have been more apt to believe them as truthful and accurate.

Another stereotypical trait commonly associated with Native people was that of stoicism, or maintaining honour while being held captive and tortured. Such an image is provided by Johnson in "As Red Men Die," a poem that tells the story of a Mohawk Chief's bravery before his Huron captors. Certain of his fate, he takes solace knowing that

> His death will be avenged with hideous hate
> By Iroquois, swift to annihilate.

And so,

> Up the long trail of fire he boasting goes,
> Dancing a war dance to defy his foes.
> His flesh is scorched, his muscles burn and shrink,
> But still he dances to death's awful brink
> ....
> Fiercer and fiercer through the forest bounds
> His voice that leaps to Happier Hunting Grounds.
> One savage yell—
>
> > Then loyal to his race,
> He bends to death—but *never* to disgrace.
> (2002, 69)

Although Johnson had already built a reputation as a performer and writer of nature poems and essays on Native issues prior to the publication of "Ojistoh" and "As Red Men Die" in 1895, their appearance as the first two selections in The White Wampum, her first published collection, indicates the attempt to meet readers' expectations of Native subject matter. By casting Iroquois figures as exotic and heroic individuals in a pre-contact setting,

Johnson not only romanticizes the past in problematic ways but also perpetuates the idea that sexuality, violence, and cruelty are all prevalent features of Iroquois society in the process. These vivid images, of course, are the moments in which literature shapes mainstream perceptions and attitudes about Indigenous peoples, images that have unfortunately persisted into the present.

Questions of authenticity and audience expectations of Native people certainly arise in "A Pagan in St. Paul's Cathedral," a newspaper article that appeared in the London *Daily Express* during Johnson's second visit to England in 1906. Assuming a voice decidedly unlike her characteristic use of standard English, Johnson uses a broken, "Indian English" style of writing to describe the paternalistic relationship between the Crown and Native peoples, in the context of both religion and politics:

> So this is the place where dwells the Great White Father, ruler of many lands, lodges, and tribes, in the hollow of whose hands is the peace that rests between the once hostile red man and white. They call him the King of England, but to us, the powerful Iroquois nation of the north, he is always the "Great White Father" ... So I, one of his loyal allies, have come to see his camp, known to the white man as London, his council which the whites call his Parliament, where his sachems and Chiefs make the laws of his tribes, and to see his wigwam, known to the palefaces as Buckingham Palace, but to the red man as the "Tepee of the Great White Father." (2002,213)

Addressing the effect of this piece, Daniel Francis concludes, "Whatever the worth of her argument about Native religion, Johnson was clearly pandering to a stereotypical notion of the Indian as an artless, childlike innocent" (1993, 120). Surely, we should expect more from an author who had written essays that dealt with similar topics in a more intelligent fashion. Johnson does, however, maintain the theme of a strong Haudenosaunee relationship to the Crown in the article, subtly reminding British readers that her ancestors had a special negotiated relationship to England that preceded the formation of Canada as a nation-state—and one that calls into question the common assumption in postcolonial studies that decolonization is always an improvement over colonial rule. But again, such a message is almost completely lost amid the simplistic language of the piece, which only serves to reinforce the idea of England as a colonial father figure to its Iroquoian wards. This kind of political positioning of the Iroquois would have certainly suited the assimilationist agenda of Canada's Department of Indian Affairs at the time, and it was because of such clichéd, weak assertions of Six Nations sovereignty that Johnson's work continued to border on undermining the political rights of the Haudenosaunee by downplaying the important political role that they had played in the development of Canada.

The time period in which Johnson lived and wrote, as well as her financial needs at the time, dictated certain limitations on her ability to address directly issues of concern for Native people. Therefore, the necessity to maintain a good working relationship with literary agents and publishers and, more importantly, audiences across Canada required her to temper any moments of anger and outrage in her work with calm reassurances of Native compliance to the larger mission of building a Canadian identity. Expressing her frustration at the need to constantly meet audience expectations, Johnson confided to a friend in 1893 that "the public will not listen to lyrics, will not appreciate poetry, will in fact not have me as an entertainer if I give them nothing but rhythm, cadence, beauty, thought" (quoted in Gray 2002, 169). Ultimately, as a single woman with dreams of publishing her work while struggling to support her aging mother and sister back in Brantford, according to biographer Charlotte Gray, "she could not afford to step off the stage" (169).

The need to fulfill expected stereotypes of Natives while conveying a tempered message about Native rights was therefore also manifested in Johnson's portrayal of the violent and warlike Iroquois as a people who were progressing from a primitive state to one of more civilized behaviour that better reflected their status as Loyalist subjects, as well as their potential to take a lead role in becoming Canada's "model Indians." But in her desire to elevate the Iroquois to such social status, Johnson repeatedly pandered to an assimilationist ideal that was likely a result of her incomplete understanding of Haudenosaunee political thought. As Terry Goldie suggests, Johnson "produced a number of texts in prose and verse which present a strong although ideologically undeveloped support of native people" (1989, 62). While she took great delight in describing the ancient

Publicity photo of Pauline Johnson during the height of her popularity in the 1890s. (Courtesy of Chiefswood Museum, Six Nations)

tradition of the Confederacy Council and especially the predominant role of women within this system, it appears that she held out little hope that the traditional government would continue to function as an independent body in the face of Canada's growing power and influence. This lack of faith in the survival of a traditional government is evident in several pieces of writing that refer to past—and sometimes present—greatness, but, as a whole, her work does not engage with the concept of Haudenosaunee peoples, or nationhood, in the future.

Johnson's most extensive description of traditional Six Nations government is contained in another article that appeared in the London *Daily Express*, entitled "The Lodge of the Law Makers" (1906), in which she compares English Parliament to the Confederacy Council. Since it is a companion piece to "A Pagan in St Paul's Cathedral," it relies on the same kind of "Indian English" to describe the workings of the Haudenosaunee government that comprises "the oldest constitutional government of America—a free Commonwealth older than any in Europe, save that of this ancient England." This curious disclaimer about England's preeminence as a political power demonstrates that Johnson was clearly catering to her audience as a means of gaining, and keeping, their attention. She also attempts to do this through positioning her speaker as a kind of Iroquois maiden fresh from the wilderness of Canada, one who can only view the world in primitive terms. "To more fully learn the wisdom of the white man's superior civilization," she writes, "I followed the wide crowded trail that leads to his council house. I knew I would find it on the banks of a river, for any trails, even in my own country whether they are beaten by man, horse, or buffalo, lead always to the edge of a stream" (2002, 216). This romanticized image fulfills a certain expectation of how "Indians" think, and concedes the simplicity of such thinking, yet at the same time cleverly leads the audience into considering the information that follows. This is a tactic that Johnson found useful in her stage presentations, and she obviously employed it in her written work as well.

While such approaches are criticized by Francis, Goldie, and others, there is no denying that Johnson was able to use her celebrity status to express opinions and present information that would have otherwise never been made available to an international readership. Consider, for example, the following critique of the short-term model of leadership that is present in parliamentary democracy:

> The Paleface ... is never content to let his mighty men rule for more than four or five years, after which time he wearies of their council fires, their lawgiving, and their treaties with other tribes; he wants new Chiefs, warriors, and braves, and he secures them by the voice and vote of the nation.
>
> We of the ancient Iroquois race can but little understand this strange mode of government. We and our fathers, and their fathers before them, have always been pleased with our own Parliament, which has never varied through the generations—save when death leaves one seat empty, and another Chief in the line of lineage steps forward to fill the vacancy. (2002, 215–16)

Despite describing the British political structure in stereotypical First Nations terminology ("Chiefs, warriors, and braves"), Johnson deftly compares the similarities of the two forms of government, and holds up the Iroquois model as more proficient due to its consistent pattern of leadership, implying a more stable political structure. Furthermore, she argues that women in Iroquois society are the true basis of power since they choose the Chiefs and, more importantly, are "listened to not only with attention, but with respect." For Johnson, the rights enjoyed by Haudenosaunee women then serve as proof that First Nations forms of government, although considered primitive by Europeans, are superior at least in that regard, for as she concludes, "I have not yet heard of ... white women even among those of noble birth who may speak and be listened to in the lodge of the law-makers here" (218).

Although Johnson has done an effective job of advocating for the political significance of women in this piece, she advocates less effectively for the Confederacy Council as a whole. While she celebrates the traditional Haudenosaunee political process and acknowledges that it "does exist in absolute authority to-day, where the chiefs who are the lineal descendants of those fifty noble families still meet, and direct the affairs of their people with no less wisdom and judgment than is displayed by these Palefaces here," she makes a curious, offhand comment that seems to undermine its ongoing relevance to Iroquois people in the present: "This is the Iroquois policy, and we practice it; but the white man knows little of the intricate workings of our inflexible league, for we are a silent people" (2002, 217). The irony, of course, is that the Haudenosaunee have been anything but silent about our political and cultural history over the years, and Johnson's own words are proof of that. Making the Six Nations Confederacy Council seem mysterious, exclusive, and "inflexible" may contribute to the exotic image of Native people and the appeal of her article, but it does very little to open up the possibility of awareness and support for the continuation of traditional government among Indigenous people at a time when they needed it most.

What, then, is the purpose, and the effect, of such a statement, and much of her political commentary in general? I would suggest that remarks such as these indicate Johnson's belief that although traditional Haudenosaunee culture is certainly valuable and noble, for First Nations to progress as a people it was necessary for them to move beyond their traditions in order to truly engage with twentieth-century Canadian society. For Johnson, this meant becoming progressive in both the political and religious realms. In short, the Grand River community needed to become more assimilated in order to find their true place within the emerging nation of Canada. Many critics have pointed out that her mixed-race identity and Anglican upbringing played a fundamental role in shaping her political views and strong support of Canadian values, but none have directly focussed on her use of language when describing Six Nations cultural practice. These are, however, the significant moments in her work that provide revealing insights about her thoughts on the continued survival of the Haudenosaunee as autonomous peoples with a unique culture and identity.

"We-hro's Sacrifice" is a short story that speaks directly to the issue of religious/spiritual practice at Grand River and serves as another example of Johnson's desire to present cultural traditions alongside more familiar beliefs as a means to measure and assess similarities and differences between Haudenosaunee and Euro-Canadian ways. First published in the American magazine Boy's World in 1907, it tells the story of a "small Onondaga Indian boy ... with as pagan a heart as ever beat under a copper-coloured skin." Again, Johnson prefaces her descriptions of Iroquois culture by noting the long tradition of belief and practice that exists among the people: "His father and grandfathers were pagans. His ancestors for a thousand years back, and yet a thousand years back of that, had been pagans, and We-hro, with the pride of his religion and his race, would not have turned from the faith of his fathers for all the world. But the world, as he knew it, consisted entirely of the Great Indian Reserve, that lay on the banks of the beautiful Grand River" (2002, 218). What is implied here is that although religion has been a feature of Iroquois society for at least as long as Christianity has been in existence, it is a pagan belief system that has been maintained because of the exclusive nature of Iroquois society and the isolated "world" that is the Grand River community. Therefore, We-hro is a devout "pagan" only because he doesn't know anything else. Such portrayal of Haudenosaunee culture, as ancient, insular, and somehow lacking connection to the contemporary world, appears to have been a recurrent theme in Johnson's later prose pieces, and distinguishes it from her earlier poetic depictions of a romanticized past.

In "We-hro's Sacrifice," then, the underlying narrative is to show the potential that this young boy has to change and grow into a more progressive-minded adult and eventually a good Canadian citizen. In order to explain this possible transformation, Johnson takes great pains to distinguish pagan from heathen, and to ensure readers that the Iroquois are not heathens in the ways that some other Native people are: "We-hro would have scowled blackly if anyone had dared to name him a heathen. He thoroughly ignored the little Delaware boys, whose fathers worshipped idols fifty years ago" (2002, 218). In establishing this difference, the Iroquois religion is presented as somehow more accessible to Western sensibilities, although it is still "othered" in Johnson's comparison of the religious life of other nations living on the reserve. "We-hro's people did not worship their 'Great Spirit' with hymns of praise and lowly prayers, the way the Christian Indians did," she writes, "We-hro's people worshipped their God by dancing soft, dignified steps, ... [to] the weird beat of the Indian drums, [and] the mournful chanting of the old Chiefs, keeping time with the throb of their devoted hearts" (219). She appears to be saying that although traditional culture continues to be practised at Grand River, there are also those who have adopted Christianity and that both beliefs exist side by side. For Johnson, this is encouraging, since it is further proof that change and compromise continue to be features of the community. What is problematic, however, is her use of phrases such as "weird beat" and "mournful chanting" to describe some of the most important ceremonial songs of the Haudenosaunee. This is reminiscent of similar descriptions that occur in other prose pieces, most notably in "A Pagan in St Paul's Cathedral," in which choral music is compared to "the melancholy incantations of our own pagan religionists" and the "eerie penetrations of the turtle rattle that set the time of the dancer's feet" (214). Although Johnson balances such moments of Native otherness with admiration for "the beautiful dignity of our great sacrificial rites" and celebrates the idea of worship through "the graceful movement of our feet" (214), I would argue that such descriptions are lost on readers who only recognize Native culture as strange and inferior to their own. To them, Johnson's writing would seem to reflect such notions and confirm Indigenous traditions as unsettling and primitive.

The colonialist agenda that was on the rise in Canada during this time is also present and conveyed in "We-hro's Sacrifice" through the character of the Superintendent of Indian Affairs, the individual who was responsible for ensuring that the policies of the Indian Act were carried out on Native reserves. In this story, he is described as "a great white gentleman, who lived in the city of Brantford, fifteen miles away. He was a kindly, handsome man, who loved and honoured every Indian on the Grand River Reserve" (2002, 220). Such an idealized depiction should be recognized as a reflection of Johnson's own feelings about such individuals and their roles, since accounts that have come from Native people on reserves in Canada over the past century indicate something quite different. It's extremely difficult to recognize Johnson's resistance to colonialism in this country when she portrays it as benevolent and compassionate at times such as this. Similarly, we are also introduced to the "Great Black Coat," the "gentle" bishop of the Anglican Church, who "wonders" why some Iroquois "have never turned Christian" but have chosen to remain "pagan" (222). Consequently, he wishes to travel to the reserve and "to see some of [the] religious dances—the 'Dance of the White Dog' ... to see if it is really *bad*" (222, emphasis in original). The crisis within this story is quickly developed when we learn that We-hro's beloved pet is the only all-white dog on the reserve, and therefore needed in order to carry out the ceremony in which such an animal is sacrificed to deliver the people's message of thanks to the Creator.[2] The title of the story is made clear when We-hro eventually consents to his father's request to give over his pet so that the ceremony can take place: "Father, you are old and honoured and wise. For you and for my people alone would I give the dog" (222).

As the Superintendent and the Great Black Coat approach the longhouse to witness the ceremony, Johnson tells us "they could hear the wild beat of the drum ... [and] could distinguish the half-sad chant of the worshippers." Throughout the story, as elsewhere in her work, Johnson is sympathetic to traditional culture and describes it in respectful ways, yet, as we can see in the passage quoted above, these customs are also held out as strange and melancholy when compared to Western religious practice. Johnson presents such moments as if the people themselves understood their religion as waning in the face of modern society. Despite her attempt to provide a Haudenosaunee perspective on religious belief, the non-Native reader of this story would most likely identify with the bishop, who is presented in a positive light as a recognized and respected leader in dominant society. Therefore, when Johnson writes, "The kind face of the great bishop was very grave. It pained his gentle old heart to know that this great tribe of Indians were pagans—savages, as he thought," most readers would understand and share this sentiment. This dismissive view of Haudenosaunee culture would then be reinforced through Johnson's brief description of the White Dog ceremony itself. "Then was a dog carried in dead, and beautifully decorated with wampum, beads, and porcupine embroidery. Oh! so mercifully dead and out of pain, gently strangled by reverent fingers, for an Indian is never unkind to an animal" (2002, 222). Regardless of her calling our attention to the gentle manner of this practice, it would still seem primitive and backward to early-twentieth-century tastes (and especially so in this twenty-first-century era of animal rights activism).

Playing upon more stereotypes of Native culture, Johnson tells us that We-hro, heartbroken over the loss of his dog, fights back his tears because "was he not taught that tears were for babies alone, and not for boys that grew up into warriors?" (2002, 222). Even though this particular story was written for a boys' magazine, and clearly addresses subject matter that would appeal to such an audience, such words still evoke the idea that Native society continues to be based upon a value system that emphasizes violence and warfare. Consequently, readers would assume that such a society needs to be brought into line and controlled through the civilizing influence of government and religion, symbolized by the presence of the Indian Agent and the Anglican bishop in the longhouse during the mid-winter ceremonies that are held at Grand River. While this story attempts to highlight the benefits of religious tolerance and respect for others' beliefs, the language that Johnson employs appears to have always favoured the social norms of dominant society. In other words, Johnson suggests that although Haudenosaunee culture has a long and ancient history that has sustained the people for thousands of years, it now needs to change in order to comply with the modern realities of living within the Canadian state. In this way, the story is not so much about the unselfish act of We-hro giving over his dog for the well-being of the people, but rather a way to show how the Six Nations exhibit great potential to become good citizens, as embodied by the young boy. Such underlying thinking is, of course, closely paralleled by the philosophy of the residential school system that was flourishing at the time, which understood that if there was any chance for Native people's survival in the future, it consisted of remaking their children into the image of what the Church and state believed they should become. Viewed this way, the scene at the end of Johnson's story could be read as quite chilling. As he observes the young boy's grief, Johnson tells us,

> the great Anglican bishop was blinded by his own tears. Then he ... laid his white hand tenderly on the head of the little Onondaga boy. His kindly old eyes closed, and his lips moved—noiselessly, for a space, then he said aloud:
> "Oh, that the white boys of my great city church knew and practised half as much self-denial as has this little pagan lad, who has given up his heart's dearest because his father and the honour of his people required it." (223)

Although We-hro is presented as a hero, it is also implied that he is ignorant of the ways of the world and that, furthermore, Iroquois society is cruel to its children, for what kind of people would require that a small boy give up his beloved pet dog to such a backward cultural practice? Johnson may have intended that this story be seen as a call for religious tolerance, but the moral ultimately fails, for audiences of any age would only recognize such a primitive custom as reinforcing the notion that Native people need to be assimilated for their own benefit, and that this transformation should take place through the guiding hand of church and state. In 1906, when this story first appeared, such an agenda was already well underway.[3]

For all of her arguments regarding the nobility of the Iroquois Confederacy, Johnson rarely, if ever, addressed the contemporary political environment at Six Nations. Although her career as writer and performer allowed her the opportunity to be an active spokesperson for the sovereign and independent status of the Confederacy, she avoided making overt political statements in favour of reinforcing a subordinate relationship to the Crown, as witnessed in her short story "A Royal Mohawk Chief," which chronicles the visit of Queen Victoria's son Arthur, the Duke of Connaught, to the Six Nations Reserve in 1869. Once again, her method of description demonstrates the attempt to effect a reconciliation between Haudenosaunee and Canadian nationalism rather than a declaration of Six Nations sovereignty: "It would be difficult to find a man more Canadian than any one of the fifty Chiefs who compose the parliament of the ancient Iroquois nation, the loyal race of Redskins that has fought for the British crown against all of the enemies thereof, adhering to the British flag through the wars against both the French and the colonists." Describing the Duke's honorary induction into the Confederacy Council, she writes "Arthur is the only living white man who to-day has an undisputed right to the title of 'Chief of the Six Nations Indians.' He possesses the privilege of sitting in their councils, of casting his vote on all matters relative to the governing of tribes, [and] the disposal of reservation lands" (1911, 129). Although Johnson remained adamant in her assertion of the immediate connection between the Crown and the Iroquois Confederacy, her understanding of this particular event was clouded by a romantic interpretation of Arthur's actual political status within the Confederacy, since his Chiefly title was purely symbolic, an act of goodwill extended by the Six Nations to the Queen. Nonetheless, shortly before her death, she published Flint and Feather: The Complete Poems of E. Pauline Johnson ([1912] 1997), which was dedicated to "The Duke of Connaught, Who is the Head Chief of the Six Nations Indians." When Johnson died in March 1913, the Confederacy Council at Grand River was actively engaged in negotiating the future of its political autonomy, which was being increasingly challenged by Ottawa. It is unfortunate that the work of the best-known voice of the Six Nations did not demonstrate more positive support for the Council's efforts to define its independence.

Although she presented stories of injustice in this country, it is no surprise that Johnson has sometimes been criticized for writing within a colonialist framework that ignored the real social and political concerns faced by her people, choosing instead to convey only a romantic view of the history of the Iroquois. Her disengagement from her community has led critic George Lyon to conclude that "it is difficult to determine to what degree Pauline Johnson grew up acculturated as a Mohawk.... [A]lthough she frequently claimed to be an Indian, as an adult she spent very little time among native people, virtually none of it among the Mohawk" (1990, 139). In other words, as her career progressed, her physical distance from the Six Nations Reserve resulted in a hollow, ineffectual activism when it came to addressing important issues of the day. Mohawk writer Beth Brant views such arguments differently, however, and places Johnson firmly in the position of a heroic Native woman who overcame the extreme difficulties of gender and racial discrimination in her time: "Pauline Johnson was a Nationalist. Canada may attempt to claim her as theirs, but Johnson belonged only to one Nation, the Mohawk Nation. She wrote at great length in her poems, stories and articles about this kind of Nationalism. She had a great love for Canada, the Canada of oceans, mountains, pine trees, lakes, animals and birds, not the Canada of politicians and racism that attempted to regulate her people's lives" (1994, 7). Brant believes that Johnson had little choice but to promote her Canadian patriotism and celebrate the natural landscape, for it was possibly the only avenue by which she could gain a voice within a national discourse that was heavily influenced by racial and gendered identity.

If we are to understand Johnson's work as being subversive in the way that Brant prescribes above, it could be argued that her best-known poem can also be seen as one of her most political, and one in which she subtly employs Iroquoian cultural metaphor. "The Song My Paddle Sings" is the most widely read work by a Native author in Canada, yet it has not been examined as a politicized statement. In her biography on Johnson, Charlotte Gray sees it as a poem that "combines two of [Johnson's] favourite themes, nature and canoeing, and describes with mounting excitement a journey through foaming whitewater" (2002, 153). Strong-Boag and Gerson provide a feminist reading and suggest that the poem "celebrates the physical prowess of a solo woman canoeist fearlessly making her way through a sensual, wild landscape that hums with its own vitality, but whose challenges invite collaboration (the paddler and her canoe become 'we') rather than the confrontation that colours the rhetoric of conquest typical of men's poetry" (2000, 153). These interpretations, while valid indeed, are missing an important symbolism that must have certainly been on Johnson's mind as she wrote this piece, and one that literary scholars and critics have overlooked for a century: the philosophy behind the Two Row Wampum. As discussed previously, the Two Row Wampum is a treaty agreement that the Haudenosaunee made with the European nations in the seventeenth century, which established and affirmed a separate-but-equal status between them, meaning that these nations were not to interfere with each other's affairs but to recognize the sovereignty of each. This was affirmed by using the metaphor of two vessels, the Haudenosaunee canoe and the European sailing ship, moving along side by side, each containing the "contents" (language, culture, customs) of its respective nation. It is also said that one cannot straddle the two vessels, or live in both worlds, without the risk of falling between them and being lost. For Johnson, a young mixed-race poet and avid canoeist eager to explore poetic metaphor, such an image would be almost impossible to ignore, especially as she most certainly would have seen herself as caught between these two social environments.

The poem begins with a failed invocation to the west wind to bring motion, or inspiration, to the narrator and her canoe. It becomes apparent that she will have to take control of the situation and begin the journey under her own power. Johnson certainly could have related to such an experience, as her identity and social status dictated that her literary career would not be easy. Therefore, her journey is a solitary one, consisting of only "paddle, canoe and I." In this sense, the poem breaks away from the metaphor of the Two Row Wampum, in which all Haudenosaunee are understood to be aboard, but Johnson, already feeling marginalized from the community, would see her own journey as an individual one. Regardless, she makes progress despite the rough waters:

> The river rolls in its rocky bed;
> My paddle is plying its way ahead.

Here, the narrator describes her paddle as the instrument of agency that creates movement, much the way her writing abilities, rather than her cultural identity as a member of the Six Nations community, are responsible for her sense of personal identity and solitary progress in the world. After this initial stage of forward progress, the narrator begins to notice rapid changes and potential dangers ahead.

> And oh, the river runs swifter now;
> The eddies circle about my bow.
> Swirl, swirl!
> How the ripples curl
> In many a dangerous pool awhirl!
>
> And forward far the rapids roar,
> Fretting their margin for evermore.
> Dash, dash,
> With a mighty crash,
> They seethe, and boil, and bound, and splash.

Such images effectively relate the power of nature and convey the threat to the narrator's personal safety (also, perhaps, the problems encountered by a young woman embarking on her literary career). But they could also speak to the rapidly changing pace of life at Grand River and foreshadow those troubles that lay ahead for Native people in the late nineteenth century. Certainly, Johnson was aware of such potential conflict, even as she quietly held onto the hope of a peaceful reconciliation process between Canada and First Nations peoples. Ever the optimist, then, Johnson predicts a positive outcome to the dangers faced not only by the narrator and her canoe but also by her own Six Nations community:

> We've raced the rapid, we're far ahead!
> The river slips through its silent bed.
> (2002, 82)

As a writer coming into her own when she first performed this poem in February 1892, Johnson seemed keenly aware of her abilities and the freedom to combine the themes of nature and storytelling in her work, merging them as a means to affirm the survival of the Haudenosaunee through the metaphor that shapes the philosophy of the Two Row Wampum. As pointed out earlier, however, this sentiment seemed to fade away later in her career, as her connection to Grand River was placed ever further behind her.

Despite its notoriety as a fixture of Canadian literature, this particular poem can also be interpreted as a covert moment of personal "revenge" for Johnson: rather than completely catering to non-Native audience expectations of an "Indian" poem and delivering it in the most stereotypical manner as in "Ojistoh" or "As Red Men Die," she chooses to cleverly craft one of her nature poems as a means to employ the canoe as a cultural metaphor about herself as a mixed-race Iroquois person, without ever having to "perform" her identity. The fact that it is the most widely read work by a Native person in this country makes it even more wonderfully invisible and ironic—much like the word *Canada* itself, which is a Mohawk word, *kanata*, meaning "village," or *Ontario*, another Mohawk word, meaning "beautiful lake."

As she confronted the social contradictions evident to her in the "Dominion of Canada" during her life, Johnson constantly faced the arduous task of negotiating her hybrid identity within her Six Nations community, in the literary world, and on the international stage. According to Goeman, "In this constantly shifting context, it is not surprising that Johnson often fluctuates in terms of her politics and beliefs, but what she provides us are complicated glimpses into what is too often disciplined into neat 'historic' packages" (44). Therefore, while her efforts were both sincere and valorous, Johnson's writing seems to strain at the edges of hypocrisy at times, as if she attempted to do too much in an era when the methods, concepts, and language of resistance, gender, and decolonization that exist today were unavailable to her. She reached out to a wide audience and, to a degree, educated them about Native people; but she was far less effective in supporting the social and political struggles of her own community, which viewed its independence as stemming from the time of the Peacemaker and encompassing a spiritual responsibility that she was seemingly unwilling to consider. Maybe she was constrained by her own financial need to continue working and therefore needed to censor her true feelings, or perhaps she really did see the future of First Nations people as one of assimilation into Canadian society. Certainly, this is a problematic conclusion to arrive at from our twenty-first-century perspective; however, it was reflective of the debate that was taking place at Grand River, and elsewhere across the country, at the turn of the nineteenth century and well into the twentieth.

Recognizing the contentiousness of her work and the reception she received as a person of mixed ancestry, Johnson occasionally spoke out in almost prophetic terms about the difficult position in which she often found herself: "You're going to say that I'm not like other Indians, that I'm not representative. That's not strange. Cultivate an Indian, let him show his aptness and you ... say that he is an exception. Let a bad quality crop out and you stamp him an Indian immediately" (quoted in Keller 1981, 234–35). Undoubtedly, the contradictory and complex nature of her writing and her persona has caused Pauline Johnson to remain an intriguing and controversial figure, and her recent re-emergence as a compelling voice in the ongoing story of First Nations, Inuit, and Métis relationship with Canada only confirms that she was not simply a novelty act during this complicated period, but an artist who had a unique conception of Canada and, most importantly, Indigenous people within Canada.

3

"An Enemy's Foot is on our Country" Conflict, Diplomacy, and Land Rights

While Pauline Johnson, Seth Newhouse, and others at Six Nations were giving voice to Haudenosaunee experience at the turn of the twentieth century, a rather significant figure in Canadian literature was also addressing issues at Grand River, but with a decidedly different purpose. Duncan Campbell Scott (1862–1947), best known as a Confederation Poet, was also the Deputy Superintendent of Indian Affairs from 1913 to 1931, the period that saw the most intense political upheaval in the history of the Grand River community. The disruption that occurred there during Scott's tenure as deputy superintendent was not a coincidence, as he had the power to directly affect the lives of all First Nations people in Canada through policies that he aggressively supervised and enforced. Since he spent the entire fifty-three years of his civil-service career employed by Indian Affairs, he was well acquainted with the social philosophies and political agenda that shaped the federal government's official policy of Native assimilation, and he was intent on seeing it carried out on the Six Nations Reserve. As a result, Grand River became the site at which political jurisdiction, Canadian literature, military intervention, and Haudenosaunee resistance of the early twentieth century intersected in myriad ways that, in fact, set the tone for many of the issues that continue to be debated today between First Nations, Inuit and, Métis peoples and the Canadian state.

Like Pauline Johnson, Duncan Campbell Scott was well aware of the contributions that the Six Nations had made to the British cause in colonial history, and he occasionally wrote of this relationship in governmental essays that demonstrated his paternalistic attitude and sometimes echoed Johnson's own prose: "In the Six Nations, … [the colonial government] was dealing with the highest aboriginal type in the northern half of the continent—a people who had armed their confederacy for peace purposes and who forced peace upon the conquered tribes; a people who had developed a form of government which suited admirably the genius of the race, and which might have developed into something higher but for the interesting and diverting hand of European civilization" (2000, 1:136). Although filled with contradictions, this passage demonstrates a consistent theme in Scott's attitudes toward the Six Nations. Because they were considered "loyal" to the British cause in the American Revolution, and because they were the "highest aboriginal type" who developed a political structure that suited "the genius of the race," he implies that the Haudenosaunee form of government had the potential to evolve into something even larger amongst Indigenous nations, but which had been diverted by the more advanced modes of European political thought.

What Scott failed to fully comprehend was that the Six Nations had achieved a highly complex political structure based on a philosophy of "the good mind." This concept of using good thoughts and words to resolve conflict is far removed from Scott's constructions of a people "who had armed their confederacy … and who forced peace upon the conquered tribes." John Mohawk states that the principal foundation of Haudenosaunee thought as put forth by the Peacemaker and contained in the Great Law is quite simple: "Human beings whose minds are healthy always desire peace, and humans have minds that enable them to achieve peaceful resolutions of their conflicts" ([1978] 2005, 32). Therefore, he writes, "human societies must form governments that will serve to prevent the abuse of human beings by other human beings and that will ensure peace among nations and peoples … by cultivating a spiritually healthy society" (32–33). This was the guiding ideology of the centuries-old Confederacy Council that Scott worked for years to dismantle in order to replace it with the more "civilized" form of government that was favoured by the more recently formed Canadian one. He finally achieved that goal, interestingly enough, with the help of several armed Royal Canadian Mounted Police (RCMP) officers in 1924. In the wake of this aggressive show of force, the Confederacy Council soon devised new ways of tenaciously asserting their sovereignty in order to challenge a decidedly indifferent Canadian government, one which was to become even less interested as the Depression merged into World War II. Nonetheless, writers and orators from Six Nations also continued to reach out in the attempt to educate an ever-widening audience about who we are as a people, while the community struggled to maintain our unique cultural values and identity despite being surrounded on all sides by modernizing, mainstream society.

"A WEIRD AND WANING RACE": DUNCAN CAMPBELL SCOTT AND THE SIX NATIONS

As discussed, Pauline Johnson often romanticized the pre-contact past and perpetuated themes of sexuality, violence, and death in Iroquois society in the process, themes that also resonate in Scott's "Indian poems" written during the same period. Scott, as a contemporary of Johnson, would certainly have been aware of her work and her strong advocacy of Native rights in Canada. Although there is no evidence of direct correspondence between them, sources do indicate that they travelled in many of the same literary circles throughout the 1890s (see, for example, Strong-Boag and Gerson 2000, 120). To Scott, Johnson must have appeared in many ways to be the ideal, assimilated Native person with her mixed ancestry, education, and embracing of a Canadian identity, even if it was a rather ambiguous and problematic one at times. From Johnson's perspective, Scott's policies were likely seen as heavy-handed but ultimately necessary if Native people were to succeed within Canadian society. More importantly, however, Scott's stature as an established figure in Canadian literature would have prevented her from being the least bit critical of him for fear of damaging her own tenuous career.

Whatever the degree of literary influence or relationship between the two, Scott's beliefs concerning the place of Native people within Canada appears to have been well entrenched by the time he ascended to power within his department in Ottawa. In 1898, both "The Onondaga Madonna" and "Watkwenies" were published, two poems that deal specifically with Haudenosaunee women. According to Gerald Lynch, they are also poems that "reveal Scott's belief in the inevitability of assimilation" and "convey his feeling that assimilation may bring with it a vengeful disposition on the part of the Indians" (1982, 42). The title of the first poem is somewhat striking in its obvious juxtaposition of pagan and Christian images. The "Madonna" holds her child while standing "full-throated and with careless pose" (Scott 1926, 230), her figure sexualized in opposition to Victorian ideas of feminine purity. Critics have pointed out that the poem's original title was "An Onondaga Mother and Child," and Lynch writes that "the change in article, from the indefinite 'An' to the definite 'The,' suggests that we are dealing here with a typical case rather than an isolated, idiosyncratic instance" (41). I would add, further, that despite the change in title, Scott was clearly singling out the Onondaga as a specific group of Native people well known at the time as the most traditional, conservative members of the Six Nations, a fact also acknowledged by Johnson in her work. Therefore, the lines

> This woman of a weird and waning race
> The tragic savage lurking in her face
> (Scott 1926, 230)

take on added significance, for not only does this image illustrate the theme of the "disappearing Indian" popular in Scott's time, it also predicts the inevitable demise of traditional, "pagan" beliefs among the Iroquois.

Like many others of his time, Scott placed much emphasis on "blood" and its importance to a person's character, particularly because ancestry affected the process of becoming Canadian. In the poem, we learn that the woman's blood is "mingled with [that of] her ancient foes" (Scott 1926, 230), an ambiguous image that alludes to unions with enemies, possibly Europeans, and maybe even rape, further evidence of violence and the "impurity" of race. Lisa Salem-Wiseman suggests that "Scott shared the common belief that Native peoples possessed an innate savagery which was transmitted through the blood; miscegenation, then, would dilute any undesirable qualities and render the Native peoples more receptive to the ways of civilization" (1996, 121). Scott himself had written that "The happiest future for the Indian race is absorption into the general population, and this is the object of the policy of our government. The great forces of intermarriage and education will finally overcome the lingering traces of native custom and tradition" (2000, 1:212). Lynch further argues that Scott foresaw a violent future in the relationship between First Nations and Canadian societies and that "the threat of further, physical violence is there throughout 'The Onondaga Madonna,' bequeathed from mother to child" (1982, 42). This is an idea that is both prophetic and unsettling in light of events such as those in Oka, Ipperwash, and, most recently, on Grand River Territory itself.

Scott's poem "Watkwenies" is reminiscent of Johnson's "Ojistoh" in its stereotypical portrayal of the violent nature of Iroquois culture in historical times:

> Vengeance was once her nation's lore and law:
> When the tired sentry stooped above the rill,
> Her long knife flashed, and hissed, and drank its fill.

Such a scene is notable because it is an Iroquoian woman (once again) who is murderous, suggesting that the entire cultural group was not above treacherous deeds and therefore to be feared. For Scott, this kind of historical imagery appears to be something of an obsession, perhaps in order to re-emphasize the need to civilize the Iroquois (which was, after all, his "day job"). In the second stanza, we are given the image of Watkwenies as an old woman, apparently now living on a reservation and dependent on the "interest money" that the Indian Agent hands out. In contrast to the sound of the "war cry of the triumphant Iroquois" that ends the first stanza, she now

> Hears, like the war-whoops of her perished day
> The lads playing snow-snake in the stinging cold
> (1926, 230).

Contained on the reservation, she can now only reflect back to an earlier time when she and her nation resisted European subjugation; therefore, the movement in the poem from the summer of her youth to the depths of winter symbolizes the "death," or "perished day," of her people's former military, and national, threat. Certainly, this marginalized position of Native weakness would have been the ultimate aim of Scott's political agenda, and it is therefore rather incriminating when it finds its way into his poetry. There are further problems within this poem as well, in the fact that the Six Nations had never received interest money, let alone the principal, for lands fraudulently expropriated by the Canadian government.[1] Six Nations lands, in fact, had never been part of the "treaty process" in this country, as they had been given to the Six Nations prior to Confederation (Dragland 1994, 40). Furthermore, Scott would have been fully aware of the fact that no payment had occurred or even been considered for those lands that the Six Nations had lost along the Grand River and elsewhere. In this way, the poem serves not as a reflection of historical truth but as yet another misleading representation of Haudenosaunee people, and Canadian history, to a Canadian audience, a representation made all the more troubling since Scott apparently considered himself a rather astute "amateur historian" (Dragland 2000, xxii).

Despite his awareness of the close political and military alliance between England and the Six Nations—or maybe because of it—Scott consistently sought to undermine its significance by downplaying historical events in his governmental reports on the topic, as he does in this document from 1914: "The council at which the Six Nations were finally persuaded actively to support the British by promises of reward and protection, and by a liberal supply of presents was held in the summer of 1777. ... [And] then began a lurid chapter of warfare in the Indian manner, with episodes of flame and the torture stake. It would be unprofitable to trace events with minuteness. It is doubtful if the Indian allegiance was of any real benefit to the British.... [B]ut Britain gained the costly prize of a savage ally" (2000, 1: 141). This piece, written shortly after he became Deputy Superintendent, reveals his dismissal of Haudenosaunee history and military importance, going so far as to characterize the Haudenosaunee as a detriment to the British cause during the American Revolution, a portrayal that stands in direct contrast to that put forward by present-day historians.[2] Accurate interpretations of Six Nations contributions to the Revolution may well have been beyond the scope of a Confederation Poet, but they are somewhat inexcusable in the

Deputy Superintendent of Indian Affairs. One cannot help but wonder, then, if the descriptions of warfare and torture in some of Johnson's work had an influence on Scott's ideas regarding England's "savage" allies. Addressing such problematic issues of race, history, and politics, Lynch points out that Scott's writing as a civil servant is all the more significant when we consider that "Scott is not only a white man writing for other white men, but … his audience is [also] the official, white, government bureaucracy" (1982, 31). As the representative of national policy regarding Native peoples, Scott also reflected what Alan Lawson sees as the profound colonial "need … to displace the other rather than replace him; but the other must remain to signify the boundary of the self, to confirm the subjectivity of the invader-settler" (1995, 28). Clearly, then, Scott was determined to assert the idea of Native inferiority and to uphold the doctrine of Native assimilation into British/Canadian society. His now-famous 1920 statement, introducing Bill 14, which would allow the government to "enfranchise" or take away Indian status without an individual's consent, stands as evidence of this desire: "I want to get rid of the Indian problem. I do not think as a matter of fact, that this country ought to continuously protect a class of people who are able to stand alone. That is my whole point. Our objective is to continue until there is not a single Indian in Canada that has not been absorbed into the body politic, and there is no Indian question, and no Indian Department and that is the whole object of this Bill" (quoted in Titley 1986, 50). The irony here, of course, is that Scott was advocating for much the same thing that the traditional leadership at Six Nations was: Native freedom from government paternalism. However, while Scott dictated assimilation and gradual absorption into Canadian society as the future of Indigenous populations, the Haudenosaunee sought to uphold the principles of the Two Row Wampum as the source of their independence from government authority and Canadian citizenship.

Throughout his career with the Indian Affairs department, Scott was highly aware of activities on the Grand River territory, primarily the Confederacy's resistance to the policies of assimilation contained in the Indian Act. In countless letters and governmental reports, he was constantly waging a battle with the Chiefs at Grand River to comply with the rules and regulations that governed the activities of First Nations in Canada. Since the Six Nations maintained a traditional government while the vast majority of other reserves in Canada were transitioning to the federally controlled elected system, Scott grew increasingly adamant that the Grand River community also be brought into line.[3] For as long as they held on to the old ways, he would have considered himself something of a failure at his job. It is interesting, then, that he chose to reproduce the "Chiefs version" of the Great Law, which was first published in 1900, as part of the Royal Society proceedings of 1911. Prefacing it with his own remarks, he once again uses paternalistic language that demonstrates his antagonism toward Haudenosaunee assertions of sovereignty, all the while furthering his career by publishing their work under his name: "The document is printed as it came from their hands and bears witness to the degree of proficiency in the use of English to which many of them have attained. The typewritten manuscript was prepared by one of the Indians, and the whole work from its shadowy basis of legend to its mechanical execution is a native production" (1912, 195). In acknowledging the ability of the traditional Chiefs to successfully complete such a text, Scott claims that their competency in the English language is because of assimilation policy, the fundamental goal of the department for which he worked, almost as if to say, "Even though they refuse to give up their traditional government, this demonstrates our success at teaching them to read and write." By this point in his career, the Six Nations at Grand River had ceased to be subjects of Scott's poetry and instead occupied much more of his time politically, as evident in many of his departmental essays, memos, and reports produced during this period.

Near the end of the First World War, the ongoing disputes between Scott and the traditional Council at Grand River began to escalate with the implementation of the Soldier Settlement Act (1917) and, especially, the introduction of Bill 14 (Compulsory Enfranchisement) in 1920. Because the Haudenosaunee had stubbornly maintained their strong views of sovereignty based upon treaties with the Crown, such federal legislation greatly angered the hereditary Chiefs, who saw these actions as direct encroachments on their rights as autonomous nations with their own property laws and citizenship codes based on matrilineal descent. In a document they produced at the time, the Chiefs stated that "the sovereignty of the Six Nations could only be terminated by an Act of submission on the part of the Indians or else by conquest, neither of which can be proved by the Canadian government" ("History," n.d., 11).

Grand River Confederacy Chiefs on the steps of the Council House in Ohsweken, 1911. (Courtesy of Deyohahá:ge: Indigenous Knowledge Centre, Six Nations)

Therefore, their immediate response to this most recent tactic by Canada was to organize a committee and hire a lawyer, A.G. Chisholm, to pursue their claim of sovereign status in the courts. In the spring of 1920, they sent Chisholm to present their case to the House of Commons in Ottawa. He was unsuccessful in his bid, but the Confederacy was persistent and prepared a document that demanded that the Supreme Court consider their claim. In November 1920, this too was denied. By now, it was clear to the people of Grand River that their claims of autonomy would not be taken seriously by Canada, and at this time they began making plans to present their case directly to their old ally, England, with whom they had established their nation-to-nation relationship over two centuries before.

The man chosen by the Confederacy to carry this message across the Atlantic was Deskaheh, a Cayuga Bear Clan Chief, otherwise known as Levi General (1873–1925). A strong orator, fluent in both Cayuga and English, he made a great impression in the English media when he made his first visit to London in August 1921 and presented the Six Nations petition to the Colonial Office. Although the Chiefs were asking the Crown to recognize their status as allies of the Crown and therefore not subjects to it, British officials chose merely to pass the matter back to the Canadian government, a tactic that has served both British and Canadian governments well when dealing with issues pertaining to the Haudenosaunee. While the response was disappointing to the Confederacy, Deskaheh's mission was a moral victory, for their grievance was finally heard on an international level, and the subsequent coverage in the English newspapers brought much negative publicity to the Indian Affairs department in Ottawa; this, in turn, helped to create some sympathetic support back in Canada.

Although tensions continued to simmer and many terse letters were exchanged between Scott's office and the Confederacy Council, it wasn't until December 1922, when an alleged shooting incident over illegal liquor sales occurred between police and reserve residents, that the government interceded with a show of force. In January 1923, a detachment of RCMP was permanently stationed in Ohsweken, presumably as a means to restore order on the reserve. An already angry Confederacy saw this as further evidence of Canada's intent to force their government, and community, into submission to Canadian rule. In a letter to Prime Minister Mackenzie King on 6 January 1923, Deskaheh complained about "the desire of the Indian Department to place and house ten members of the Mounted Police with horses upon Indian lands without a colour of justice, right, or cause" ("History," n.d., 26). Meanwhile, the Dutch, who had entered into the very first Two Row Wampum treaty with the Haudenosaunee in the seventeenth century and had shown support for the Six Nations sovereignty case since Deskaheh's first visit to Europe, were planning to present the petition on their behalf before the recently formed League of Nations. Neither the English nor Canadian governments were in favour of this intervention, however, and they were quick to deter the Dutch from bringing such issues of "domestic concern" before an international organization, going so far as to remind the Dutch "that they too had colonized peoples who could raise a similar protest" (Titley 1986, 121). The Dutch soon withdrew their official support of the Six Nations' cause at the League.

As always, the Confederacy remained adamant that their status claim was valid, and in August 1923 Deskaheh travelled to Europe once again in order to maintain pressure on an international audience.[4] By this point, the Confederacy was well aware that European audiences responded much more favourably to Native causes when actual Native people were there to present them. This time, Deskaheh was also armed with "The Redman's Appeal for Justice," a pamphlet that "outlined the historical basis of the Six Nations' claims and urged that the League secure for them the following: 1. recognition of their right to home rule; 2. an accounting by the British and Canadian governments of their trust funds; 3. freedom of transit across Canadian territory to and from international waters" (Titley 1986, 121–22). Of course, such demands and allegations greatly embarrassed and angered Scott, who believed they were merely indicative of the "vanity and general ignorance" of the Iroquois. He warned, "if the Government fails to take the fullest measures consistent with justice and fairness to suppress this agitation, it will weaken our administration of Indian affairs in Canada" (in Titley 1986,118). Nearly fifty years after the Indian Act was established, the Canadian government finally agreed with Scott's approach to dealing with the Six Nations Confederacy.

Consequently, "justice" and "fairness" were extended to the Confederacy Council on 7 October 1924 when Colonel C.E. Morgan—a former colonial administrator in South Africa who was now stationed on the reserve—and approximately twenty armed RCMP officers "officially" removed the traditional Chiefs from the Council House at Six Nations, under Scott's orders, to be replaced by an elected-band-council system as set forth in the Indian Act. Although they were taken by surprise and alarmed at the show of force, the Confederacy Chiefs were not altogether unprepared for such tactics. Significantly, no violence occurred, as the Council firmly believed that such action on the part of Canada was completely unwarranted and invalid. In fact, the Secretary to the Confederacy, Art Anderson, casually recorded the event that day as if it were of little importance: "Col. CE Morgan ... read a lengthy proclamation desolving [sic] the Six Nations Council of Chiefs and appointing a day for an election day under a clause of the Indian Act" (1991, 200). Even though the Chiefs proceeded with their usual agenda, they soon learned that their traditional government was, as far as Ottawa was concerned, no longer the recognized government at Grand River. Shortly afterward, the *Toronto Star Weekly* reported the event along with the following editorial comment: "those who have pride in the history and traditions of the Six Nations, much as they desire to see progress among the living descendants of the great confederacy of the Six Nations, mourn the official passing of the oldest continued parliamentary body on the American continent, ... a body which because of its decisions did much to bring about the supremacy of the Anglo-Saxon on the North American continent" (in Titley 1986, 126). The paternalistic tone of this piece, though expressing regret over the measures that the Canadian government took to achieve its ends, manages to remind readers that North America continues to embody colonialist value systems that were helped along, ironically, by the Haudenosaunee. It is also illustrative of popular opinion at the time and reflects a society that was in support of Scott's goal of creating a homogeneous Canadian national identity. Stan Dragland suggests that, "As poet and nation-builder, Scott the temperamental moderate had few ideological resources for envisioning anything but a uniform Canada purged of a distinct Native population" (2000, xxv).

Deskaheh and others at Grand River obviously had very different ideas about nationhood, and strongly resisted any notions of the Haudenosaunee relinquishing their identities in order to become Canadian citizens. This was a central theme in his most famous speech, broadcast on a radio station in Rochester, New York on 10 March 1925:

> My home is on the Grand River.... You would call it Canada. We do not. We call the little ten miles square we have left the "Grand River Country." We have the right to do that. It is ours. We have the written pledge of George III that we should have it forever as against him or his successors, and he promised to protect us in it.
>
> We didn't think we would ever live long enough to find that a British promise was not good. An enemy's foot is on our country, and George V knows

it for I told him so, but he will not lift his finger to protect us, nor will any of his ministers. One who would take away our rights is, of course, our enemy. ([1925] 2005, 48)

At the time of this speech, Deskaheh was living in exile in the United States after returning from Europe, having been denied entry back into Canada due to his agitation at the League of Nations. He was also quite ill and realized that he would not likely ever see the Grand River country again. However, he continued to seek support for Six Nations sovereignty by any means possible and took every opportunity to remind North Americans of the relationship between the Haudenosaunee and the Crown, and the responsibility of England to support their old allies. In referring to Canada's recent military occupation and overthrow of the traditional government at Grand River during this speech, Deskaheh deliberately invokes the language of war, so fresh in the minds of Americans and Canadians alike. He points out to his audience that the occupation at Grand River was not unlike German aggression, and that their inaction constitutes a failure to respond to the solidarity Six Nations members had shown to Canada and the United States in the First World War, when "many of our young men volunteered and many gave their lives for you. You were very willing to let them fight in the front ranks in France." Why, then, he asks, are England and the United States now so unwilling to assist and protect the Six Nations when the "enemy's foot is on our country"? Aware that many people listening to him speak had very little conception of who the Haudenosaunee were and the extent to which they sought to maintain their autonomy, Deskaheh knew that he needed to sensationalize the issue somewhat and that talk of the Great Law and early North American history would likely have little effect on their sympathies. Therefore, he chose to keep the Six Nations claim in the present moment and at the level of the common person by invoking within people their own sense of justice and fairness. "I do not mean that we are calling on your governments," he said, "we are tired of calling on the governments of pale-faced peoples in America and Europe. We have tried that and found it was no use. They deal only in fine words—we want something more than that. We want justice from now on" (48). It is apparent that the Cayuga Chief believed that while governments may not consider the Six Nations claims of sovereignty, a people that had just gone through the experience of World War I might have some compassion for a small group of Natives that was being oppressed within its own country.

Taking advantage of this particular moment in history, Deskaheh realized the importance of appealing to a younger generation of people who might have a different perspective on the role of their governments and, more particularly, the ways in which history, politics, and conflict affected their lives. By this point in the narrative of North America, the "Indian" was an all-but-forgotten piece of the past, since the United States and Canada were more concerned about nation building in a postwar world than reflecting on previous, perhaps uncomfortable, aspects of Indian policy. Deskaheh knew that this history was laid out in writing, however, and was confident that enough incriminating information remained, despite its inaccuracies and biases, to demonstrate the extent to which Native nations were subjected to oppressive policies and great injustices in the loss of their territories. Therefore, he urged his audience to seek out this information in order to determine for themselves if what he said was true, and to take an active position as members of a democratic society:

> Do not take my word, but read your history. A good deal of true history ... has got into print now. We have a little territory left—just enough to live and die on. Don't you think your government ought to be ashamed to take that away from us by pretending it is part of theirs?
>
> You ought to be ashamed if you let them. Before it is all gone, we mean to let you know what your governments are doing. If you are a free people, you can have your own way. The governments at Washington and Ottawa have a silent partnership of policy. It is aimed to break up every tribe of red men so as to dominate every acre of their territory. ([1925] 2005, 49)

By continuing to use the rhetoric of war, Deskaheh makes it clear to his listeners that their own governments were and are guilty of the same offences that provoked global military conflict only a few years earlier. Furthermore, he suggests that the Canadian and American governments are actually collaborating on their mutual desire to take control of Native lands in North America.

As a means of emphasizing the hypocrisy of the fact that these agendas are conducted using "friendly" terminology designed to mislead the public into thinking that Native people want and need to be absorbed into mainstream society for their own benefit, Deskaheh challenges his audience to reconsider the Iroquois perspective on citizenship. "If this must go on to the bitter end," he declares, "we would rather that you come with your guns and poison gases and get rid of us that way. Do it openly and above board. Do away with the pretense that you have the right to subjugate us to your will. Your governments do that by enforcing your alien laws upon us. That is an underhanded way" ([1925] 2005, 49). Furthermore, he makes a distinction between Native people choosing to embrace certain features of twentieth-century life and the way of life that is imposed upon them against their will. "We want none of your laws and customs that we have not willingly adopted for ourselves," Deskaheh states, claiming that Haudenosaunee people still have political and social agency that should not be seen as acquiescence to dominant society. In fact, social and political influence works both ways, he argues, since "you have adopted some of our [customs]—votes for women, for instance," referring to the recently successful suffragist movement in the U.S. and Canada. The irony is that when the Confederacy Council was deposed at Grand River, Haudenosaunee women lost the right to vote in the elected-council system after centuries of having a political voice under the Great Law and in the Confederacy system, around the time non-Native women achieved this right for the very first time. Aware of such injustices incurred in the name of federal policy regarding Native nations, Deskaheh concludes, "We would be happier today, if left alone, than you who call yourselves Canadians and Americans" (49). In reiterating the distinct identity of Haudenosaunee people, he continues to remind his listeners that Native people do not want to be subsumed by those who seek to displace their lands, government, and traditional cultures under the guise of betterment and progress.

Understanding the recent events on Grand River, he was also well aware of how governments had begun to use "new practices" as a means to gain control of Native communities and identified this process, now theorized as internal colonialism, as yet another underhanded way that Canadian and American governments were copying the British "policy of subjugating the world" (Deskaheh [1925] 2005, 50). Making subtle reference to the effects of education and assimilation on First Nations communities, he suggests that younger generations of Native people were now being co-opted into a mainstream belief system that was the new form of bribery and coercion. The governments of Canada and the United States, he explains, "know that our remaining territory can easily be gotten from us by first taking our political rights away in forcing us into your citizenship, so they give jobs in their Indian offices to the bright young people among us who will take them and who, to earn their pay, say that our people wish to become citizens with you and that we are ready to have our tribal life destroyed and want your governments to do it. But that is not true" (49). Although he does not elaborate further on the effects of "white man's" education, he acknowledges that Native people can become corrupted when they achieve positions of power and implies that this is exactly what the government wants. As a traditional man, Deskaheh was fully aware that the teachings of Handsome Lake strongly warned against the dangerous effects of Western education for Haudenosaunee people, for it could lead to such abuses of individual power and cause disruptions to our collective well-being. But he also realized the value of being educated, since it enabled Native people to understand and negotiate with those who would otherwise seek to deceive them. "We are not as dependent in some ways as we were in the early days," he says. "We do not need interpreters now. We know your language and can understand your words for ourselves and we have learned to decide for ourselves what is good for us" (52). Once again, he stresses the existence of Six Nations agency in the face of external forces that would seek to overwhelm us.

Deskaheh did realize, however, the limits of the Haudenosaunee ability to resist the oppression of large governments without outside help and this was the reason for his trips to Europe, as well as the radio address that night in Rochester. Like Joseph Brant before him, Deskaheh understood that the very governments that had promised to protect and secure Haudenosaunee rights were the same power structures that were seeking to take them away, and that Native people needed the outside world to know what was happening to their nations. But unlike the struggle of Brant's time, the Six Nations now had access to much broader, international organizations, as well as new technology, such as radio broadcasts, that allowed our voices to be heard by a wider audience. In addition, the Confederacy Council repeatedly sought ways to engage the federal government on its own terms by raising the issue of treaties and agreements in the courts. This, of course, met with predictable outcomes. "We appealed to Ottawa in the name of our right as a separate people and by right of our treaties," Deskaheh stated, "and the door was closed in our faces. We then went to London with our treaty and asked for the protection it promised and got no attention. Then we went to the League of Nations at Geneva with its covenant to protect little peoples and to enforce respect for treaties by its members, and we spent a whole year patiently waiting but got no hearing" ([1925] 2005, 50). Such tactics of silence and delay on the part of governments proved to the Haudenosaunee that these officials did not intend to negotiate in good faith when it came to recognizing past agreements and political alliances. Unfortunately, this continues to be governmental policy in the present day, most recently witnessed in the Douglas Creek Estate dispute near Caledonia, Ontario, a specific land claim that Six Nations filed with the Canadian court system in June 1987.

Despite the Confederacy's best attempts to maintain their sovereign status by following proper protocol at the national and international level, they were only met with higher levels of opposition by Canada. When the traditional Chiefs resisted the implementation of the Soldier Settlement Act at Grand River in 1919, Deskaheh explained, "We knew that would mean the end of our government. Because we did so, the Canadian government began to enforce all sorts of dominion and provincial laws over us and quartered armed men among us to enforce Canadian laws and customs upon us." The reason for this occupation of their lands by RCMP officers was quite obvious to the people at Six Nations, and few were surprised when armed officers finally moved in to remove the Confederacy Council in October 1924. Deskaheh claimed that this military action was carried out "to punish us for trying to preserve our rights." Ever the proud nationalist, he refused to recognize the legitimacy of this action by a foreign invader: "the Canadian government has now pretended to abolish our government by Royal Proclamation and has pretended to set up a Canadian-made government over us, composed of the few traitors among us who are willing to accept pay from Ottawa and do its bidding" ([1925] 2005, 50). Such strong sentiments opposing the federally imposed elected-council system, and denying its legitimacy, have been an ongoing feature of political viewpoint and debate at Grand River ever since.

Along with his harsh words for those "traitors" who had cooperated with Canada and enabled the government to dismantle the Confederacy, Deskaheh was critical of the "Ottawa government" who held false assumptions about those who maintained their traditional beliefs at Grand River. After describing how Canadian officials had recently come to Six Nations "under pretense of a friendly visit" and stolen several ancient wampum belts belonging to the Confederacy, he says that Ottawa then thought "we would give up our home rule and self-government, the victims of superstition." This was not the case, Deskaheh argues, and, in fact, "any superstition of which the Grand River people have been victims are not in reverence for wampum belts, but in their trust in the honor of governments who boast of a higher civilization." Throughout his speech, such moments of sarcasm and humour emerge, especially when he is being critical of government hypocrisy. Elaborating further on the theft of the wampum belts, he says, "these false-faced officials seized and carried away those belts as bandits take away your precious belongings. The only difference was that our aged wampum-keeper did not put up his hands—our hands go up only when we address the Great Spirit. Yours go up, I hear, only when someone of you is going through the pockets of his own white brother. According to your newspapers, they are now up a good deal of the time" ([1925] 2005, 50). In making this reference to the amount of crime in American society, Deskaheh points out that modern, civilized society is a violent and dangerous place that merely reflects the actions of its political leaders, who believe that they are superior to the primitive culture of Native people, and therefore entitled to steal from them.

In the case of the Six Nations, such theft claimed not only land and political rights, but a large amount of money as well. While the Chiefs at Grand River had been aware of a misappropriation of a substantial amount of their funds for many years and had made several complaints, they had never received an acknowledgment of it from either England or Canada. Although Deskaheh had brought attention to this fact while campaigning across Europe and at home, Canada repeatedly dismissed such accusations as false. The government continued to ignore this claim until Colonel Andrew Thompson was hired by Duncan Campbell Scott to conduct a private investigation into the political affairs at Six Nations; he filed his report in November 1923, and it included confirmation of the validity of this grievance. Brian Titley writes that, "between 1834 and 1842 almost $160,000 of Six Nations' funds had been invested in the stock of the Grand River Navigation Company without consultation with the Indians. All of it had been lost." Titley continues, "Ottawa refused compensation because the incident had occurred prior to the granting of responsible government," while the British, "insisted that the matter was a purely Canadian affair" (1986, 124). As far as the Six Nations are concerned, however, the Crown was responsible, since it was with them that the Confederacy had dealt initially. As Deskaheh pointedly remarked: "We entrusted the British, long ago, with large sums of our money to care for when we ceded back parts of their territory. They took ... that money ... to use for their own selfish ends, and we have never been able to get it back" ([1925] 2005, 51). Such unfair dealings did little to boost Haudenosaunee confidence in their so-called allies, and by 1925 the traditional Chiefs at Grand River realized that they were more politically isolated than ever.

It was for this reason that Deskaheh was now appealing to the general public as a means of promoting awareness of government injustice, and in the hopes of creating support among the voting population that could possibly influence political change: "If you think the Iroquois are being wronged, write letters from Canada to your ministers of parliament, and from the United States to your congressmen and tell them so. They will listen to you, for you elect them. If they are against us, ask them to tell you when and how they got the right to govern people who have no part in your government and do not live in your country but live in their own. They can't tell you that" (53). As suggested earlier, he deliberately avoided any overt mention of the Great Law or other aspects of Haudenosaunee culture in order to construct his argument in the common terms of justice and human rights. He then called upon members of mainstream society to closely consider their roles as members of a powerful nation. "Do you believe—really believe—all peoples are entitled to equal protection of international law now that you are so strong?" he asked. "Do you believe—really believe—that treaty pledges should be kept? Think these questions over and answer them yourselves" (52). The significant point here is that he is not instructing people on what, or how, to think of these matters, but simply letting them consider the consequences of allowing their elected government to break promises. In doing so, he is then asking that they apply this thinking not only to the case of the Six Nations but also to their political relationships to other nations and to the promises that their government has made to its own citizens.

As a means to further advance his argument, Deskaheh specifically calls upon the women to reflect upon what he is saying and reminds them of their recently acquired political influence, as well as the responsibility that they have in the raising of children: "You mothers, I hear you have a great deal to say about your government. Our mothers have always had a hand in ours. Maybe you can do something to help us now. If you white mothers are hard-hearted and will not, perhaps you boys and girls who are listening and who have loved to read stories about our people—the true ones, I mean—will help us when you grow up, if there are any of us left to be helped" ([1925] 2005, 52). By making reference to the role that women have always played in the social and political structures of Haudenosaunee society, Deskaheh once again reinforces the idea that modern society is merely catching up to that which always existed in Iroquoian culture. In these subtle ways, he seeks to demonstrate that powerful governments are constantly appropriating Indigenous people's lands, monies, and cultural systems as well, to the point where he questions whether there will be anything left to take, or anybody left to take it from.

Given all that had happened to the Six Nations at Grand River since 1784, and the direction in which things appeared to be headed at this time, Deskaheh's hopes for the future well-being of the Haudenosaunee were less than optimistic:

> If you are bound to treat us as though we were citizens under your government, then those of your people who are land-hungry will get our farms away from us by hooks and crooks under your property laws in your courts that we do not understand and do not wish to learn. We would then be homeless and have to drift into your cities to work for wages, to buy bread, and have to pay rent, as you call it, to live on this Earth and to live in little rooms in which we would suffocate. We would then be scattered and lost to each other and lost among so many of you. ([1925] 2005, 52)

This is a significant moment in his speech, for it forecasts much of what was to occur to the people at Grand River for the next several decades. Due to an expanding population and limited opportunity on the reserve, along with a preponderance of wage economy jobs in the surrounding cities of Hamilton, Buffalo, and Detroit, many members of the Six Nations community slowly began emigrating off-reserve, beginning in the 1920s. For a culture that had always been centred upon family and collective values, such a change signalled a profound shift within the community. Deskaheh and other traditionally minded people at Grand River would have certainly been concerned about the effects of such changes, not just in terms of cultural survival, but because it would also weaken our abilities to resist further encroachments on our lands and political rights. However, this was not the first time in the history of the Haudenosaunee that people felt we would not be able to withstand drastic change to our social structure, nor would it be the last.

Throughout his speech, Deskaheh stresses the importance of understanding history and, more importantly, being aware of how significant the dominant ideology can be within society. Therefore, he urges the young people in his audience to consider the history of their nation and how they were taught in their schools to celebrate those who founded their country and its ideals, but he also encourages them to realize how Native people had suffered under those ideals. For Deskaheh, this irony exists in the fact that Americans learned a great deal about the concepts of freedom and democracy from Native peoples, yet denied it to them almost immediately upon gaining their independence from England. Addressing these issues of history and entitlement, he states, "Boys, you respect your fathers because they are members of a free people and have a voice in the government over them and because they helped to make it and made it for themselves and will hand it down to you." But, he says, if "your fathers ... were mere subjects of other men's wills, you could not look up to them," since they "would not be real men then" ([1925] 2005, 52). This is the dilemma that now faced the Haudenosaunee, according to Deskaheh, who declares, "The fathers among us have been real men. They cry out now against the injustice of being treated as something else and being called incompetents who must be governed by other people—which means the people who think that way about them" (53).

Realizing that older people in his audience were perhaps too entrenched in their attitudes about Natives belonging to primitive cultures that were unlikely to survive in the twentieth century, Deskaheh sought to influence the younger generation, who might possibly be interested in seeing the world, and their position within it, differently. It is notable that this approach is not so far removed from the philosophy that guided the residential school system in Canada and the U.S. at the time: target the youth as a way to create the desired change in a people.

As he nears the end of his talk, Deskaheh begins to employ a decidedly Haudenosaunee rhetorical strategy in his effort to build support for his cause. By reminding the young men in his audience that they are the future of their nation, he urges them to consider the great responsibility that comes with power—one of the central themes contained in the Great Law:

> Boys—think this over. Do it before your minds lose the power to grasp the idea that there are other people in this world beside your own and with an equal right to be here. You see that a people as strong as yours is a great danger to other peoples near you. Already your will comes pretty near to being law in this world where no one can whip you. Think then what it will mean if you grow up with a will to be unjust to other peoples, to believe that whatever your government does to other peoples is no crime, however wicked. ([1925] 2005, 53)

In calling upon the young men to use their minds and reflect upon the concepts of tolerance, justice, and peace, his words echo those of the Peacemaker when he travelled among the warring nations of the Haudenosaunee centuries before. The Peacemaker's message was that "all men whose minds are healthy can desire peace … and there is an ability within all human beings, and especially in the young human beings, to grasp and hold strongly to the principles of righteousness" (Mohawk [1978] 2005, 33). Already aware of the tremendous influence that the United States was beginning to establish around the world, the Cayuga Chief provides words of caution and restraint that were passed down to him, and that, interestingly enough, resonate now more than ever in America and beyond.

Because he recognized the seriousness of his political activism, Deskaheh understood the lengths that governments might go to in order

Chief Deskaheh (Levi General). (Courtesy of Deyohahá:ge: Indigenous Knowledge Centre, Six Nations)

to quell Haudenosaunee claims of injustice to their nation. If Canada had already denied him entrance back into the country, what else could it be capable of? Regardless of the possible consequences, he remained defiant and committed to the cause, urging others to carry it on if, and when, he was no longer able. "Tell [this story] to those who have not been listening," he asserted. "Maybe I will be stopped from telling it. But if I am prevented from telling it over, as I hope to do, the story will not be lost. I have already told it to thousands of listeners in Europe—it has gone into the records where your children can find it when I may be dead or be in jail for daring to tell the truth." Like the Chiefs who had committed their ancient, oral traditions to print a quarter-century before, Deskaheh wanted his words recorded so that they would be available to those who came after. Therefore, he was not about to waste an opportunity to reiterate his message: "This story comes straight from Deskaheh, one of the Chiefs of the Cayugas. I am the speaker of the Council of the Six Nations, the oldest League of Nations now existing.... It is a league that is still alive and intends, as best it can, to defend the rights of the Iroquois to live under their own laws in their own little countries now left to them, to worship their Great Spirit in their own way, and to enjoy the rights that are as surely theirs as the white man's rights are his own" ([1925] 2005, 53). Although modern society was largely responsible for the demise of traditional cultures, languages, and ways of life, the technology that it brought did provide opportunities to reach out to larger numbers of people and to preserve that which might have been lost, or silenced, by the dominant society. This irony was certainly not lost on Deskaheh, whose final words that night were: "I could tell you much more about our people, and I may some other time, if you would like to have me" (54). Unfortunately, he fell seriously ill shortly after this speech and died on the Tuscarora Reservation near Lewiston, New York on 22 June 1925, exiled from the Grand River territory.

Although the sovereignty movement did not end with his death, as Canada had hoped it would, it was dealt a serious blow, for no individual was able to effectively capture the imagination of the international audience quite the same way that Deskaheh had. Although delegates from Grand River made visits to England and Geneva on two other occasions, in 1929 and 1930, their grievances received considerably less attention. In fact, the second group even had to resort to borrowing money from the Salvation Army in London to pay for their voyage home (Titley 1986, 132). As the Great Depression raged throughout the country and on the reserve, politicians were even more disinclined to listen to the claims of Native people who insisted on their independent status, and the Chiefs and their supporters had less money to pursue it. As far as Ottawa was concerned, the Six Nations' struggle for independence was over.

In 1939, a now-retired Duncan Campbell Scott wrote an essay entitled "The First People," which included the following passage:

> The Six Nations, the Iroquois Confederacy, were [in the past], as they are now, the exponents of all that is admirable in the Indian character and there are a few who still think of alliance as the basic relationship. But only a few; it took the stern realities of the Revolutionary war and all the struggle to establish and maintain themselves on the Grand River to make them realize that they were subjects of the Great Father and no longer partners in sovereignty. The idea of a law stronger than their own tribal laws prevailed and spread abroad wherever contact was made with aborigines. (2000, 2:465)

Obviously, Scott was convinced that he had effectively done his job with regard to dismantling the traditional government at Grand River and that over time the Six Nations people would be the better for it, once they realized their "proper" status within Canadian society. What Scott and the Department of Indian Affairs had not counted on, however, was the stubborn determination with which the Council had maintained its existence, with the wide-scale support of the reserve population, despite not being recognized by the federal government (Shimony 1984, 157). The persistence with which the Confederacy at Grand River has asserted its independence is proof of the Haudenosaunee understanding of the supreme, sacred importance of the Great Law. Although Scott and others believed that the ancient form of government would simply disappear after 1924, the Confederacy Council at Grand River refused to acknowledge Canada's right to strip it of its authority, and has continued to appoint Chiefs in the traditional way and to meet on a regular basis. In fact, it has often been at the forefront of Indigenous political movements throughout the past century and has emerged as a strong presence in the dialogue surrounding First Nations self-determination today.

Blinded by their arrogance and prejudice, government officials simply could not recognize the importance of Native peoples' spiritual beliefs, not just in their religious practices, but also as they pertain to community, identity, and political structure. Although large numbers of Indigenous people have converted to Christianity over the years, a large majority of those continue to maintain cultural practices and devise ways by which to combine the two belief systems, which is yet another example of the ancient principle of adapting to their surroundings. Such practices are not to be confused with assimilation, as Scott believed; he felt that, after doing away with structures like the Confederacy Council, an elected system of government and Christianity would work side by side to ensure that traditional Iroquois society would simply fade away. He was wrong, for he did not understand the deep commitment that the Haudenosaunee have to recognizing their responsibility in this world and acting upon it. As Craig Womack asks, "Are some creeds, especially ones that relate to tribal traditions and political strategies such as sovereignty, worth staking oneself down and defending?" (1999, 205). For Deskaheh and many others at Grand River, the answer was, and continues to be, "yes." Furthermore, one must remember that the messages contained in the Great Law are not intended solely for the Six Nations, but are said to be available to any nation and peoples who would care to listen and consider their worth. John Mohawk describes the guiding principle of the Great Law as understanding that peace "was the product of a spiritually conscious society using its abilities of reason that resulted in a healthy society. The power to enact peace (which requires that people cease abusing one another) was conceived to be both spiritual and political" ([1978] 2005, 34). This was also a fundamental message in Deskaheh's speech, and one that resonated again in 1939 as the world was on the verge of another global conflict.

As they did during the First World War, several dozen young men from Six Nations volunteered for active duty with the armed forces in both Canada and the United States. Interestingly enough, both elected and hereditary Councils supported the war effort, but the Grand River Confederacy was a little more hesitant to support the cause of these "foreign" nations until the Grand Council at Onondaga, New York travelled to Washington and served notice that the nations of the Haudenosaunee had also officially declared war on Germany in 1941.

"TRAILS OF PEACE": THE POETRY OF BERNICE LOFT

At the outbreak of World War II a young woman from Six Nations named Bernice Loft (1902–1997), who often went by her Mohawk name, Dawendine, was quietly writing speeches, essays, and poems that were based on Haudenosaunee traditions. Although her writing was not published until 1995, it stands as a unique and important contribution to the literary community at Six Nations and beyond. Because Loft was fluent in Mohawk, Cayuga, and English, her understanding of cultural practices was far more substantial than Pauline Johnson's, although she was certainly influenced by the famous poet's work. In fact, there were many similarities between the two women. Like Johnson, Dawendine travelled throughout Ontario during the early 1930s "in traditional Mohawk dress," and told stories and gave lectures and presentations on Six Nations culture (Stacey, Smith, Colwell 1995, 17). It is apparent that she also did so as a means to support herself and her ailing father, traditional Mohawk Chief and noted Native rights organizer, William Loft. One newspaper at the time, *The Simcoe Reformer*, called her "a specialist in the folklore and history of her race, and ... well fitted by education and understanding of the likenesses and differences between the first residents of the Dominion and its white inhabitants, to act in the capacity of interpreter of the legends, customs, philosophy of life and practices of her people in a manner that must make for a better appreciation by her fellow Canadians" (Stacey 1995, 143). When her career as a public speaker was interrupted by her marriage to Arthur Winslow in 1937 and their subsequent move to Massachusetts, she eventually turned to the written word and continued her work as an "interpreter" of Haudenosaunee culture.

Such cultural translations are evident in several pieces of poetry written during the Second World War, which invoked elements of Iroquois tradition, nationalism, and the responsibility of the Six Nations to defend their homes, their allies, and ultimately global peace. In "Awake America," she makes reference to the eagle who is said to guard the "great tree of peace," and whose duty it is to warn the people when the threat of danger approaches:

> Louder, faster comes the beat of the drums
> The war-drums of America
> Age-old chant of the Iroquois,
> Calling to arms all nations
> From the Atlantic to the Pacific.
>
> Gwan-an! Gwan-an!
> High in the heavens the scream
> Of the eagle carries the cry "awake";
> The four winds of the Earth
> Carry it all over the land.
> (1995, 49)

Married and living near Boston when the war broke out, Winslow later said that she began writing as a way to maintain a connection with her home at Six Nations, since she felt much "nostalgia or loneliness for those whom I had left and known so long. I was trying to describe them because it was one way to bring back certain things" (1995, 20). As a result, many of her poems contain Haudenosaunee subject matter, and in this particular work she connects the image of the eagle referred to in the Great Law with the "American eagle" as the national symbol of strength and freedom. Like Pauline Johnson before her, Winslow is quick to remind her audience that the Six Nations have a long shared military history with England and the United States, as well as a tradition of conflict and resolution that predates European arrival on this continent. Although quite subtle, this poem serves to show that America was not the first nation to use the eagle as an important representation of national identity and character, and, more importantly, that the Haudenosaunee make the ideological distinction between protection and aggression.

These themes are also evident in "Warriors of the Iroquois (Of the Silver Covenant Chain)," a poem that calls forth the relationship between the Haudenosaunee and the British Crown as national allies in times of war. Despite the treatment that the Six Nations had received from England following the Revolution and, most recently, during Deskaheh's campaign to have our sovereign rights recognized, Winslow makes it clear that the Haudenosaunee continued to respect the agreements that they had made with England many years ago, even if their allies did not. As described earlier, one of the most important of these treaties dates back to the early eighteenth century and is known as the Silver Covenant Chain, which promised friendship forever between the Haudenosaunee and the British. It is because of this treaty that young men from the Six Nations are required to assist the Crown in maintaining peace. Winslow writes,

> Many years has peace been kept,
> But the silver covenant chain
> Must clear and shining remain
> And a nation's honour intact be
> ....
> Listen, to the scream of the eagle
> And the throb, throb, throb of drums.
> Great White Mother o'er the sea
> We are coming. The Iroquois are coming.
> (1995, 59)

In volunteering for service far out of proportion to their population, the Haudenosaunee demonstrated that they continued to uphold their agreement with the Crown. Winslow understands this, and seems to offer this poem as a challenge to the English to remember their responsibilities to the Six Nations, so they too can maintain their "honour" as the Six Nations have done.

Because she came from a family that was largely traditional and had a long history of military service, she was taught Haudenosaunee philosophies on conflict and peace. While the circumstances that led to the war in Europe were vastly different than those experienced by the Haudenosaunee in pre-contact times, the traditional concept of peaceful nations having to protect the balance that exists between right and wrongful human behaviour still remained. Winslow suggests that this was merely an ancient cycle in human history that the Great Law provides possible solutions for. In "Wampum White," she writes,

These trails were run of old. These
Blood-stained paths o'er all the world
Were trod by others in recent years,
Blood and tears and aching hearts have been
The bitter harvest of other wanton, wasteful years.

Oh, infinite blindness of man!
How shall we teach thee the age-old truths,
The uselessness, futilities of wars; that hate,
Greed, and power mis-used can only sear
Not cleanse the hearts of men?

(1995, 50)

Since the theme of recurrent warfare is a strong motif within Haudenosaunee oral tradition, she recognizes the parallels between those ancient stories, the most recent conflict, and what had taken place in Europe only twenty years before. With such violence and suffering occurring yet again, the world needed to understand that it must somehow learn to break this cycle of perpetual conflict, just as the feuding Iroquois nations had done centuries before. She asserts, then, that the Haudenosaunee have a responsibility to instruct the world about the uselessness of war—which only creates further violence through hatred, revenge, and abuse of power—to solve differences.

Because the Haudenosaunee are a culture based upon the concepts of peace, power, and righteousness, ideologies that arose only after years of rampant chaos and violence among our people, we believe that we do have something to offer the global community. The Haudenosaunee concept of "power," in particular, seems at odds with how the West came to understand it in the twentieth century, as defined by destructive technologies. For the Haudenosaunee, power is not to be viewed in terms of military strength; rather, it is seen as "power in all the senses of the word—the power of persuasion and reason, the power of the inherent goodwill of humans, the power of a dedicated and united people, and, when all else failed, the power of force" (Mohawk [1978] 2005, 34). It took the horrific events of the Second World War to make the Western world understand that the trajectory of complete global destruction was possible if nations and peoples did not come together to find other ways to resolve conflict. John Mohawk says that it was at this time that the rest of the world first became aware of the principles already found in traditional Haudenosaunee thinking: "The vision of the Peacemaker that all the peoples of the world would live in peace under the protection of a law that required that hostilities be outlawed and disputes offered a settlement process is yet today an exciting prospect. When the idea of a United Nations of the world was proposed toward the end of World War II, researchers were dispatched to find models in history for such an organization. For all practical purposes, the only model they found concerned the Constitution of the Five Nations" (38).

Following the war, Canada realized the significant contribution that First Nations and Métis people had made throughout the conflict, and also began to understand the extent of the oppressive nature of Indian Act policy in the country. Consequently, a movement to repeal several pieces of legislation, including those banning ceremonies, instituting compulsory enfranchisement, and forbidding Natives to hire lawyers, was quietly underway. These policies and several others, all remnants of Duncan Campbell Scott's administration at Indian Affairs, were taken out of the Indian Act in 1951. Despite these amendments, this "new" version of the Indian Act still closely resembled the policies contained in the 1898 version. What is more troubling is that this same body of legislation that was drafted in 1951 continues to be the foundation of policies and procedures today. Throughout it all, the Grand River Haudenosaunee remained committed to the idea of their independence and pride in their heritage, regardless of what transpired in Ottawa.

In a poem simply entitled "Six Nations Reserve," Winslow celebrates a place where nature and tradition served as a continuous reminder that the Haudenosaunee's place in history was ensured, so long as the people remembered to protect the legacy of their past:

Oh blessed plot of land, the Iroquois Reserve,
Bought with blood and unwavering loyalty,
What need of deed or sign of fealty
Since forever upon your country's heart
Is engraven the integrity of a nation,

The honour of a people?
Guard well, then, this your heritage,
For in the great wampum belt weaving
Of this awakening Canadian nation
Your echo shall move on to eternity.
(81)

As much as she continued to hold up the importance of history and culture throughout her career, Winslow's life and work were complicated
by the tensions that emerged at Grand River after the imposition of the
elected-band-council system in 1924, as well as by her marriage to a wealthy,
non-Native man. According to historian Cecilia Morgan, "Loft lived and
worked within both Iroquois and white society at a time when the formal
divisions between the two had been sharply drawn by the colonial state.
And these divisions affected all aspects of her life, including her social and
cultural position and her political and national status." As a result of such
a problematic positioning in both her work and her personal life, Morgan
suggests, Loft-Winslow's "interstices between these two locations could be
stimulating for her creatively but also ... extremely painful and ambiguous
for her personally" (2003, 7). Much like Pauline Johnson, Winslow appears
to have made little impression upon the Grand River community while she
was at the height of her performing career, although her written work speaks
strongly about upholding history and a sense of Haudenosaunee political independence in ways that Johnson's work did not. While her collected
poems and essays were not published until 1995, evidence of her largely
forgotten legacy, they demonstrate tremendous significance in their reaffirmation of a literary voice at Grand River in the mid-twentieth century. A few
short years later, in 1959, the seemingly tranquil place that she wrote about
became the scene of a heated internal conflict that was the result of Duncan
Campbell Scott's actions thirty-five years before.[5]

On 5 March 1959, approximately 1,300 supporters of the hereditary
Chiefs forced their way into the Six Nations Council House in Ohsweken and
demanded that the traditional Chiefs be reinstated as the rightful government. The Council House, originally built by the Confederacy in 1863 but
used by the elected band council Chief and Councillors since 1924, was

Confederacy Chiefs and supporters displaying Two Row and Silver Covenant Chain wampum belts at Six Nations, May 1955. (Courtesy of Deyohahá:ge: Indigenous Knowledge Centre, Six Nations)

occupied for seven days and nights by mostly young traditionalists who advocated for Haudenosaunee sovereignty and an end to the Indian Act at Grand River. Not only did this cause considerable tension with reserve residents who supported the elected system, it also caught the attention of the local media, which ran several pictures of the event, most of which featured images of the physical conflict that erupted when the RCMP were ordered to remove the occupiers.[6] Although most news reports described this event as taking place between the traditional longhouse community that supported the Confederacy and the Christian members of Six Nations who supported the band council, this was not the case. As Annemarie Shimony argues, many Grand River Haudenosaunee "believed that church and state were separate institutions, meaning that adherents to the Longhouse religion did not necessarily have to support the council of Chiefs—a secular organ of government—nor did adherents to the Confederate Council necessarily have to practice the Longhouse religion" (1984, 159). After the overthrow of the Confederacy in 1924, the emergence of activist groups such as the predominantly Christian "Mohawk Workers" shared common goals with the traditional community at Grand River, namely, to re-establish the traditional Haudenosaunee government as prescribed under the Great Law of Peace. Despite religious differences, both groups firmly believed that the key to the sovereign status of the Grand River Territory lay with the presence of a traditional, pre-contact social and political structure. While this kind of resistance to the state and political ideology would make headlines a decade later with the emergence of the "Red Power" movement, these young Haudenosaunee, largely guided by the influence of Deskaheh, were already engaged with political activism and decolonizing at the local level, an activity that still continues on an almost daily basis at Grand River.

4

Displacement, Identity, and Resistance *Grand River in the Era of "Red Power"*

Under changes to the Indian Act in 1961, Native people were given the ability to vote in federal and provincial elections. Although this was seen as great "progress" by Canadians and many First Nations across the country, at Six Nations the majority of members continued to resist the imposition of Canadian governmental authority and urged the community not to participate in either election process. This remains the case to this day. In the early 1960s, the residential school system was still very much in place around the country, and First Nations, Métis, and Inuit people continued to face discrimination daily outside their communities. While the civil rights struggle was still in its early beginnings, and the various protests that marked the decade had yet to occur, the "uprising" at Six Nations in 1959 was perhaps the earliest example of an ideological shift that was occurring among young Indigenous people upset with the status quo of government mistreatment. As the 1960s progressed, increasing numbers of these Native youth became more educated and vocal about the racism and injustice that their people had endured, which led to the emergence of student activist groups across the U.S. and Canada. This wave of "Red Power" activism also resulted in the formation of the American Indian Movement (AIM) in 1968, and in the famous occupation of Alcatraz Island in the San Francisco Bay in November 1969, led by Richard Oakes, a Mohawk from Akwesasne.[1]

Because of its large population, its geographic location with access to wage economy jobs and educational opportunities, and its long history of contact with mainstream Canadian society, Six Nations in the 1960s was a unique Native community whose members had a diverse range of social and political interests. With the diaspora of Haudenosaunee people travelling to urban centres such as Detroit, Toronto, Buffalo, and Rochester to find employment in factories after the Second World War, Grand River began to embody a wide array of perspectives regarding our history, cultural representation, and future vision for the community. Against such a backdrop of social change, this chapter will focus on four artists and writers who produced work that demonstrates the diversity of Six Nations voices in the mid-twentieth century.

"AIN'T GOT NO HOME": THE SONGS OF ROBBIE ROBERTSON

As the events of the 1959 "uprising" were taking place in Ohsweken, a fifteen-year-old with close ties to the Six Nations community was making a name for himself playing guitar in the less reputable bars and taverns of Toronto. Jaime Robbie Robertson was born 5 July 1944 to Rosemary Chrysler, a Mohawk woman from Grand River, and an alleged Jewish mobster from Toronto named Klagerman ("the Six Nations meets the six Tribes," as one of his friends put it years later). His father was allegedly killed in a shootout while Robbie was still an infant, and soon afterward his mother married the man from whom he got his name. In many ways, Robertson was a product of the displacing effects of the Indian Act and a member of the generation of Native people that Deskaheh, thirty-five years earlier, had predicted would arise: a young person growing up apart from his community and therefore "lost" in his cultural identity and to his people. While this narrative of displacement and disconnection is one shared by hundreds, if not thousands, of Six Nations members, Robertson soon became the most successful and well-known artist with connections to Grand River. Known for being part of The Band, recording and touring with Bob Dylan, socializing with Allen Ginsberg and Martin Scorsese, and appearing on the *Ed Sullivan Show* and *Saturday Night Live*, in a cover story in *Time*, and in several movies, Robbie Robertson has been a counter/pop-culture icon for nearly five decades. Millions of people may not know of his heritage, or even his name, but songs like "The Weight" and "The Night They Drove Old Dixie Down" are instantly recognizable around the world. Curiously, he kept his Mohawk identity well concealed until 1987, when he released his first solo record, *Showdown at Big Sky*, but this late revelation only makes his story, and his body of work, all the more compelling.

While it may be more suitable, perhaps, to address Robertson's later material, which is almost wholly concerned with Native themes and musical content, I'm more interested in the consistent themes of loss, isolation, and questing that appear in his most famous and enduring work from the late 1960s, and which coincided with the emergence of the Red Power movement. These themes are what best distinguish his lyrics from those of his contemporaries during a time in which rock music began to be taken more seriously; these songs lend themselves to a suggestion of Native aesthetic and narrative style. Cultural critic Greil Marcus writes that Robertson's lyrics frequently employ a sense of the outsider looking to find or reconnect with a community or with the mythologized "vision" of America itself. Marcus argues that this is due to The Band's outsider status as Canadians who had first "fallen in love with the music" that originated in America, but who soon "fell in love with the place itself." "They felt more alive in America," he writes, "they came to be on good terms with its violence and its warmth ... American contradictions demanded a fine energy, because no one could miss them; the stakes were higher, but the rewards seemed limitless. The Band's first songs were a subtle, seductive attempt to get this sense of life across" ([1975] 1997, 45). Given his background and distance from his home community, Robertson perhaps had an even more finely tuned sense of outsider perspective than did his white, working-class bandmates and he sought to immerse himself in a social and historical landscape in which the possibilities of identity or recreating himself were wide open. He just needed to find his lyrical voice and write himself into an American consciousness. Such an approach to his earlier lyrics, as opposed to his more recent output, also raises the important question of whether Native artists have to always address Native themes to make their work authentic, powerful, or important.

To build upon this idea, I want to also raise Philip Deloria's argument about Native "unexpectedness" in North American society. According to Deloria, Native people have made major contributions to popular culture in the United States (and Canada), but because mainstream society does not expect Native people to behave or perform in particular ways, these contributions go unnoticed or unmarked. Rather than celebrate these contributions as great achievements made by Natives, they are instead seen as anomalies that result in a person's Native identity being erased. Deloria argues that "Native actions have all too often been interpreted through the lens of Euro-American expectation formed, in many cases, in ways that furthered the colonial project." Therefore, unique and talented Native voices that challenge the status quo have been overlooked and forgotten, as "ideology and domination have made certain histories unable to be spoken" (2004, 7). Robertson's keeping his Mohawk identity a secret during the 1960s and 1970s,when such ancestry would have most likely been celebrated by fans and critics alike, suggests an initial fear of being branded an "Indian" at a time early in his career when such things were, in his own words, "better left unsaid" (1993, 10). Such statements are obviously a reflection of the racism and discrimination felt by Native people, and evidence of colonial attitudes still very present in the 1950s and early 1960s.

Robertson was first exposed to the guitar on summer excursions to Six Nations, when his mother would take him to visit relatives who were avid musicians and singers. Shortly afterward rock and roll music was everywhere on the radio. Robertson stayed up late at night to listen to stations like WLAC from Nashville that were powerful enough to be heard in Toronto, and which first exposed him to soul and rhythm-and-blues music. He began writing songs as a teenager. They were mainly of the '50s rock and roll variety, with titles such as "Hey Boba Lou" and "Someone Like You." These were, however, good enough to gain the attention of Ronnie Hawkins, a well-known rock and roll musician in Toronto, who recorded them and sent Robertson to New York as his "song consultant" when he was a mere fifteen-year-old to meet with Jerry Leiber and Mike Stoller, two of the best-known pop-music writers of the day. After working his way through the ranks of Hawkins's backup band, The Hawks, and touring a circuit that included southern Ontario and the southern United States, Robertson was already known as an exceptional guitarist by the age of nineteen. Years later, he told an interviewer that despite all this musical success, "I thought, there's something missing in my life ... Finally I realized it was knowledge. So without thinking I knew what to do: I started reading—all kinds of things. I was reading Zen and I was reading Faulkner, Hemingway and just anyone who wrote about the South. I had a view of what that whole situation there was like. It was very enlightening to me" (1989, 108). Coming to learn of a place through its literature certainly gave Robertson a particular perspective on the United States and clearly came to be an influence on his songwriting skills as well. Undoubtedly, the South was also a rich terrain from which to understand the sense of collective loss and social breakdown that was shared by Native people at this time, and which was beginning to be vocalized by young people recently empowered by their Indian identity and struggles for justice.

Through a series of unlikely events, Robertson and The Hawks were recruited by Bob Dylan in August 1965 to become his first-ever electric backing band. Tours of the United States and England followed, with intense booing from an audience upset with Dylan's new electric approach. Robertson and his bandmates persevered, and channelled these negative responses into some of the most legendary and profound musical performances that were "light years ahead of [their] time in terms of power and majesty," according to Rob Bowman (2000). This particular period of Dylan's career is often touted by critics as the "seminal moment in the history of popular music," as it signalled the shift from the soft folk and pop that dominated the radio to a more aggressive, electric sound, with lyrical content that now allowed rock music to speak for a generation of youth raised during the Vietnam War. Robertson was also maturing both as a musician and a songwriter. Greatly affected by Dylan's influence, he began to approach songwriting in a truly original way that was "less direct, more enigmatic; [where] part of the picture was left incomplete" (Bowman 2000). In an interview with Rob Bowman, Robertson stated, "More than anything else ... I remember the barriers coming down. There were rules in songs in what you could do up until the experience with Bob" (Bowman 2005, 27). "That's the door that [Dylan] opened," he acknowledges, "but at the same time I was just as influenced by Luis Buñuel or John Ford or Kurosawa. I got this hunger for education and knowledge because I hadn't gone to school since I was 16. I started to read a whole lot and I started to see these kinds of films. I got into all kinds of mythologies [that] ... influenced me in a style of storytelling" (Bowman 2000).

When The Band released its first record, *Music from Big Pink*, in the summer of 1968, very few people knew that these were the same musicians who had backed Dylan during his famous tour two years earlier. Adding to their mystique was the large picture contained in the album package, a group shot with the band dispersed among thirty or so family members, including various parents, aunts, uncles, and cousins, taken at bassist Rick Danko's family farm near Simcoe, Ontario (and some twenty minutes from Six Nations). Whereas most music of the day was very loud, electric, and psychedelic sounding, The Band's first release started slowly and quietly, countering the expectations of what a rock band should sound like. This, combined with its "anti-image" of being photographed in decidedly un-hippie-like attire among extended family, demonstrated that this was a group that was not interested in pandering to the style of the day. As Robertson stated in an interview, "We were rebelling against the rebellion. Whatever was happening. If everybody was going east, then we were going west and we never once discussed it" (2005, 35). Although The Band at this time was very much a collective of talented musicians and songwriters who all made significant contributions without an identifiable leader, it was Robertson who had envisioned the shape of the album from a production standpoint and who crafted what soon become their trademark style. "I wanted to discover the sound of The Band," he stated, "I wanted these pictures in your mind. I wanted this flavour ... This is emotional and this is story telling. You can see this mythology. This is the record I wanted to make" (Bowman, 2000).

Robertson wrote four of the songs on this album, the most famous of which is "The Weight" (1968b), sung by Levon Helm. A song rich in imagery and ambiguity, it tells the story of a nameless narrator who ventures into "Nazareth" and encounters a series of characters who all expect something from him, when all he wants to do is rest and escape whatever unnamed trouble he is attempting to flee. Greil Marcus calls this character "the quester" and suggests that he is the unifying voice of the album, a person on a journey through an America that has changed considerably over the past decade. This is undoubtedly the effect that Robertson and his bandmates were hoping to achieve, as they attempted to capture the emotions of a country that was very different from what they had first encountered when they toured the southern States as teenagers less than a decade before. (Such world-weariness seems remarkable when one remembers that four members of the band were still in their mid-twenties.) Marcus writes, "if the music is part of the story, it is also the landscape against which the story takes place. Blurred at the edges and unsure of its center, this America is still a wilderness—the moral, social wilderness that is left even when the natural wilderness is gone" ([1975] 1997, 49). Who better to comment on a country deep in the throes of various social revolutions than four young men from southern Ontario and one bona fide Southerner? In the middle of this was, of course, one Native artist too ashamed or fearful to admit his identity (or perhaps just too overwhelmed with his larger musical vision to really care).

One compelling reference to a place with particular interest to Six Nations is the song "Caledonia Mission" (Robertson 1969). With its mysterious images of a young woman who has learned fortune-telling from the "old wives" and a man whose magic "might be real," it is quite easy to associate this song with Six Nations due to its close proximity to Caledonia, Ontario. Of course, by now we have come to see that Robertson is more concerned with metaphor and imagery in his lyrics than linear, direct storytelling. However, some critics have argued that this song does indeed refer to the Caledonia that is located on Highway 6 halfway between Hamilton and Port Dover, and which the Hawks would have travelled through numerous times in the early 1960s on their way to and from gigs. Seen this way, the song could indeed be a cryptic retelling of an actual or imagined event that involved some kind of escape or rescue from the sacred or secular authorities in or around "Caledonia." Peter Viney suggests that the song is also a reference to the time when The Hawks were busted by the RCMP for pot possession at the Fort Erie border (1997). In the context of an album rife with Christian imagery, however, one cannot help but try to interpret "mission" in its religious, rather than its literal, sense, especially with the lines

inside the mission walls
down in Modock, Arkansas.

To further complicate matters, in the live version of "Caledonia Mission" that appears on the 1971 album *Rock of Ages*, Rick Danko sings the lines

inside the mission walls
on the riverbank of Caledonia

which would seem to positively identify Caledonia, Ontario, and the Grand River which flows through it, as the location. The problem with this reference, of course, is that there is no mission in Caledonia. Perhaps Robertson and Danko simply juxtaposed a series of images in order to relate a somewhat whimsical story of romance, imprisonment, and escape that could have taken place in Ontario or Arkansas, or neither. Whatever the intended meaning, however, Robertson clearly chose to reference a town well known to the Six Nations community, and one which has been closely associated with the Grand River since its founding as a mill town in 1847.

Another Robertson composition that The Band is famous for is "The Night They Drove Old Dixie Down" (1969). In the best poetic fashion, it manages to capture the emotional spirit of defeat and despair felt by the South after the Civil War in three brief verses and a two-line chorus. Robertson says he was inspired to write the song after spending so much time in the Southern States where the deep sense of loss was still felt 100 years later. Like any substantial work of poetry, it also resonates in other contexts. In this case, Dixie could be seen as a comment on the futility of the Vietnam War, or as a reference to the American Indian nations who had fought against the United States in their struggle to retain their homelands and way of life. Since anti-war activism and the American Indian Movement each had a high profile presence within the counterculture at this time, it is no surprise that the song was an immediate classic. It is to Robertson's credit that he was able to convey a sense of confusion and loss that has a universal quality without raising the spectre of slavery and racism associated with the Civil War. But it is Levon Helm's phrasing and inflection that really makes this song work, for when he sings the relatively simple lines,

You take what you need and you leave the rest
But they should never have taken the very best
(Robertson 1969)

the feeling of suffering at the hands of another's greed or wanton destruction is palpable, whether it be through the exploitation of the land, natural resources, or human life.

At this stage in their career, The Band were sometimes criticized as being overly nostalgic, unwilling or unable to comment on the profound social changes taking place around them. Making note of this criticism in the cover story in *Time* in January 1970, Jay Cocks defends their musical approach and its effect on some of their audience: "The thoughtful young have led the way in declaring disenchantment with the present. But for the perceptive and rebellious, no slickly packaged nostalgia will provide escape or inspiration…. In pop music, they are now turning toward The Band" (1970, 44). In a quote in the article, Robertson reveals the possible reason for such an impact on listeners more accustomed to hearing the concerns of youth when he discusses where he draws his inspiration from: "I'm knocked out by older people. Just look at their eyes. Hear them talk. They're not joking. They've seen things you'll never see" (44). Interestingly, he echoes a sentiment that has long been held within Native cultures, the importance of elders and listening to their stories as means of gaining knowledge. And given their own personal experience of "paying dues" in the music business for ten years, Robbie and his bandmates certainly recognized the value of story and the lessons to be learned from the past. If anything, they were not as arrogant as their contemporaries who believed that they were a part of the Age of Aquarius that was about to change the world. Therefore, Marcus sees the value of such songwriting as a means to frame the past for a generation that had been separated from its history. Referring to "The Night They Drove Old Dixie Down," he suggests, "The [song] leaves behind a feeling that for all our oppositions, every American still shares this old event, because to this day none of us has escaped its impact, what we share is an ability to respond to a story like this one" (56). To this I would add that the story of the so-called Indian Wars of the American West could be included in this reflection on American history. In 1970 such discussion was only just beginning to emerge, but it is a significant one because this is precisely the story that has subsequently become so important to Robertson's career over the past twenty years.

The themes of loss, injustice, and displacement also figure prominently in "Acadian Driftwood" (1975), one of the most popular songs from The Band's later period. An historical narrative that tells of the Acadian migration to Louisiana following the defeat of the French by the British on the Plains of Abraham in 1759, the song is a close cousin to "The Night They Drove Old Dixie Down." Once again, Robertson is able to capture a depth of emotion through story that is unique in rock lyricism. According to Bowman, "Robbie's ability to create a fictitious historical voice that speaks so eloquently for several thousand real ones is a rare gift" (2005, 78). Robertson himself says he was inspired by a film based on the Acadian displacement, in which he saw connections to other historical events like those portrayed in "The Grapes of Wrath, where people just have to move, have to go somewhere to find a new home. Plus there was a parallel in this to my own story of going from Canada down to the deep South. I'm taking the side once again of the underdog ... , looking at the story from the side that didn't win" (Bowman 2005, 78). The irony is obvious here, of course, in that Robertson sympathized with other groups of people in other times and situations, but did not appear to recognize the displacement and suffering of his own ancestors, or the larger story of Native displacement in American history.

But one could argue that "Acadian Driftwood" does set the groundwork for the Native subject matter that emerged in his work a decade later. As the unnamed narrator tells of what befell the Acadians after the British victory, there is a sense of a defeated people's lives being forever changed at the whim of a foreign government:

The war was over and the spirit was broken
The hills were smokin' as the men withdrew
....
They signed a treaty and our homes were taken
Loved ones forsaken
They didn't give a damn.
(Robertson 1975)

Whereas "The Night They Drove Old Dixie Down" told a story with brevity and emotion, relying on Helm's singing to achieve the desired effect, "Acadian Driftwood" is a much longer song that suggests the need to tell a bigger history of a people torn from the land by violent circumstances. For despite the defeat in the Civil War, Southerners were not forced to leave their homes and properties to relocate hundreds of miles away as the Acadians were, or as countless Native nations were as well. Robertson also chooses to tell this story since it is little known in North American history, yet speaks to so many marginalized groups that are often lost in the bigger picture of the nation's narrative, including those who left their homelands under similar circumstances to immigrate to the United States.

As the narrator laments the home he left behind, it is apparent that the land and the natural climate of the South are alien elements to him that must be endured as a kind of punishment, as if being displaced weren't enough:

> Everlasting summer filled with ill-content
> This government had us walkin' in chains
> This isn't my turf
> This ain't my season
> Can't think of one good reason to remain.

While the lyrics tell a tale of suffering and injustice, the music itself gains a certain joyful, Cajun quality that suggests the gradual evolution of that musical genre, with its strong French influence. It also suggests the possibility of eventual return (which was the case for some Acadians). At the very least, the music serves to keep those memories and that hope of return alive, as evident in the chorus:

> Acadian driftwood
> Gypsy tailwind
> They call my home the land of snow
> Canadian cold front movin' in
> What a way to ride
> Ah, what a way to go.
> (Robertson 1975)

Barney Hoskyns sees the song as a kind of turning point in the story of The Band, and Robertson in particular: "It was as if Robbie had finally lived outside Canada for long enough to see it through the same romantic lens he'd used to view the American South a decade before" (1993, 318). After fifteen years of touring and recording, The Band had indeed come full circle, redefining an approach to popular music that bridged the folk, country, and rock worlds and would eventually become labelled "roots" music or Americana. The irony is obvious given their Canadian backgrounds, but more importantly, perhaps, it was Robbie Robertson's talents as a guitarist, songwriter, and producer that firmly placed an "unexpected" Native American influence onto American consciousness and popular culture for all time.

On Thanksgiving weekend 1976, The Band gave their farewell concert at the Winterland Arena in San Francisco. It included a star-studded list of performers who came out to show their acknowledgment and appreciation of a group of musicians who had been releasing records for only eight years, but who had played together for close to twenty. Muddy Waters, Van Morrison, Joni Mitchell, Neil Young, Bob Dylan, and many more all played with The Band that night, a testament to the respect that these musical legends had for the group of men from southern Ontario and West Helena, Arkansas. The entire four-hour event was filmed by Martin Scorsese, a close friend of Robertson, and released as The Last Waltz in 1978. The film went on to win an Oscar that year. Although they claimed otherwise at the time, it turned out to be the last time that The Band ever played together.

In 1987, Robertson released his highly acclaimed solo record, Showdown at Big Sky, and it was during the promotion of this album that he revealed his Mohawk heritage and connection to Six Nations.[2] Although this took many people by surprise, most at Grand River quickly took great interest and pride in the record and his career in general (including my eighty-seven-year-old grandfather, who made a point to go out and buy the record himself). Coming three years before the Oka Crisis, it did not ride the "wave" of celebrity interest in Native issues at that time, but it did open the door a little in regard to media coverage of such issues.

While Robertson was a key figure in the counterculture of the sixties, providing a soundtrack to many of the events of the time, all but a few family members at Six Nations were unaware of his Mohawk identity. But the Six

Nations community was certainly affected by this tumultuous period, and many were direct participants in various ways. Because of the close ties between Grand River and other Haudenosaunee communities in New York State, a number of young men joined the U.S. Army and took part in the Vietnam War, once again in disproportionate numbers to the population. And the political awakening of young Native people across the United States and Canada did not go unnoticed at Grand River either. In July 1969, a number of young Confederacy supporters once again took over the old Council House in Ohsweken and occupied it for three days, demanding that the traditional council be restored. Unlike the "takeover" of 1959, however, the RCMP did not become involved, and members of the community eventually resolved the situation under their own terms by convincing the occupiers to leave peacefully. Although tensions faded, the debate over the "rightful" leadership of Grand River continues to this day, but in less openly confrontational ways.

THE FEATHERED U.E.L.'S AND FORBIDDEN VOICE: DIVERGENT PERSPECTIVES

As the 1960s gave way to the 1970s, First Nations issues remained a high-profile topic in the media, with politicians scrambling to address the "Indian problem" through the Liberal Party approaches made popular at that time by Prime Minister Pierre Trudeau. Of course, these proposed changes to the Indian Act, including the infamous "White Paper" of 1969, proved to be largely ineffective, if not insulting, to Native people. However, these policies had the positive effect of motivating a large number of young, educated First Nations, Métis, and Inuit people to become writers and activists who challenged government hegemony. Most notable among these were Vine Deloria Jr. (Standing Rock Sioux), who published *Custer Died for Your Sins: an Indigenous Manifesto* in 1969, and Harold Cardinal (Cree), whose *Unjust Society* (1969) was a direct response to Trudeau's new policy on Indian Affairs in Canada. The National Indian Brotherhood also rose to prominence at this time, later changing its name to the Assembly of First Nations. A community always well known for its diverse "conservative" and "progressive" populations, Six Nations also continued to receive considerable attention from anthropologists and sociologists. In response to these changing attitudes and the increased interest in Native issues, culture, and politics, a group of writers and spokespeople began to emerge from within the Grand River community, giving voice to history and culture in ways decidedly unlike those of the non-Native academics who sought to study and analyze us.

Two books in particular—*The Feathered U.E.L.'s* (1973) by Enos Montour, and *Forbidden Voice* (1971) by Alma Greene—are noteworthy because they were both published in the midst of this awakening political consciousness, but could not be any further apart in narrative approach and content. Consequently, their respective subject matter represents the religious division within the Grand River community and would appear to reinforce the conclusion that this conflict between traditional and Christian culture is the sole defining feature of Six Nations for the large majority of scholars. But such a reading only accounts for the surface, for if one reads more deeply into both texts a much more nuanced message emerges. Simply put, despite religious and cultural differences, the people of Six Nations have a shared understanding of their distinct history and the expectation that they should be treated fairly by the British Crown, as well as the Governments of Canada and the United States. Although Montour and Greene convey this message from decidedly different perspectives, both were likely influenced by the political environment of the period and encouraged by a publishing industry eager for the latest book by a Native author.

As a Methodist minister on the reserve, Montour chooses to focus his historical fiction on people and events associated with the Chapel of the Delawares, a wooden-frame church that still stands on the reserve (and which recently celebrated its 150th anniversary). In making this church a central "character" in his work, Montour is able to document events over a 100-year period as they revolve around this particular building. While generations of people come and go, the church is witness to many changes on the reserve, from its beginnings as a "rough wilderness" to the advent of mechanized farming and the industrial age, and to wars, both local and distant. In chapters that alternate between his own perspective on historical events and those that follow the mostly fictional activities of four generations of the Logan family, from the grandfather who fought in the American Revolution to his grandsons and great-grandsons who fought in the First and Second

World Wars, Montour seeks to provide an accessible "people's history" of the Grand River community.

As the story opens, we are introduced to fifteen-year-old Hiram Logan, who the author describes as "a mixed up Delaware boy" sitting in front of his parents' log cabin in the years following the War of 1812, when "his Loyalist people had just become settled in the Canadian bush." After being made aware of the time and setting, we also quickly come to learn of the boy's source of confusion: "He had seen his dad's canoe crossing to the Longhouse side of the river. He knew there was some sort of weird ceremony at that Indian religious centre. The Longhouse religion was supposed to be a force in every Indian's life, yet he could never warm up to it" (Montour 1973, 7). From the outset, Montour describes the difference between Christian and "Indian" religions in an historical context, and although he treats longhouse traditions with some amount of respect, it is also very clear which religious belief he favours for the community. As Hiram continues to sit outside of his house, he can hear "from across the river ... strangely disturbing sounds, the monotonous beat of the tom-tom, mingled with shouts and singing," while "on his side of the river a Methodist revival service was starting ... [and] the singing of revival hymns floated back to him [and the boy] found them strangely stirring" (8). In addition to using the Grand River as a symbol of religious division, Montour also presents these differences along gender lines. Hiram's father is a Revolutionary War veteran who is closely connected to the "old" ways and to the history of the Six Nations, while his mother was "taken from her bush home and given whiteman's learning" (8) at a Lutheran boarding school. As a result, Montour tells us, "she did not feel at home in the Longhouse ceremony which she attended occasionally with Hiram's father" (9). Despite their different views on religion, however, the author also makes it clear that mother and father are comfortable in their own beliefs and do not quarrel over them, as if to say that the two traditions can coexist peacefully. Moreover, Hiram is the figure who continuously embodies the changing attitude toward history and religion and, ultimately, suggests more progressive beliefs among those at Grand River.

Through Hiram's unnamed father, the reader learns of the promises made to the Six Nations by the British prior to the Revolution, when General Haldimand told them, "Assist the King now and you will find it to your advantage. Go now and fight for your possessions and whatever you lose of your property during the War, the King will make up to you when peace returns." Convinced by these assurances, Hiram's father told him that the Six Nations and other allied nations such as the Delaware decided to ally with the King and "marched into battle on the side of the British and under the Union Jack" (Montour 1973, 9). After the British defeat, Montour tells us, Joseph Brant met with Haldimand to remind him of the King's promise to the Six Nations. While he does not go into the terms of the Treaty of Paris, and its omission of any mention of the Haudenosaunee or their allied nations, Montour does stress the significance of the Haldimand Deed: "Captain Joseph Brant actually obtained the Title Deed to this territory for the Indians in the autumn of 1784, under the Seal of Royal Authority. They were given the land because they did not forsake their Great White Father, the King.... It was clearly indicated, in the terms of the award, that this was a gift which the Mohawks and other tribes of the Six Nations with their posterity, were to enjoy forever." Clearly, Montour places much emphasis on the Loyalist inter-pretation of Six Nations involvement with the Crown, and makes no mention of the sovereign status of the Confederacy. Consequently, Brant is reinforced as the individual who is the primary leader behind the Six Nations establish-ing themselves at Grand River, where "they were all Loyalists who would never forsake their Great White Father, the King" (10). Such descriptions obviously contradict many others at Six Nations who view our relationship to the Crown as being very different, but it is also important to note that many at Six Nations would have shared Montour's interpretation of a Loyalist tradition at Six Nations, a situation that often paralleled religious beliefs. In general terms, the Christian members of the reserve favoured an historical narrative that emphasized loyalty to the Crown (and subsequently to Canada), while the traditional community remained in support of the sovereign inde-pendence of the Confederacy Council. This debate around the exact nature of Six Nations ties with the Crown persists to this day. But despite the acknowl-edged difference in religious affiliations and political loyalties, the belief that the Six Nations were an independent people who had a unique history and relationship to the Crown is made quite clear throughout Montour's text.

In order to emphasize this point, he devotes considerable time to chron-icling the significant military contributions that the Six Nations community has made, largely in support of the British, and later, to Canada. Not only were the Six Nations a formidable presence in the American Revolution and the War of 1812, Montour continually reminds the reader, but they were also involved in the lesser-known Fenian Raid of 1866. At that time, a group of approximately fifty men marched from Six Nations to Hamilton along the Plank Road to volunteer their services. According to Montour, "They had not been called up and language difficulties made it hard for them to grasp the trend of events. One thing they knew was that their beloved 'Canady' was in danger and they wanted to help" (1973, 51). Although these men saw no action in the conflict (as the fighting was over before they arrived), he describes their willingness to serve as a demonstration of their commitment to a fledgling Canada and therefore a confirmation of their Loyalist beliefs. He also sees such sentiment as being reaffirmed at the outbreak of the First World War, when five men from Six Nations immediately volunteered in August 1914, including Cameron D. Brant, a direct descendant of Joseph Brant. These men joined the "Mad" Fourth Battalion and were all killed early in the war. Several months later, the 114th Haldimand Rifles, one-third of whom were from the "Loyalist Six Nations Reserve" (99), were organized and sent overseas in June 1917. For Montour, such ongoing support of the Crown serves as the primary theme of his text, and one which is most clearly evidenced by the more than 200 years of military service of the "Feathered" United Empire Loyalists. What he does not discuss, however, is the intense debate that occurred at Grand River during the First World War, as the Confederacy Council, stressing Haudenosaunee sovereignty, opposed any involvement by Six Nations members, proof that not all at Grand River were in support of the conflict, as Montour would like his readers to believe.[3]

After setting an historical context, Montour's focus becomes the story of how various individuals at Grand River emerged to demonstrate their ability to overcome the barriers of racism, discrimination, and poverty to compete with, and eventually succeed in, the "whiteman's world." Such stories are often closely associated with the theme of assimilation—although Montour never uses the word—and he devotes much time to describing how various Six Nations members contribute to making their community more progressive. Not surprisingly, these stories revolve largely around Christianity and education. After telling of how the early construction of the Cherry Hill

Methodist church in 1856 suffered from vandalism by traditionally minded members of the community who "were upset and angry about what they called, 'this show of whiteman's religion'" (1973, 23), he makes similar reference to the opposition to establishing a school in the new church. "Not all Indians welcomed the schools. Some oldtimers felt it was a step in the wrong direction. They did not need whiteman's book to read. The forest, with its many nature signs, was all the book [sic] they needed." At this point in Six Nations history, before the establishment of Confederacy-run day schools, churches were the sites of early efforts to educate school-age children, and Montour closely aligns these initiatives with the political sympathies of those Native people involved: "Being Loyalists of the most unchanging type, their early schools were graced by large wall pictures of Queen Victoria and from a rough, partly peeled pole, the Union Jack floated proudly" (26). From Montour's perspective, these signs and symbols of loyalty to the Crown demonstrate the close connection between religious and political alignment with the project of progressivism on the reserve.

But he is also quick to point out another significant barrier to Native education as being the racist attitudes of those in "the Indian Department and of some church leaders," who "doubted the Indian child's ability to absorb knowledge" (Montour 1973, 28). Into this scenario he introduces the real-life figure of Augustus "Gus" Jamieson, a driving force behind the establishment of schools on the reserve, the hiring of qualified teachers, and the modernization of the curriculum to meet Ontario standards, all of which took place at Six Nations between 1906 and 1924. Montour describes him as "a man of many parts, a builder of schools and a 'Do it yourself' architect" (28) who once declared, "To the best of my ability, I will endeavour to show them that they are mistaken in the notion that Indian children can not gain knowledge and make progress." Montour makes note of the kinds of tributes that were paid to Jamieson after his death, by Native and non-Native leaders alike, words that reflected hope for a future via the education of Native youth: "Most progressive; A Man of Vision; the Founder of Education on the Six Nations Reserve" (29). Accolades such as these are clearly important to Montour, as he is concerned with stories that celebrate those members of Six Nations who demonstrated the ability to cross racial boundaries of religion, politics, and education in order to reconcile the differences between

Native and non-Native society. Throughout his book, he focuses on people and events at Grand River that effectively illustrate the intersection of Native society with mainstream values as a means to prove the "progress" of the Six Nations community and to counter the image of a static, unenlightened, and exclusive people.

Curiously, however, Montour maintains a noticeable distance from any substantial discussion of the Mohawk Institute in Brantford during this discussion on Native education, as if he is unable to reconcile the assimilationist agenda of the residential school project with his own religious perspective and the unwavering belief in the abilities of Natives to succeed on their own terms. Writing in the early 1970s—some two decades before the abuses that took place at residential schools were fully brought to light—Montour appears to praise the efforts of such institutions to further the advancement of Native youth and, in the process, contradicts our present-day understanding of what these schools were truly about. Describing the state of education at Grand River at the turn of the twentieth century, he declares, "Most of the literate Indians had done some time in the Mohawk Institute, a church boarding school for needy natives, established in 1831. Really bright, ambitious children were sent there to better their chances of getting an education" (1973, 116). Knowing what we do now, such statements are inaccurate, if not completely false, accounts of the quality of education that was available to Native children attending the Mohawk Institute, also widely known as the "Mush Hole," during this time. They also appear to contradict Montour's own description of church leaders' attitudes toward educating Natives, noted above. Significantly, however, Montour does contradict even himself when he provides a subtle, and rather chilling, description of the school environment that argues against his own otherwise positive characterization of student life. "On Sundays," he writes, "these uniformed inmates marched to the historic Loyalist Mohawk Chapel, where they were exposed to religion" (117). Along with the idea that literate Natives had "done some time" at the Institute, he is obviously aware on some level of the prison-like quality of life at residential schools, but like others in his time, he fails to be critical of such treatment.

Regardless of Montour's awareness of the exact nature of the experience of residential schools for Native youth, he appears to view such measures as necessary if Native people are to rise above their marginalized position in Canadian society. This is a sentiment that is particularly evident in the chapter entitled "Through Penury to Achievement," in which he details the life of Doctor Edward Davis, the reserve's first Native MD, who also attended the Mohawk Institute. By telling how the young "Eddy worked half a day on the school farm and attended school the other half" (reference to the manual labour that students also had to provide) and succeeded by applying "himself to his lessons with unflagging zeal," Montour points to the opportunities that can be accessed through commitment and hard work. Assuredly, there is little to argue against in that regard, but the author then suggests that this kind of ambition is precisely what Native people are lacking and what prevents them from rising above their social state. Echoing stereotypical attitudes of the day, Montour states: "At fifteen, he returned to the Injun Bush. Eddy Davis was looking for more worlds to conquer; in this he was unlike the usual little Institute graduate who usually reverted to careless and leisurely ways" (1973, 117). Sounding very much like Duncan Campbell Scott and others of the era who believed that residential schools provided the best opportunity for Native people to be assimilated into life beyond the confines of Native reserves, Montour appears to criticize those who "reverted" back to life within their communities after being given the chance to make use of the education they had received. In this way, Edward Davis's dreams of becoming a Doctor, and his success, become emblematic of what Natives can achieve if they only work hard enough—and forget the treatment they endured at residential school.

But where Montour does differ from the popular assimilationist rhetoric of the day is in his understanding of the prejudice that Native people faced in the early twentieth century. For this reason, he describes the academic achievements of Davis as especially noteworthy in the context of "racial discrimination, some social ostracism, and unkind remarks" (1973, 118) that he endured while enrolled at Caledonia High School. Once in Medical School in Toronto, Davis found himself an outsider once again. "He lived in a garret eating prunes, beans, and stale bread," Montour tells us. "With only one suit to wear, he felt uneasy among the wealthier classmates. Poverty was the wrong background for taking a course at university" (119). Aware of the barriers that Davis faced in his desire to enter the medical profession,

Montour relates his story as an inspirational one that speaks to the value of Native people refusing to accept a lower social status; at the same time, he describes the difficulties of such aspirations for a Native person. Although guilty of employing stereotypes of the "lazy Indian," Montour does address the issue of discrimination in the education system from a Native perspective and manages to celebrate the achievements of Native people at the post-secondary level. "Today, many Feathered Ones have followed in [Davis's] footsteps, getting education the hard way. College records show their names in law, science, pedagogy, medicine and theology. All came up through the same path of penury to achievement" (120). While Montour could certainly write such things in the early 1970s with a fair sense of optimism, it can be argued that discrimination at the post-secondary and professional levels is an unfortunate problem for Indigenous peoples that continues to this day. Dr. Edward Davis is undoubtedly a Native pioneer in the medical profession, but very few Native people have been able to find success in this field 100 years later, despite the fact that the overall health and wellness of First Nations, Inuit, and Métis people lags far behind the Canadian standard.

Although Montour avoids overtly political messages in his work, he does devote a short chapter to discussing the story of Deskaheh's struggles to oppose Canada's overthrow of the Confederacy Council and assert the sovereignty of the Grand River Haudenosaunee in the early 1920s. While respectful of the man and his efforts, Montour also makes a subtle yet distinctive connection between Deskaheh's religious beliefs and the idea of progress at Six Nations. He describes Chief Levi General as "an ordinary, run-of-the-mill Indian farmer" who had "come under some church influence, but his heart was in the Longhouse." As a result, Montour continues, "He believed in the old primitive way of life and in the hereditary Chiefs rather than in the elected Council. He felt that the Indian had lost everything by trying to live like a whiteman." Such a pronouncement indicates Montour's bias against the maintenance of Haudenosaunee traditions, which he sees as a kind of primitivism; he completely dismisses the significance of the political stance that Deskaheh took during his lifetime. What Montour fails to acknowledge here is the fact that Deskaheh was completely aware of and very politically engaged with the "white world" around him. Instead, Montour describes him as a conservative who can merely fret over the apparent, and seemingly inevitable, decline of the ways of the "old timers." "As a leader in the Longhouse ceremonies," Montour tells us, "he was called upon to do much meditating and lonely worrying. The word Deskaheh means a socio-religious leader. As such, he sat at the centre and handled the tom-tom in the quarterly Longhouse Festivals" (1973, 125). Writing fifty years after the fact, Montour still echoes the language used by Pauline Johnson a century earlier when she described longhouse activities; although Deskaheh was certainly an esteemed speaker at the Sour Springs Longhouse, his name itself does not refer to this position. Such inaccuracies are evidence of Montour's incomplete understanding of cultural practice and apparent indifference to their importance.

Like many people at Grand River during this time, Montour sees the removal of the Confederacy Council as an event necessitated by what he considers backward conservative culture, by illiteracy, and by the (perceived) incompetence of the hereditary Chiefs. At no time does he discuss the philosophical content of the Great Law or its ancient roots based upon an oral tradition that emphasized careful deliberation and peaceful dialogue. After noting how returning veterans from the First World War led a movement to depose the traditional leadership in favour of "a more modern, democratic form of council," Montour explains that "the council carried on its business in the Indian languages, as they met to handle the affairs of their six thousand people who lived in the heart of industrial Ontario." Obviously, he saw such a situation, in which a primitive form of government existed within a "civilized" space, as absurd and in need of change. But always the moderate, he describes the traditional leadership in polite, understated terms: "The Council carried on its business to the best of its natural ability. A formal education was not one of the requirements for membership in the Hereditary Council" (1973, 126). It is clear that Montour believes that the key to the development and growth of the Six Nations community revolves around Western education and a modernized form of local government. From his perspective, it was inevitable, and ultimately beneficial, that an elected band council was put in place at Six Nations, despite its implied recognition of the ultimate political authority of the Department of Indian Affairs to oversee daily life at Grand River.

Yet apart from these subtle and not-so-subtle criticisms, Montour does pay tribute to the sheer determination that Deskaheh displayed in his attempts to bring the political struggles of the Six Nations (and all Indigenous peoples) to the global stage. Marvelling at his tenacity, Montour describes how the Chief "dug up treaties, quoted history, and led delegations to Ottawa. Then, when he didn't seem to be making progress in Canada, he formed a delegation which crossed the ocean to England where they presented their claims to the throne ... [and] knocked on the doors of the League of Nations." In the process, Montour concludes, Deskaheh "sacrificed his money, health, and finally his life, working for the cause." While he no doubt supported the change to an elected council, Montour does acknowledge the harsh and unfair treatment that Deskaheh received at the hands of the Canadian government for simply standing up for what he believed in. Commenting on Canada's refusal to allow a gravely ill Deskaheh entry back into the country after travelling to Europe, Montour calls such action "the unkindest cut of all" (1973, 128). But he does identify one positive outcome in this otherwise futile struggle: the establishment of the annual Border Crossing celebration that takes place every July in Niagara Falls. This event, directly inspired by the political work of Deskaheh and initiated by his good friend Clinton Rickard of the Tuscarora Reservation in New York, celebrates the provisions of the 1794 Jay Treaty that allowed Native people free passage across the U.S.-Canada border. Montour concludes that this particular day is evidence that "Deskaheh did not work or live in vain. Today, the Border Crossing ceremony is celebrated by all Indians of every political view or opinion. Educated or illiterate, all join in celebrating the victory so dearly bought" (129). Once again, Montour emphasizes the distinction between two "kinds" of Native people (i.e., progressive and conservative) but sees this particular event as one that transcends internal differences and creates cohesion and unity based upon collective rights and an assertion of pride and identity.

Along with chronicling the lives of various Six Nations people and their achievements, the text recounts some social customs and practices unique to the Grand River community. This includes the annual event known as Bread and Cheese Day, which, along with the Border Crossing celebration, is a social occasion with distinct political roots. It is also significant to Montour's text because it highlights the close connection between the Crown and the Six Nations, coinciding as it does with Queen Victoria's birthday—the queen who, during her reign, began the tradition of passing out sizable portions of bread and cheese in a symbolic gesture of gratitude to the Six Nations for their military service to England. He explains that May 24 "was a gala day among the Indians, the day the Loyalists who came from the United States under Joseph Brant got token reward. They liked all things British, and good Queen Victoria was especially revered" (1973, 44). After her death, the custom was carried on by the hereditary, and later the elected, council, and despite its overt echoes of colonialism it remains a popular and extremely well-attended event to this day.

Although the large majority of people at Grand River view Bread and Cheese as a community event in which any connection to the Crown has been all but forgotten, Montour goes so far as to say that "It marks an ancient tradition; it is the Feathered Loyalists' birthright" (1973, 46). Such a conclusion is highly exaggerated, but it does serve to underline Montour's intention to portray the Six Nations reserve as a homogeneous community that revels in its Loyalist history. Rather than discuss the diverse and complex interpretations of history and politics as they relate to Grand River, he seeks to provide an account of events more agreeable to the casual reader, and not necessarily one intended for a Six Nations audience.

Although it is far from a definitive historical text, Montour's work is one of the very few that provide an account of life at Six Nations from a community perspective told in anecdotal form, and for this reason it is a highly unique and interesting text, especially when one considers that it was published at a time when Native people across North America were becoming more empowered politically and culturally. The Feathered U.E.L.'s, however, reflects a decidedly assimilationist perspective that is in opposition to what most Native people were espousing in the early 1970s. Although Montour was not alone in his opinions at this time, such views would all but disappear within a few short years due to a much stronger assertion of Native rights within First Nations communities.

For all of his assimilationist rhetoric, however, Montour cannot resist including elements of Native "otherness" in his book that would be of interest to outside readers (and quite possibly fulfill certain expectations). Amid the quaint and poignant sketches of life at Six Nations, then, are moments in which Montour points to Haudenosaunee culture as being markedly different, and strange, when compared to that of their white neighbours.

Traditional beliefs and ceremonies are the primary difference, of course, but because he is not a participant in longhouse activities he provides very little detail about this particular cultural distinction. Instead, he relates several stories of "everyday life" that stand in contrast to the individual stories of those who had made their mark beyond the boundaries of the reserve, as if those who remain on the reserve were marked by a distinct sensibility not found in mainstream society. As mentioned, this contrast most often manifests itself in the idea of the educated and progressive versus the illiterate and conservative Six Nations member, but it occasionally emerges in other ways as well. In a chapter entitled "Things that Go Bump in the Night," he engages the topic of "an eerie, supernatural visitation to the home of John R. Lickers, an Indian schoolmaster" (1973, 65) as a means to illustrate some reserve residents' easy belief in supernatural events. After describing how household items began moving of their own accord in broad daylight—pictures swayed on the walls, and fires spontaneously broke out in the home—he relates how the Indian agent (J.E. Cameron), the reserve's medical doctor (Dr. N. Holmes), and "university specialists" all visited the residence but could find "no reasoned explanation ... of this eerie, reserve manifestation" (66). According to Montour, "superstitious Indians simply called all this uncanny activity Jistiggly, meaning night-flying weird creatures in the Mohawk language or Cheepii in the Mohican [Delaware] dialect meaning ghostly haunters. It wasn't too hard to convince the native Indians of the reality of this disturbing presence. They readily believed in haunted houses, demon possession and in strange occurrences in nature that were bad signs for them and their friends" (67). What makes this story interesting is Montour's juxtaposition of the respected schoolteacher with such unexplained events, as if these kinds of things can also happen to an educated (i.e., "progressive") person in an environment where such activity is considered rather commonplace by many of his "conservative" neighbours. Although he does not express this sentiment explicitly, Montour seems to suggest that the reserve is home to many such beliefs that are either remnants of eroding cultural superstition or further proof that some residents still hold fast to a belief system that is quite unlike the enlightened Euro-Canadian view of the world that surrounds them.

This mysterious, foreboding tone of Native otherness is a prominent feature of *Forbidden Voice: Reflections of a Mohawk Indian*, written by Alma Greene

(Gah-wonh-nos-doh) and published in 1971. (While the book is essentially an "as told to" autobiographical narrative, ghostwritten by a non-Native collaborator, Greene is given sole authorship.) Although it appeared only two years before Montour's work, the two texts differ completely in terms of tone and content. Whereas *The Feathered U.E.L.'s* is filled mostly with uplifting stories of the old days and humorous tales of reserve life, Greene's book is a much darker work that relates stories of murder, ghosts, and witchcraft. In addition, it contains several black-and-white illustrations that depict scenes from these stories, pictures that include headless horsemen, skeletons, and dismembered hands, among other such disturbing images. To a large degree, it is these illustrations that give the book its ominous look and feel, but because they were done by a non-Native named Gordon McLean, we must also consider whether his own sense of what Greene was conveying gave way to a Eurocentric bias of what Native culture was about. In other words, did his own fears of the "other" and primitive culture manifest themselves in his visual interpretation of the stories? Whatever the case, Greene's tales are an intriguing mix of folklore, history, and culture that serve as a highly illuminating counternarrative to Montour's version of life within the Six Nations community.

Like Montour's book, *Forbidden Voice* begins with a descriptive "snapshot" of the reserve told from a child's perspective and moves toward the present. As both works progress, this narrative device often has the effect of nostalgic lament, as if the "good old days" of the community were behind it and what remains is an inferior version of what the culture and people once were. Unlike Montour's story, however, Greene concerns herself with an account of the traditionalist community at Grand River, particularly the Mohawk nation. By positioning herself within this context, Greene becomes for the reader a figure of insider knowledge and authority. She states, "As a small native girl of the Six Nations, Forbidden Voice was a princess of royal blood, heiress to her mother, who was a [Turtle] clan mother to a Chieftainship title.... The little girl's father was also a Mohawk of the Wolf Clan ... he gave up his time for the good of the council fire, he could act as interpreter and secretary and many times represented the Confederacy Council as one of the delegation on an important mission" (1973, 12). This curious, disjointed narrative style in which Greene refers to herself in the third person, as Forbidden Voice, is consistent throughout the book and would seem to confirm the presence of an outside writer, particularly when such glaring mistakes such as the following occur: "a clan mother ... must not marry a man of a different clan" (12). Of course, the exact opposite is true, according to traditional "law," and is something that Greene would have been fully aware of. Regardless of such inaccuracies and the question of authorship, her "presence" within the work is more fully pronounced than Montour's, as demonstrated by the following: "Forbidden Voice is an old lady now, and this book shall reveal the things she has seen and heard which have never been told before" (17). A statement such as this is clearly meant to appeal to a non-Native audience hungry for "authentic" remnants of First Nations culture and spiritual beliefs, information which Greene—or the publisher—is happy to provide.

What follows, then, is a diverse collection of stories, prophecies, reminiscences, and historical sketches of Six Nations history as filtered through Greene's experience as a Mohawk clan mother and traditional healer. Her abilities as a seer are recounted early in the text when she describes her encounter with a small deer, "no bigger than the dogs," which only she could see, beginning when she was four years old. At that time, her mother was alarmed at her insistence that such an animal existed and "consulted an old Indian Chief. He told her not to interfere, for the little girl had been favoured and blessed. The tiny deer, which few people have ever seen, was actually a sign that the time would come when she would help her people in sickness and give counsel in their distress" (1971, 20). Having been identified as a medicine person from an early age, she was instructed in the use of medicinal plants and other curative customs. She also gained an awareness of other, more malevolent practices such as charms and witchcraft. Both of these cultural elements are featured prominently in the book, and, as mentioned earlier, the illustrator takes a particular interest in the strange and more macabre stories that are presented. Greene also devotes considerable time, however, to discussing the significant relationship of Haudenosaunee culture to the plant world and provides several herbal remedies and practices to aid in everything from digestive problems to heart conditions and cancer. This sort of information, now known as Traditional Ecological Knowledge (TEK) or herbology, was virtually unknown to all but a very few outside of Indigenous communities at this time, and since the 1970s has, of course, become an increasingly respected field in the medical world. She also makes note of the spiritual importance of tobacco to the Haudenosaunee, for "burning it was a protection and a remedy and a prayer to the Creator" because the "Creator had given his people a promise that whenever they burned the sacred tobacco he would hearken to them" (24). The significance of these plants was not lost on the artist either, apparently, as he provides detailed depictions of them.

In addition to traditional cultural practice, Greene provides brief historical outlines of the formation of the Confederacy, the Code of Handsome Lake, the role of the Haudenosaunee in the American Revolution, the relocation to Grand River, and the subsequent erosion of the land base provided by the Haldimand Proclamation. Like Six Nations writers and orators before her, she also reiterates the sense of outrage over promises made by the British before and after the Revolution, which were only forgotten and broken by their successors:

> The Six Nations had been given the lands in the Grand River Valley and had moved there from the United States and had rekindled their Great Council Fire in their new home. But the treaty of pledge, which had been executed on April 7, 1779, had promised the Six Nations not just land to replace what they had lost but the same status as before the war, which meant the right to be an independent nation; to be allies of the English, not British subjects; to be brothers of the sovereign with their own equal sovereignty.
>
> And now what had happened? Their lands had been sold or stolen; the Canadian government treated them as silly children for whom it was quite all right to make laws without consultation; and the white men called them heathens. (1973, 127)

Statements such as this are significant because they serve as further proof that many at Six Nations had not forgotten their historical alliance with England, although both the Crown and Canada were largely oblivious to such a relationship by the 1970s. Although Greene and Montour could not be further apart in political and social perspective, both authors agree that the Grand River Haudenosaunee had a unique and binding agreement with the Crown, one that differed significantly from the Crown's relationship with other First Nations, and one that needed to be remembered and honoured in the present. In this way, both texts are quite consistent with the political awakening that was taking place on reserves in the 1970s.

Another interesting element of Greene's work is her occasional discussions of Christianity and Mohawk traditionalism and the ways in which she negotiates similarities and differences between the two. Although we know her father was a Pine Tree Chief with the Confederacy Council, she tells us that he was also "a lay reader in the Anglican church, and the first English Forbidden Voice had ever heard was her father reading the Bible on Sundays" (120). As a child, Greene's "mother had taught her a prayer in Mohawk to repeat every night before she went to bed. All it said was 'God the Father, God the Son, God the Holy Ghost; Creator of the sun, the moon, the stars and the earth. Amen'" (122–23). As she grew older, Greene reflected on these words and understood that although "its form was Christian ... its spirit seemed ... more like a true Mohawk prayer" (122). She realized that this simple prayer paralleled the longhouse "festivals [that] were held according to the moon and their purpose was to thank the Creator for the seasons and for the ripening of each crop as it came on." She continues, "this was her people's ancient religion, and it began to seem to her the purest way of worship. Wasn't it better than always asking the Creator to do something or to give something more than He already had?" (123). While this mixture of religious practices may seem odd or confusing to most Christian thinkers, such blending and merging of beliefs was not uncommon among Native communities throughout the twentieth century (nor is it uncommon in the present), and Grand River was no exception, despite the divisions emphasized by Montour. Greene, coming from a part of the reserve that was heavily populated by Christian Mohawks would have certainly been exposed to both traditional and Christian belief systems, and her approach to spiritual matters reflects such a confluence. She does note, however, that her father eventually left the Anglican Church in disgust when he learned of its role in taking Six Nations lands during the nineteenth century.

Joseph Brant was, of course, closely tied with the presence of Anglicanism at Grand River, and he is singled out on more than one occasion for criticism in Greene's text. In rather scathing terms, she suggests that he is to blame for altering Haudenosaunee society forever, not only politically but culturally as well: "Forbidden Voice wondered what it would have been like for the Mohawks if there had never been a Captain Joseph Brant, though everyone seemed to think of him as an illustrious warrior.... For Brant, who was not even a Chief but just a Mohawk warrior, was the one who had got the Six Nations mixed up with the white man and who had helped talk the Six Nations into fighting for England. And he was the one who had been so eager to see the Mohawks become Christians that he had destroyed their longhouse" (1973, 127–28). The debate about Brant's legacy is a frequent one at Six Nations; although very few outside of the community are aware of his controversial reputation at Grand River and among other Haudenosaunee as well. While the popular perception of his loyalty to the British forms the basis of The Feathered U.E.L.'s, for example, and resulted directly in Brant's image appearing on a commemorative loonie coin in 2007, most people at Six Nations protest vehemently when labelled "Loyalists." Greene's statements, then, reflect how Six Nations history is often contested from within the community and demonstrate how the "accepted version," written for decades by non-Natives, needs to be questioned and re-evaluated in order to provide a greater understanding of the exact relationship between the Grand River Haudenosaunee and the British Crown. Therefore, her assessment of Brant's influence, and her distancing of his reputation as a Loyalist from the rest of the Six Nations, can be viewed as a significant decolonizing moment performed at the height of the Red Power movement.

Although the narrative style throughout Forbidden Voice indicates an author other than Greene, the last two pages appear to be written in the first person. "I have had a long life," she states, "and I am a grandmother now, and these are the memories and stories I have hoarded all that long time up till now. But these are not all my stories or memories. Some things I know I would not tell to anyone, except perhaps my little granddaughter if she becomes a clan mother in her turn. And I think some of the things I know I would not tell even to her" (1973, 156). With this statement, Greene addresses the significance of the oral tradition as it exists within twentieth-century Haudenosaunee culture. Aware that her audience has an interest in "Indian stories," she makes it clear that some stories are not for outsiders, some are for those who require specific knowledge (such as her granddaughter as a potential culture carrier), and some are perhaps too powerful or dangerous to share with anyone. While she has certainly committed to print many stories that had not ever been told beyond the boundaries of the reserve before, Greene is at the same time aware of the limits of such storytelling and knowledge-sharing. Her work is therefore an example of a transitional period in Native communities (and Native Studies) in that it follows the time during the 1930s, 40s, and 50s in which people at Six Nations shared information about traditions and culture rather freely, and precedes the contemporary period in which much Native cultural content is now largely considered "off limits" to people from outside the culture and to non-Native audiences in general.

Long recognized as the "breakthrough" work by an Indigenous writer in Canada, Maria Campbell's *Halfbreed* appeared the same year as *The Feathered U.E.L.'s.* While by no means as popular as Campbell's text, the books by Montour and Green are, however, very similar to *Halfbreed* in that they contain personal stories about a specific community that convey "insider" histories, relate cultural practices and beliefs, and address political injustice at the hands of the Canadian government. It is also significant that the two writers from Six Nations were much older than Campbell, and this fact demonstrates that the movement to tell, and to write, these stories for a larger audience was not confined to a generation of young activists who were frustrated and angered by the long history of Canadian colonialism and mistreatment, but that such sentiment transcended age, region, and cultural group. It also speaks to the interest in First Nations, Métis, and Inuit stories by publishers willing to produce such works in the early 1970s as they recognized a growing interest in "authentic" Indigenous voices at this time. Furthermore, the politically charged works by authors in Canada such as Harold Cardinal and Howard Adams that dominated Native and Métis writing during this period would eventually give way to more introspective and literary works by the early 1980s. While this latter development signalled a distinct shift in the approach to articulating Indigenous issues, it was also quickly apparent that literature—theatre and poetry especially—was highly effective as a means of resistance in the movement to decolonize First Nations, Métis, and Inuit peoples by empowering individuals and communities. Although visual art by Indigenous people also began to find a wide audience during this time, literature soon became the primary expression of political resistance and social commentary by increasingly vocal First Nations, Inuit, and Métis writers as the 1980s progressed; they soon also found audiences beyond Indigenous readers.

DANIEL DAVID MOSES: SOME GRAND RIVER POETICS

Daniel David Moses (Delaware, b. 1952), a self-described "farm-raised Indian boy" from Grand River, aspired to be a writer from a young age and set out to learn his craft through the conventional means of university training throughout the 1970s. This included degrees in creative writing and fine arts from York University and the University of British Columbia, accomplishments which would have made fellow Delaware Enos Montour quite proud. But after graduating, Moses felt confined by the restrictions of such training and realized he "had also absorbed a number of … prejudices about the nature of literature" (2005, 8). While working a series of odd jobs in and around Toronto in the early '80s, he continued to write and eventually began to pursue his own literary voice and technique. "Working at last independently," he states, "with no institutionalized threat of failure and no constant contact with current academic and literary fashions, I began to work haltingly toward a way of writing that could express more of what I felt" (10). Around this time, he also met Anishinabe poet and storyteller Lenore Keeshig-Tobias and Cree musician and playwright Tomson Highway, both of whom were engaged in similar artistic pursuits. In 1986, the three would form the core of what became known as the "Committee to Re-Establish the Trickster," a group of Indigenous writers and artists committed to asserting culture through creative expression and "dedicated to the idea that the Trickster is emblematic of our different worldview and the different literature connected to it" (149). This was the official beginning of the explosion in First Nations, Inuit, and Métis writing that continues to this day, and which has resulted in the emergence of Native presses and Native literature courses in almost every university and college in Canada.

Moses's first published collection of poetry, *Delicate Bodies* (1980), was followed by the play *Coyote City* (1988), which was nominated for the Governor General's Award for drama. Notably, the play bears an interesting resemblance to many of the stories in *Forbidden Voice*, since Johnny, the lead character in *Coyote City*, is a ghost. This particular approach was an almost unconscious one and was rather perplexing for Moses himself, who later wrote: "Why was I afraid to decide that the ghost was as much a character as the rest? My intuition told me I had to make that proverbial imaginative leap if the play was to work. I had to believe in the ghost as much as I did in the [other characters] if I was to do justice to the story, the play and the audience" (2005, 6). Like Montour a decade earlier, Moses struggled to acknowledge and make sense of the understood presence of such entities within his community and within his work; and he also realized that, as an educated person, he should perhaps "know better." But being a poet, Moses also ruminated upon this issue further in order to understand the persistence of belief, place, and story:

> I grew up on a farm on the Six Nations lands along the Grand River near Brantford in southern Ontario. I grew up nominally Anglican in a community of various Christian sects and of the Longhouse, the Iroquoian traditional religious and political system. These form the largely unarticulated base of my understanding of the world.
>
> I grew up on occasion hearing ghost stories rooted in that community, stories I only paid small attention to, because I was being educated to have— let's call it—a western mind, to balance being a good Judaeo-Christian with being scientific.... How could I possibly believe in a character, write a character who was a ghost? (6–7)

Interestingly, Moses draws a distinction between his understanding of the Trickster and what constitutes a "ghost" story, as if one kind of story can more easily and readily exist in First Nations literature and the other cannot. I would argue that such a moment illustrates the difference between what is perceived as superstition and what is accepted as "culture," but ultimately both are constitutive of the same body of beliefs held by First Nations about the world around us. Thus, such embarrassment about cultural beliefs can be viewed as moments of residual colonial shame that were quite present in First Nations, Inuit, and Métis communities well into the later part of the twentieth century. Moses is certainly not alone, for such feelings are a symptom of the impact of Christianity and Eurocentric thinking upon generations of Indigenous peoples, most notably evident by the need to *re-establish* the Trickster.

Moses relates that once he got past the expected, Western conventions in his approach to writing stories of Native people, and got to the way that the stories "wanted" to be told, his poetry soon became full of "irony and humour," and his plays began to demonstrate an improvement in their "dramatic monologues, implied dialogues, the half-heard discussions of several voices" in ways that were "exciting and intriguing" (2005, 10). These characteristics, of course, all indicate a renewed sense of the power of language and an increased emphasis on oral tradition and performance, and in this way closely reflect First Nations, Inuit, and Métis modes of expression and communication that are unique, and recognizable, to their communities. This shift was not lost on those involved with the Committee to Re-establish the Trickster, and Moses gives particular credit to Keeshig-Tobias, who for years had been "consciously looking for ways to write about being a Native person [through] ... studying [Native] storytelling, folklore and presentation" (10–11). Moses describes a specific moment in the evolution of his writing, one that had a very significant local resonance as well: "Seeing [Keeshig-Tobias] recite one poem to a rapt audience crowded into the Trojan Horse coffee shop on Danforth Avenue, a poem by 'Mohawk Poetess' E. Pauline Johnson, reconfirmed my taste for the oral. (It was perhaps an original taste since Johnson had been the one poet I had heard talked of beyond the school-yards of my childhood)" (11). What makes this scene particularly notable is not only the ability of Johnson's poetry to affect an audience in Toronto nearly a century after her death, but also the impact it had upon another writer from Six Nations who had all but forgotten her work and who now realized how it could serve to empower his own.

Like Johnson, Moses grew up in close proximity to the Grand River (literally across the river, in fact, from Chiefswood, Johnson's childhood home) and it is no surprise that it serves as the central image in one of his more powerful poems, "Some Grand River Blues," a piece that shares similar qualities with "The Song My Paddle Sings." Both are rather sombre yet ultimately affirming odes to the ability of nature to inspire and uplift the human spirit. Instead of the individual, first-person narrator in Johnson's piece, however, Moses's poem is a dramatic monologue, with the speaker addressing a second person in the effort to "lift" his or her mind from a state of melancholy or sadness:

> Look. The land ends up
> in stubble every
> October. The sky
> today may feel as
>
> empty. But just be
> like the river—bend
> and reflect it....

This image of the land after harvest is a familiar one along the rich farmlands of the Grand River, and while it does indicate the coming of winter, this emptiness also signifies that the harvest is complete and that nature has once again provided for the people so that they will be sustained through the long, cold months ahead. As an agricultural society, the Haudenosaunee have always placed great importance on the seasonal cycles. These are also the predominant patterns that form the basis of the traditional ceremonial calendar, which closely follows the process of growth, death, and renewal that takes place continuously within the natural world. For Moses, such ebbing and flowing of life is also paralleled within each of us emotionally, physically, mentally, and spiritually, and he instructs his companion to

> Just remind
> yourself how the land
> also renews
> (2000, 1)

evoking the Indigenous belief that humans are also elements of the natural world and therefore often affected by similar forces of decline and regeneration on an individual level of well-being.

Another significant feature of Moses's poem is the way it oscillates between the images of land, water, and sky, which are mirrored on emotional and physical human levels. With the desolation of the land after harvest and the "empty" October sky reflecting the mental and emotional state of his companion, the speaker notes the similarities between the veins in our bodies and the river, since water is often referred to as the "lifeblood" of Mother Earth in Haudenosaunee philosophy. In this way, human beings are connected further to the natural world and the land itself is perceived as a living entity. After urging his companion to "be like the river," the speaker points out that

> Those
> blues already show
>
> through the skin inside
> your elbow—and flow
> back to the heart....
> (2000, 1)

These lines connect the physical and the emotional with their reference to veins as rivers of blood that flow to the heart, the organ closely associated with emotions. Here, Moses is also alluding to the "blues" as an emotional state, as well as having "the blues" in a musical sense, which is of course conveyed by the title.

This interconnection of land and water, body and emotion, then, becomes the central image at the end of the poem, in which Moses effectively evokes the relationship between self, place, and healing. After we learn that "a few passing // Canada geese" have excited his companion with thoughts of a similar flight or escape, the speaker seeks to reassure his friend that their migratory journey is not a fleeing, but merely the act of adapting to a change in environment.

> Your heart
> started beating with
> their wings the moment
> you got sight of them
> —but that's no reason
> to fear it will still

when they disappear.
Look away now. Let
loose. See? The river's
bending like a bruise.
(2000, 1–2)

The impulse to take flight and flee a situation is not an acceptable method of
dealing with a difficult situation, and the central message is to understand
that emotional pain will recede so long as we do not hold onto that which
afflicts us but rather let it "loose" and "bend" to accept it. Moses also rein-
troduces the image of the river as a feature of the body to suggest that, while
trauma will often leave a physical or emotional scar, such hurt will soon fade
and be cleansed/carried away by the flow of blood/water. What makes this
poem especially compelling is the way Moses infuses the Grand River with
great stability, power, and resiliency; it remains as seasons change and generations come and go. One can therefore gain wisdom and gather strength
by reflecting on the "lessons" it can provide. This is, of course, particularly
resonant for the Six Nations community, whose identity and sense of place
is so closely intertwined with the Grand River. Despite their distance across
the years, this is a fact that is not lost on either Pauline Johnson or Daniel
David Moses.

Although he is always quick to identify Six Nations as his home, Moses's
literary vision has carried him across North America, and his achievements
in the field of Native literature have been profound. Much like Pauline
Johnson's, his literary work may not be widely known at Grand River, but
his influence is felt by many young Indigenous authors who see his work
as transcending specific cultural boundaries to speak to the wider project
of creating a First Nations, Inuit, and Métis aesthetic in poetry and theatre.
Consequently, his career has reflected the transition of Native writing from
the recounting of stories and cultural beliefs, as seen in Montour and Green,
to the emergence of a full-fledged, recognized body of Native literature that
is studied at the post-secondary level. Moses may not always address cultural themes familiar to Haudenosaunee audiences, but his appreciation of
storytelling and the power of words are most certainly shaped by his experience growing up at Grand River, where the sense of "haunted" and hidden

histories that demand to be told is quite strong. As demonstrated in this chapter, the diversity and richness of these traditional narratives, both sacred and secular, are what gave rise to the wide array of literary perspectives that emerged from the Grand River community in the latter half of the twentieth century. And with the Oka "crisis" of July 1990, the diversity of voices would grow larger still.

5

"Linking Arms Together"   Six Nations of the Grand River from Oka
to the Twenty-First Century

The explosive events around the expansion of a nine-hole golf course onto traditional Mohawk lands near Oka, Quebec, in the summer of 1990 are well known as a watershed moment in recent Canadian history. This land dispute, and the resulting three-month conflict between the Mohawks of Kanehsatake, the Sûreté du Quebec, and the Canadian Armed Forces, has been the subject of countless articles, books, political analyses, and a few well-produced documentaries.[1] What has been less reported on and studied, however, is the significance of this event within Haudenosaunee communities, as well as the important role that Haudenosaunee women played at this time. Because the Kanehsatake Mohawks are part of the Six Nations Confederacy, all Haudenosaunee people were especially affected by the situation at Oka, and although there was widespread support from Indigenous peoples across Canada (and the U.S.), the clash with police and the Canadian Forces had particular meaning for all seventeen Haudenosaunee communities, who saw our collective land base being threatened yet again. Grand River, being the most populated, became heavily involved with organizing demonstrations and raising funds, in addition to the hundreds of members who ventured to Kanehsatake to show support and assist in any way they could. As the seat of the Confederacy Council in Canada, hereditary Chiefs from Grand River played an active role in negotiations, not only with the Canadian government, but also with the Mohawk Warriors, a militant group of mostly Mohawk men and women whose political views often conflicted with the Confederacy Council's responsibility to uphold the principles of the Great Law of Peace.

It was a tumultuous time during which Haudenosaunee people argued over the appropriateness of using armed force to defend our lands and sovereignty, but which also made people reconsider the traditional concepts of peace and of dialogue as a means of resolving conflict. The diverse understandings of what it meant to be Haudenosaunee in the late twentieth century was openly discussed in healthy, empowering ways, and like thousands of First Nations, Inuit, and Métis across Canada who shared this experience, we too became much more aware, and proud, of our Indigenous identities in ways that had not existed prior to 1990. While the writers and artists discussed in this chapter all address the themes of Haudenosaunee consciousness in the late twentieth century from a wide range of cultural and community perspectives, they each demonstrate that divergent opinions on these matters often arrive at the same destinations. What is most important, therefore, is that we keep the thinking and the dialogue alive, in whatever form, and do not lose sight of the unique connections between our histories, traditions, and communities as the sites of our cultural continuity.

BACK ON THE REZ: PERSONAL HOMECOMINGS/ COMMUNITY RECONNECTIONS

As Daniel David Moses was forging a literary career for himself and opening up opportunities for other Native artists during the 1980s, Brian Maracle (Mohawk, b. 1947) was involved with Native politics and journalism in Vancouver and Ottawa. Both were aware of a new, awakening consciousness around Native issues in Canada, and both lived away from their community, working to promote positive change in their respective fields. Despite being a part of this exciting time, Maracle writes, "Living away from the reserve for so long, cut off from the land, the people and the culture, left me with a nagging sense of loss" (1996, 15). Raised in an era when Native people were forced to leave their communities to find employment and opportunity in the city, Moses and Maracle were not unlike thousands of others living off their reserves. While the majority did not return to live permanently, visiting only for weddings, funerals, and holidays (and some not at all), others eventually made their way back to resume their lives among family and friends. Brian Maracle's book *Back on the Rez: Finding the Way Home* is the non-fictional account of just such a return, made all the more interesting as it takes place in a post-Oka environment in which many of the old expectations and attitudes about being Native in Canada had changed dramatically since he had left. "During my life in mainstream society," he writes, "I earned two college degrees and achieved minor success in native politics and journalism.... In October 1993, I left a career on the fringes of Parliament Hill to start a new life back home on the Six Nations reserve. After forty years away, I returned—alone—to live in a battered log house in a community where I had few relatives, fewer friends and no job" (5).

What makes his work especially engaging is the way that he employs his journalistic training and political experience along with his "outsider" status to construct a narrative about life at Grand River in the 1990s that is at once objective and subjective in tone and content. Because of his time away, Maracle is able to "report" on the situation at Six Nations from a distance, but he also has an obvious, deep connection to his subject matter built upon family ties and the inclusion of cultural content. While some of the text is taken up with his musings as a modern-day Mohawk Thoreau adjusting to daily life in his cabin in the reservation woods, it is his observations on local politics and the erosion of Haudenosaunee languages within the community that emerge as the most striking elements of *Back on the Rez*.

The book chronicles the events of his first year after returning to Grand River, with the four chapters structured after the seasons in order to evoke the significance of the yearly cycle of Haudenosaunee life. Each of the four chapters is also titled in Mohawk (i.e., "Tsiteyotenerahtatenyons—'When the leaves are changing'"), demonstrating Maracle's emphasis on the continued use of our languages in small but meaningful ways. Narrated as a series of vignettes and editorial-style commentary, with topics ranging anywhere from the emerging tobacco industry on the reserve to visits with his Gramma Lillian and play-by-play accounts of the annual snowsnake tournament, his text is effective in capturing the subtle features and intricacies of the Six Nations community as it was in the early 1990s.

As such, two of the earlier pieces cover the passings of Onondaga elder Reg Henry and his Aunt Vi, illustrating the sad reality that as we move forward as a people we are also reminded of what we lose every year in terms of knowledgeable elders and older family members. It's a situation all too familiar to any First Nations community struggling to retain a connection to traditional identity. What makes the loss of such individuals so alarming is the vast amount of cultural and historical information that goes with them. Maracle captures this pressing concern quite eloquently when he relates that one of the reasons he made his decision to move back to Grand River "was to be able to spend time with some very special people—the old timers on this territory, who have many things to teach me about the people, the culture and the history of this place" (1996, 28). But shortly after his return he attends the funeral of his old friend Reg Henry, whom Maracle had met as a boy forty years earlier while living in Rochester, New York, and who had also found his own way back to Six Nations to become a highly respected traditionalist and Cayuga language teacher. Maracle states that Reg's "[language] work was so precise that the method he used to write the Cayuga language, with its distinctive spellings, accents and punctuation marks, was adopted by the local school system, universities, government and Cayuga speakers everywhere and is now known as the Henry orthography" (29). The sad irony of Reg's passing so soon after Maracle moves back home is not lost on the author, and has no doubt been a motivation in his own efforts to revitalize Haudenosaunee languages at Grand River, which is the work that he still carries on.

Although most of the older members of his family spoke Mohawk, like the vast majority of his generation, Maracle did not grow up speaking the language. He says that "even though I began to study the language more than twenty years ago, I never learned anything more than a few expressions and a little of the vocabulary" (1996, 256). This is an experience commonly shared by adult language learners, in which the difficulty and lack of progress causes most to be frustrated and eventually give up trying to learn. After relocating to Six Nations, however, Maracle found the opportunity to dedicate himself to more intensive language classes and soon realized that he was gaining more than just the ability to speak the language of his ancestors. "What thrills and intrigues me about learning the language is the insight it provides into Kanyen'kehaka [Mohawk] culture and psychology," he states, and "learning the language is helping me to learn more about my own people" (260). This excitement in discovering the linguistic differences between Mohawk and English sentence structure, coupled with his journalistic knowledge of the way the English language works, leads Maracle to assert that language is a highly effective means of defining the distinctions between Indigenous and Western worldviews. He writes, "In Kanyen'kehaka ... context takes first priority. Only when the action is placed in context does the individual appear, and this, to me, reflects in a small way why Indian societies are the way they are: why they are egalitarian, why the people are modest and why the environment is revered" (264). This he contrasts with the "English-speaking world [that] ... is so self-centred and narcissistic ... because the individual—politically and grammatically—always comes first" (263).

These are bold statements, to be sure, and we must be cautious when comparing the way we are as a people today who speak English as a first language with those of our grandparents and great-grandparents who were raised as native speakers and who "lived" a language. What Maracle is saying, I believe, is that despite our lack of use, understanding, and thinking in our languages, there are still fundamental cultural beliefs that persist in the ways in which our communities continue to function in the present, regardless of what language is spoken. As a result, First Nations value systems are uniquely different than those of the rest of Canadian society, as witnessed by the ongoing conflicts around issues such as land rights, resource management, and education, to name just a few. These sometimes unconscious, embedded cultural values are the kinds of things that the media and Canadian politicians do not recognize, let alone respect, since they put little if any thought to the importance of Native languages as having significant ideological meaning, and influence, in the present.

Maracle's concern is that, over time, our own people will grow further away from a full understanding of our culture as our languages continue to erode and fall into disuse. This is particularly evident to him in the way that the Six Nations band council fails to comprehend the significance of language when posting jobs within the community. Upset that their ads do not require applicants to speak one of the languages, even if the position involves working with older people, Maracle says that he doesn't "want to think that the council figures that the languages are so far gone that they aren't worth saving. Those thoughts are just too infuriating to contemplate. But what other explanation can there be?" (1996, 272). He speculates that the council does not see that saving the languages is their responsibility, as this is the domain of the schools and/or the parents. While this speculation may be true to a degree, Maracle maintains that languages are in such a crisis that the elected leadership of Six Nations needs to recognize their regeneration and retention as a priority. He lists several possible methods by which languages can be utilized inexpensively on a daily basis so that they are visible to the community and suggests that "members on the council could make it a personal priority and set an example by learning the language themselves and using it" (274).

For Maracle, such action would demonstrate courageous and committed leadership that would earn the respect of the entire community. He does not see language as simply the domain of traditionalism but as a key component of our Indigenous identity, regardless of religious beliefs—to lose our languages would have tragic consequences for all. "The chain of cause and effect is very clear," he concludes. "Once we lose our language, we lose our culture. And once we lose everything that sets us apart from mainstream society, we will surely lose the little land we have left" (1996, 275). Echoing this idea of language as a method of resistance and a decolonizing force, Taiaiake Alfred argues that "it seems impossible to imagine a way out of the European imperial reality using conceptual tools (languages) that represent the very framework being challenged" (2005, 248). "If indigenous languages are the tools we will use," he continues, "then indigenous narratives are the foundations upon which our indigenous identities and resurgent cultures will be reconstructed" (249). Both Maracle and Alfred agree that language and politics are inextricably linked in these ways, both understand the responsibility of leadership to demonstrate this fact to their community, and both are critical of ineffective leaders who fail to support language initiatives when our languages are on the verge of disappearing forever.[2]

Although his disdain for the elected council at Grand River is consistent throughout the book, his years of experience in Ottawa also make Maracle aware of the frustratingly ineffective nature of Native political systems as dictated by the federal bureaucracy. Because he knows the tremendous systemic obstacles they face daily, he is not entirely anti–band council either. In fact, he comments that, based upon his observations over five months, he feels that "the Chief and council appear, for the most part, to be motivated by a sincere and selfless desire to help others," and that "they honestly believe they are working in the best interests of the community." He cautions, "hard work and good intentions are not enough," but understands that "the people who run the elected system are not the problem either. They are basically good people who have been sucked into an oppressive, destructive and alien system that will never meet the needs of the people here" (1996, 228). What he fails to explain, however, is that most First Nations communities, including Grand River, do not fully realize the extent to which the elected system is controlled by Ottawa, and that this is often the cause of extreme tensions between leadership and community members. Consequently, people will often criticize and condemn their leaders for their incompetence rather than engage with the very real, difficult work of decolonizing themselves, their families, and their communities. This was certainly the case in the mid-1990s when Maracle was writing, and very little has changed with regard to the potential for Native self-determination within First Nations communities, except that people are now more aware of what their councils have to contend with and are therefore, perhaps, slightly more sympathetic.

Of course, a significant difference between other First Nations communities and Six Nations is that Grand River still has a traditional government in place that could be the answer to the ineffective nature of the federally controlled elected council. The problem, however, according to Maracle, is that even though many community members understand the spiritual and historical significance of the Great Law and the Confederacy Council, most do not regard it as having legitimate, or practical, authority in the present (at least at the time of his writing). Among those who do, he notes, there exists a commitment to traditional ways not found in those who support the band-council system. Describing the audience at a Confederacy Council meeting, Maracle writes, "it's my guess that most of them don't understand the language well enough to know exactly what was being said. Yet they sat there all day long. That's the kind of loyalty money can't buy. That's the kind of dedication that will ensure that the Great Law will outlast the Indian Act" (1996, 173). Despite his admiration for the Confederacy, Maracle is also quite aware of its internal disputes and the complaints of its inaction and its inability to make decisions quickly. While this can be attributed to cultural protocol and limited political authority, he does point out that when faced with an immediate threat, such as when a band member began construction on a tire recycling plant in the early 1990s, the Confederacy was able to quickly mobilize and "stopped a multi-million-dollar high-tech project dead in its tracks in no time at all." He believes that such a strong political show of force indicates that the Confederacy Council functions most effectively when faced with a direct threat, and that because "the Confederacy does not face imminent peril on any other front right now, there is nothing forcing the Chiefs to work together." He writes, "I'm tempted to agree with one Chief who says the reason the Confederacy can't accomplish anything is because the Onkwehonwe have it too good, that things are too easy" (210). This rather interesting perspective stands in direct contrast to what most First Nations people would believe their experience to be but is certainly worth considering. If we are to recall the very real crises that Native people endured throughout much of the twentieth century, including residential schools and the most oppressive policies of the Indian Act, then life at Grand River in the 1990s would certainly seem relatively calm in comparison (aside from Oka and its aftermath). However, the events at Douglas Creek Estates ten years later would definitely present an immediate danger, one that propelled the Confederacy into necessary action once again.

At one point in his book, Maracle reflects on his first year back at Six Nations and realizes how his understanding of the challenges that face Native people is enhanced by his physical presence within the community. After giving a presentation at a CBC media conference regarding First Nations issues, he writes that his return home "allowed me to speak with more passion and greater confidence because I was speaking from within the circle of our existence. More important than that, however, is the fact that living on a reserve has broadened and deepened my knowledge, it has brought my view of the world into sharper focus and it has strengthened my convictions" (1996, 237). Maracle's ability to look at his own community with a certain amount of detachment allows him a unique perspective on what needs to be done in order to resolve some of the problems that plague the Six Nations community. Foremost among these is the division between the elected and Confederacy councils. Although he acknowledges that it would not be simple, he supports a plan that had initially been proposed by the Confederacy Council in 1991, in which the Confederacy would be responsible for such things as "land claims, taxation, treaties, membership, hunting and fishing issues, while the band councils [sic] would provide municipal services and administer [federal] government programs" (300). It may have taken fifteen years, but the elected council did indeed hand authority back over to the Confederacy to negotiate land claims after the Reclamation at Kanonhstaton in 2006, proof that the band council recognized the Confederacy's jurisdiction over land and the treaties that it made with the Crown more than 200 years before. Even more significant is the fact that the federal government also recognized the Confederacy's legitimate authority to do so. In addition, the Confederacy has also recently taken on more active roles in monitoring development activities along the Grand River as well as in negotiating membership issues with regard to recent measures concerning border security and the requirement of passports for travel between Canada and the United States.

Realizing that the complex nature of politics, internally and otherwise, is an almost overwhelming situation for most people to contend with, Maracle also prescribes certain measures that ordinary citizens of Six Nations could undertake as a means to make the community a better, and healthier, place. These include planting a garden, learning and using the language, becoming more familiar with the traditional ceremonies, and aspiring to achieve "the traditional pattern of thinking and behaviour that once governed our lives—the principle of the good mind." Harkening back to this ancient concept that sustained our people for centuries, he believes that such a balanced, positive approach would unite people around our common experience as Haudenosaunee rather than focussing on that which divides us. In this regard, his suggestions ring true not only for the Grand River community, but also for all First Nations people. "[C]onquering the problems we face won't depend on self-government, economic development, feasibility studies ... government programs or government money," he writes. "The only thing that will win our struggle will be our culture—specifically our clans, languages, ceremonies and traditions. We may never solve our legal, economic, social or political problems, but if we can fortify our culture at least we will be physically fit, morally strong, emotionally healthy and spiritually fulfilled" (1996, 303). This is echoed more recently by Alfred, who believes that such a return to traditional values is vital to the decolonizing process. He states, "we transcend colonialism and begin to live again as Onkwehonwe when we start to embody the values of our cultures in our actions and start to shed the main traits of a colonized person: thinking of ourselves before others and projecting our imaginary fears and harmful attitudes onto situations and relationships." Alfred concludes that "when clear, calm minds and strong bodies are connected, we have whole persons again, and working together we become strong and dignified nations" (2005, 165). Such an understanding of the strength of balanced individuals and communities is deeply embedded in Haudenosaunee oral traditions, and both Maracle and Alfred make these connections evident in their work.

Maracle admits, however, that he is "more than a little uncomfortable making all the foregoing suggestions because I don't want to sound like a bossy, lecturing know-it-all," but understands that he is "not saying anything that I haven't already heard many other Onkwehonwe say many times before" (1996, 303). The significance here is that Maracle uses his abilities as a writer in order to articulate such ideas into a book, thereby becoming, in a sense, the collective voice of the Grand River community rather than an individual author expressing his own conclusions. Knowing that his book would be read by a diverse audience of both Haudenosaunee and non-Haudenosaunee people, Maracle understands that he is taking something of a risk in writing about his community in such a direct way, but he also understands the critical state of our languages and culture. Therefore, he issues such statements as a challenge to others at Grand River to contribute to strengthening their community.

Near the end of Back on the Rez, Maracle writes, "My fondest wish is to see a Kanyen'kehaka [Mohawk] longhouse built in this territory because we desperately need one." The lack of such a cultural base has prevented many Mohawks at Grand River from learning their languages and ceremonies, he believes, and has "weakened and impoverished the present generation." He continues, "we owe it to our children and to future generations to give them what we were denied, and a Kanyen'kehaka longhouse will help immeasurably in doing just that" (1996, 301). Acknowledging that "it wouldn't be easy to establish, given the shortage of people who speak the language, and know what to do," Maracle argues that "it certainly is worth doing and the good thing is that there are many people around who are willing to learn and willing to help" (302). As proof of his deep commitment to reviving cultural tradition, Maracle has been instrumental in achieving this particular goal, and along with several other dedicated Mohawk people, oversaw the construction of the Mohawk longhouse in 2004. Equally important is his establishment of adult immersion courses in the Mohawk language, which have operated successfully at Six Nations, despite being seriously underfunded, for the past ten years. Still living in the 150-year-old "battered log house" that he moved back to in 1993, Brian Maracle is clearly an example of what can be done to revitalize First Nations languages and cultures when one dedicates oneself to the task.

THE "GOOD MESSAGE" IN THE TWENTY-FIRST CENTURY:
CHIEF JAKE THOMAS'S TEACHINGS FROM THE LONGHOUSE

Following the events at Oka in July 1990, there was a reawakened interest in Native cultural traditions, as increasing numbers of First Nations people were once again proud of their histories and heritage, as images of warriors and talk of Native rights, land claims, and resistance appeared daily in the media. While this upsurge was strongly reminiscent of a similar movement twenty years earlier with the occupation of Alcatraz Island and the emergence of the American Indian Movement (AIM) and Red Power, at Six Nations the effect was heightened by the fact that the Mohawk community of Kanehsatake was directly involved and that the Confederacy Council was called upon to negotiate with the federal government during the Oka conflict, proof that traditional structures were still in place and being used as an effective political resource. This resurgence of tradition in contemporary politics, along with the newly created language immersion schools on the reserve and the understanding that our cultural carriers were becoming elderly and passing away, provoked many to actively begin seeking out traditional knowledge that had been denied to them by mainstream pressures to assimilate or by parents and grandparents too ashamed or embarrassed to pass on their language and culture.

One of the people whom many relied on to assist them in this recovery of cultural knowledge was Jacob "Jake" Thomas (1922–1998), who carried the Chief's title, Deyonhwe'ton, (Cayuga, Snipe Clan). He was "raised up" as a Chief in 1973, the same year he became an assistant professor with the Native Studies Department at Trent University, where he taught courses on Iroquois language, culture, and traditions until his retirement in 1990. During this time, he also established the Jake Thomas Learning Centre at his home on Six Nations, where he held classes on woodcarving, wampum making, history, and ceremonial speeches in order to ensure that these practices were carried on in the community. He also held several recitations of the Great Law—in Mohawk, Cayuga, and English—that, for many, was the first and only time they had heard this ancient narrative in its original, spoken form. Although he was soundly criticized by many in the traditional community for delivering the Kaienerekowa in English, Thomas continued to do so, stating that it was important for people to hear the philosophies contained within it, regardless of what language was used.[3]

While Thomas produced many small publications through his learning centre on various subjects pertaining to Haudenosaunee language and culture, his only book-length work, *Teachings from the Longhouse*, was published in 1994 in collaboration with Terry Boyle. According to Boyle's introduction it was Thomas who approached him about working on this project together, stating simply: "He needed a writer and I was ready for the teaching" (1994, 6). He emphasizes that "the information contained in this book includes principles that need to be considered for natives and non-natives to develop a good mind, to honour all things, and to practise no criticism and no judgement." The information he is referring to is what is known as the Gaihwi'yo, or The Good Message, or Code of Handsome Lake. As discussed earlier, this is the series of visions and teachings that were given to the Seneca Chief Skanyadai:yo' (Handsome Lake) beginning in 1799, and which eventually became the basis for what is now sometimes known as the "longhouse religion" among the Haudenosaunee. Although the Code had previously been published in various forms for almost 100 years, Boyle explains that "in preparing this text of the Code of Handsome Lake, we used a script written in 1918, which came from the oral tradition in the Onondaga language. Chief Jacob Thomas had already transcribed the script into English, but the text was not expanded, and it was not in circulation as a published work. He had done the translation for the benefit of his people who no longer spoke their native language" (7). Thomas obviously felt the need to make the Code of Handsome Lake, like he had done with the Great Law, accessible to those who did not understand an Iroquoian language. Even more notable is the fact that he chose to work with a non-Native writer who could make such material available to an even wider audience. At a time when tensions between First Nations and Canadian society were highly strained, and fewer and fewer Haudenosaunee fully understood their own cultural traditions, Thomas offered his words as a means to promote a more healthy and positive understanding of tradition and responsibility, not only among all people but in relationship to the natural world as well.

It is clear that Oka was on Thomas's mind, and more specifically the actions of the Mohawk Warrior Society, who had captured the imaginations of Native and non-Native alike at the time. Aware that many people were sympathetic to their cause, Thomas warned that there was more to the Warrior Society than most realized, and that their belief in taking up arms and supporting gaming activities on reserves were in direct contradiction to the teachings in both the Great Law and the Code of Handsome Lake.

> The Warrior Society claimed to be acting in accordance with the Great Law by protecting their people. If they were protecting their people, why did they turn their guns on their own people? At Akwesasne in 1989 two native people were killed during a crossfire attack between pro-gamblers and anti-gamblers, but no one really knows who did it. The Warrior Society members call themselves traditional, but they are warriors. They are very powerful today, and if you question them you could be threatened. I was one of the few people who stood up and said, "If you want to shoot me go ahead. I have something to die for." Four years ago the Warrior Society threatened to shoot me if I didn't watch myself. I received this message twice. (1994, 144)

Thomas's defiant tone demonstrates his firm convictions about the significance of traditionalism around the events at Oka, and also that the spiritual philosophies contained in the Great Law and the Code of Handsome Lake were not to be compromised to serve the political agenda of a minority of people who put "their own self-interest ... before the benefit of all nations" (142). This included the Warriors' backing of the emerging cigarette industry that was bringing millions of dollars into Haudenosaunee communities in Quebec and at Grand River in the early 1990s, something that Thomas identified as harmful to the people since it promoted greed, competition, and conflict among members who, according to the Great Law, were to help and support one another. He therefore took offence at the fact that most Warriors cited the Great Law as the basis of Haudenosaunee sovereignty, which gave them the right to engage in trade across borders and not to recognize the authority of either Canada or the U.S. to impose taxes on cigarettes and alcohol or legislation on gaming activities on reserves. The threats against his life illustrate the extent to which the Warriors were willing to go to silence those who challenged these political beliefs. Such moments convey that while Oka was an empowering event for many First Nations, it was also an extremely difficult time for Haudenosaunee leaders like Thomas who were responsible for upholding tradition in the face of a militant body of their own people who felt differently about what culture and sovereignty meant in the late twentieth century.

As difficult as this was, Thomas also understood that Haudenosaunee oral tradition recognized and allowed for such situations of internal division—and that it also contained the potential for solving such problems. Addressing the social tensions that had arisen in the wake of Oka and the presence of the Warriors on Haudenosaunee territories, he states, "This is what happens when a nation no longer follows its traditional teaching. There is disunity, violence, and warring. But there is still the possibility of change if we can practise a good mind once again." For Thomas, the key to achieving a collective state of balance, of having a good mind within a community, was reliant upon an understanding of traditional culture. "The answers are there if people would only listen," he asserts. "The teachings are there for people to follow to make you a better human being" (1994, 145). The problem, however, is that people have become "narrow minded" in their everyday thinking and "this is why we are so divided today and lack unity. Our people are educated to be self-sufficient, but this takes away from a good mind. They

Chief Jake Thomas interpreting wampum string during the wampum repatriation ceremony at Onondaga Longhouse, Grand River, 1988. (Photo by Tim Johnson. Courtesy of Deyohahá:ge: Indigenous Knowledge Centre, Six Nations)

are looking out for themselves, rather than the nation" (146). What is significant here is his mention of education as a detrimental force in the lives of Haudenosaunee, particularly in the context of the Code of Handsome Lake, which strongly warns against "white man's education" as a form of indoctrination into Western society, seen most explicitly in the assimilation of Native people, as well as the rapid rise of Warrior-style capitalism and its detrimental effects upon First Nations communities. While one could conclude that this attitude is simply reflective of Thomas's call for a return to traditional teachings and conservatism, such a conclusion would be inconsistent with his seventeen-year-long career as a university professor. What, then, is his understanding of education or, more specifically, epistemology and "think-ing" from a Haudenosaunee perspective?

The answer, I believe, is evident in the way Thomas invokes the impor-tance of respect and generosity throughout his statements in *Teachings from the Longhouse*. Although these words are not used directly in the text of the Code as presented in this work, they are concepts that are implied through-out, as invisible tenets that do not make the literal or metaphoric translation into English. Therefore, his attempt to bridge traditional philosophies with modern modes of communication—producing books and teaching at the post-secondary level—demonstrates his commitment to sharing these Haudenosaunee ideologies with a larger audience as a means to improve relations between Native and non-Native peoples, and to improve the quality of life in First Nations communities. This is an approach that Vine Deloria Jr. recognizes as a distinctly Native method of dealing with Western educa-tion systems: "A solid foundation in the old traditional ways enables students to remember that life is not scientific, social scientific, mathematical, or even religious; life is a unity, and the foundation for learning must be the unified experience of being a human being" (1999, 142). In sharing his vast knowledge of Haudenosaunee history, culture, and philosophy, Thomas maintained that Indigenous ways of understanding and respecting the world, and all people's roles within it, were useful lessons that everyone could benefit from, despite the fact that our own people had been taught otherwise over the long history of assimilation wrought first by the church and then by the policies of the state. For this reason, he reached out to any and all who would listen, as all had a stake in retaining traditional Haudenosaunee teachings, especially around issues pertaining to the sustainability of the natural environment.

Indeed, an important aspect of Haudenosaunee philosophy is based upon assisting others, and Thomas does much to explain this willingness and desire to educate:

> In our culture everyone has a purpose. No one arrives in this world without a purpose. That is why the Creator gave us a culture. He meant that we should keep that culture going.... The Creator has given each of us gifts to help one another. We should be generous and do so.... Some people have the gift of

thinking in a small way; those who have been given the gift to think in a larger way should help those people who have less. This is what it is to be generous with one another and to help one another get along in peace in this world. (1994, 134)

For Thomas, this is a belief that is lost not only to mainstream society in the twentieth century but also to Haudenosaunee communities who were being affected by the sudden infusion of material wealth via tobacco and gaming, and who had begun to mistake a traditional understanding of sovereignty and nationhood with capitalism and individualism. In the brief passage above, he merges the central philosophies of the Great Law with the Code of Handsome Lake as a comment on what he sees as the erosion of cultural values hastened by the allure of "easy money." In this new environment of greed, consumerism, and individual wealth, Thomas fears that Native people will eventually forget the importance of the collective well-being of clan and nation in favour of a more isolated, Western conception of self, family, and community.

As a method to counter this destructive movement away from traditional kinship relationships, he asserts that Native people need to be honest when articulating their past and to acknowledge the negative along with the positive aspects of their historical identity. To fail to do so would be to fall into the trap of European civilizations that have largely hidden the truths of their colonial pasts. In one of his most strongly worded critiques, Thomas states:

When we talk of our traditions, we never hide the truth of our history from our children. We are honest about our faults and share this with our people. But do white people do that? We speak the truth to help our people become better human beings. Whites keep real history away from their people. They hide the poverty, theft, and murder from others. Instead of learning from the past and changing it, they create repetition by denying historical truths.... White people will not admit to these wrongs in their past, so they can look good in the present. But people do not learn this way. People need to know the truth about their families and nation to gain peace of mind. (1994, 147)

Although aimed directly at dominant society, Thomas's words also serve to address the situation within Haudenosaunee communities which were then caught up in the rhetoric of Warrior Society resistance to Canadian authority in the wake of Oka. By taking an unpopular anti-Warrior position at this time in stating that "they do not follow the Great Law" (142), Thomas certainly opened himself up to intense criticism from his own community, but he understood the necessity of articulating the "truth" about traditional philosophies as opposed to those who would misinterpret them to suit their own political agendas. Therefore, he offered his knowledge as a means not only to educate but also to caution Native people —Haudenosaunee in particular— not to overly romanticize the past, but to be more engaged in thinking deeply about what those oral traditions meant and how they could best be applied in the present. As one of the few remaining individuals at Grand River who understood ceremony, history, and tradition as a fluent Iroquoian speaker in the 1990s, Jake Thomas was a remarkable teacher and spokesman who was not afraid to use whatever means necessary to convey the ongoing relevance of Haudenosaunee thought and philosophy in the present day. He did this for our benefit and for all those who choose to listen.

TRADITIONAL TEACHINGS FOR CONTEMPORARY TIMES

Published in 1995, Mohawk author Richard Green's *Sing, Like a Hermit Thrush* is a short novel that is generally considered children's literature, telling the story of thirteen-year-old Darrin Captain, a young Mohawk boy "coming of age" one summer on an unnamed Native reserve. However, despite Green's disclaimer that "[a]ny resemblance to actual localities, events, prophesies and persons living or in the Spirit World is coincidental," most anyone from Six Nations would instantly recognize Grand River as the location of the story, along with several events and perhaps a character or two. Told from young Darrin's perspective, the reader is closely involved with his often-comical struggle to understand adults, relationships, girls, bullying, traditional culture, and most importantly, how to live with his "gift" of vision, or foresight. Written at nearly the same time as the books by Brian Maracle and Jake Thomas, *Sing, Like a Hermit Thrush* is, by contrast, a fictional tale of optimism and youth, dealing with the themes of family and culture as experienced by a younger generation somewhat oblivious to the political impacts of the Oka crisis. In fact, it is difficult to tell exactly when the novel takes place— the '70s, '80s, '90s?—since there are no direct references to dates or current events, perhaps to reflect the consciousness of a young boy on summer vacation, but also a deliberate narrative approach by Green to create a timeless quality to the story in order to convey its larger theme.

Although the novel avoids political issues, Green was well aware of the environment in which he was writing in the 1990s; he understood literature, whenever it is produced by a Native author, is often a political act. Born in Ohsweken in 1940, Green travelled extensively as a young man and found himself in San Francisco shortly after the American Indian Movement (AIM) occupation of Alcatraz Island began in November 1969. He took part in various demonstrations around that event and went on to work as a freelance writer and journalist in California for a number of years, covering mostly Native issues. He returned to Six Nations in the early 1990s, where he taught creative writing courses and continued to write fiction and non-fiction until his death in 2012. His first self-published work, *The Last Raven and Other Stories*, is a collection of short stories that appeared in 1994, dealing with characters and events closely associated with Six Nations and nearby Brantford, Ontario. This was followed by *Sing, Like a Hermit Thrush*, also self-published, which continues Green's focus on reserve life and the cultural beliefs that still resonate within families and the community in general. His frequent use of Mohawk language in the story demonstrates his belief, like Maracle, in employing the language whenever possible as a means to encourage others, especially younger readers, to recognize and understand it as a viable means of communication, and as a subtle form of decolonizing the written text. Ricara Features, the publishing company he established, which specialized in local and emerging authors, is another expression of his commitment to decolonization through literature.

The story from which the book takes its name is an explanation of how the small bird known as the hermit thrush got its unique song. By coming to understand the story within the story, the reader learns, along with Darrin, that all people have special gifts or talents that they should not be embarrassed by, nor should they abuse them or be arrogant about them. Rather, they are to use them in such a way as to help others whenever they can, much like Thomas describes in *Teachings from the Longhouse*. We are given an indication of Darrin's uniqueness very early in the novel when he experiences a "strange dream" while playing with a friend. In this waking dream, he witnesses what seems to be a competition between various birds to see who can fly the highest. Coming back to reality before the competition is finished, Darrin wonders what the outcome was, but quickly takes his strange experience in stride. We learn that this is not the first time such an occurrence has happened to him, and that he has had other episodes in which he "saw" things that hadn't happened yet. Green makes the reader realize that although Darrin has the gift of a seer, he doesn't yet understand his own ability and instead feels he has a problem: "[T]hese vision things seemed to be happening more frequently. They were getting out of hand. He'd have to tell somebody. He'd have to get help" (Green 1995, 15).

In order to do so, Darrin first talks with his traditionally minded grandfather, who understands his gift as well as his confusion, but who feels he is not knowledgeable enough to help his grandson. He suggests that the young boy visit with Truman Cloud, a medicine man who lives by the river. Although Darrin is willing, he is also hesitant to talk with this old, traditional person whom his family seems to be somewhat afraid of. Here, Green captures many people's aversion to traditional culture at Six Nations. While they acknowledge and understand its significance, they are still affected by the assimilating influence of Christianity and avoid contact with "Old Indian stuff" (Green 1995, 49) as much as possible. Nevertheless, driven by his desire to find out about his visions, Darrin eventually makes his way to Truman's cabin, which is full of things seemingly consistent with a traditional person: a snapping turtle hanging from a tree, glass jars full of dried roots, nuts and corn, as well as horse tails and "braided, weed-like things" (76). Although nervous about these strange objects, Darrin soon feels comfortable enough with the old man and tells him about his "problem." After listening, Truman replies reassuringly, "Others have shared your dilemma" (77). He then proceeds to tell Darrin the story of the hermit thrush, who travelled on the back of an eagle in order to ascend high into the Sky World and bring back the most beautiful song to be heard on earth. However, Truman says, when the little bird returned he "became concerned that Eagle would be angry. He was afraid Eagle might even decide to kill him. The other [birds] would either be mad at him or be jealous of his best song." The old man asks, "What do you think he should do?" After reflecting for a few moments, Darrin replies, "I dunno" (78). Truman explains that the hermit thrush "knew he had good camouflage and could scarcely be seen in the forest.... So he found a thick grove of bushes all around. Here, he could do his duty and share his beautiful song. He could sing and feel proud that he was different from all the others" (79). While this is the story that was foreshadowed earlier in the novel, Green makes the reader aware of its significance by repeating it a second time so that its message is emphasized again. This is especially important as the novel is aimed at a younger audience, who are asked to consider the story of the hermit thrush as one dealing with jealousy and conflict, but also one concerned with understanding personal responsibility and, above all, humility. The scenes between Darrin and Truman Cloud are also notable since they encourage Native youth to visit with their elders, to reassure them that it is OK to approach older people and learn from them, despite what those around them, including their own families, may think about traditional culture.

As a work that appeared amid a wave of post-Oka literary activity dealing with the empowerment of Native culture and identity, Green's novel is most effective in reaching a younger audience. And while not available to readers beyond the Six Nations community, this novel certainly speaks most closely to those at Grand River. With references to the Ohsweken fairgrounds and the old Community Centre (built in the 1920s and torn down in 2005), dusty side roads leading to the Grand River, and the annual Six Nations powwow at Chiefswood Park, Green obviously writes with a sense of place and nostalgia, but also with an eye to the future. This is evidenced by young Darrin's ability as a seer as well as his respect for Native language and traditions. Conscious of writing a story that would capture the attention of younger readers, Green includes much that would appeal to such an audience (baseball, bullies, first kiss, etc.), along with occasional moments directed specifically at young Haudenosaunee. Describing Darrin's participation at the Grand River Powwow, traditionally a Western Plains gathering and now very popular among all First Nations (and with tourists alike), Green explains Darrin's grandfather's refusal to attend this event with him: "because the dancing competition prizes were money. Instead, he preferred the old way. He drummed the [Haudenosaunee] water drum and danced with Darrin at Longhouse socials. He told Darrin to always use the gifts that the Creator provided. Never forget your own dances and songs" (1995, 92). Here, Green reminds young people that dancing and singing were not competitive events originally, but gifts that the Creator had given to the Haudenosaunee in order to communicate with the natural world. Therefore, our songs are to be sung with reverence, humility, and respect, for they give us our unique cultural identity and ensure our survival as a distinct people, while connecting us with our ancestors.

Creative writing was just one mode of expression employed by First Nations in the wake of the events at Oka, and as the 1990s progressed, significant achievements also began to be made in documentary and film production. As Indigenous communities sought to represent their stories in more meaningful and accurate ways than portrayed by the media on the nightly news, the Aboriginal Peoples Television Network emerged, along with filmmakers such as Alanis Obomsawin, Loretta Todd, Christine Welsh, and several others. At Grand River, one such artist and filmmaker also began making a name for herself by lifting Haudenosaunee culture off of the page and making it come alive in visual form.

THE CREATIVE POWER OF TRADITION: THE FILMS OF SHELLEY NIRO

Born in 1954, Mohawk artist and filmmaker Shelley Niro first became known for her photography that playfully, yet powerfully, juxtaposed traditional Haudenosaunee themes and images within a contemporary social context. One of her most popular series of photos, *Mohawks in Beehives* (1991), arose out of her response not only to the Oka Crisis but also to the first Gulf War. Remarking on this intense period that saw the intersection of Native issues, violent conflict, and media representation, Niro felt that as a Native person, "it was almost like your personal existence has no meaning at all." As a means to reassert a modern First Nations identity lost in the compelling visual imagery of violence so often associated with Native people, she chose Brantford, Ontario, a site of special significance to the Six Nations, as the backdrop for a series of photos that show her sisters vamping in "loud clothes and louder makeup" in front of the statue of Joseph Brant, the individual from whom the town takes its name. According to Comanche scholar Paul Chaat Smith, these photographs serve to "symbolically reclaim Joseph Brant's town, not with banners and rifles, but with obsolete hairstyles, attitude, and costume jewellery, the bigger the better.... Mohawks in Beehives is about taking things back, taking control, and seizing power by refusing victim status" (1998, 110). Given Brant's historical legacy among the Six Nations and in Canada, and the fact that Pauline Johnson wrote a poem specifically for, and attended, the unveiling of this very statue in 1886, Niro's work resonates on several levels, the most important of which is to demonstrate that the Grand River Haudenosaunee are well aware of how their past has been represented by others and how they are actively engaged in a continuous, creative dialogue about their present and their future.

Although Niro is a multimedia artist whose dozens of photos, paintings, and installations all speak to contemporary Haudenosaunee identity, this discussion will focus on three films that demonstrate the trajectory of her approaches to representation and cultural survival from the period following Oka to the present. The first, co-directed with Anna Gronau, was titled It Starts with a Whisper (1993) and was produced to coincide with the 500th anniversary of the "discovery" of North America by Christopher Columbus. It premiered on New Year's Eve 1992–93 at the Iroquois Lodge in Ohsweken, the seniors' home at Six Nations. This may seem like an odd choice of venues until one realizes that the film is ultimately intended as a celebration of the survival of Indigenous people in the Americas after 500 years of sustained contact with the aggressive forces of colonial power—and who better to understand this reason for a party than 100 Native senior citizens who had lived through some of the most oppressive policies that the Indian Act had inflicted upon First Nations?

The twenty-five-minute film features Shanna, a young Haudenosaunee woman who struggles to reconcile her modern identity with what she has learned of her ancestors' past and who is affected by the negative representations she sees in the media regarding Native people in the present. On a road trip with her aunts to Niagara Falls for the weekend, she becomes upset with their teasing and frivolity that contrast sharply with her more "serious" worries about the present state of First Nations communities. Her anger is evidence of the frustration she feels as a result of the constant pull between the demands of her career in the city, the expectations of her family on the reserve, and her internal conflict over these matters. Her inability to laugh and enjoy her aunts' company indicates Shanna's growing distance from family and community, brought on by her relocation to the city and her reliance on the media as a source of information, as well as her need to address the historical trauma and pain she is experiencing as a sensitive, young Native person.

Although Oka is never mentioned explicitly in the film, it is still a large presence in the story because it is the event that provoked thousands of young people like Shanna to want to learn about their history and cultural past, making them more politically aware and often angry as a result. The importance of the Meech Lake Accord for First Nations rights is also represented in the film, as Niro was able to persuade Elijah Harper to make a cameo appearance, despite his celebrity status and her extremely low budget. Produced in the wake of these two media events from the "Indian Summer" of 1990, combined with the significance of the 1492–1992 anniversary, It Starts with a Whisper is a subtle but highly political film; however, it is the humour that Niro employs that truly makes it a compelling work, particularly for Native audiences. As Paul Chaat Smith argues, "It is without a doubt the most serious Indian comedy ever made" (1998, 111). Although the comedic elements do not always emerge deliberately but are sometimes the result of the cheap effects, costuming, and sets necessitated by financial limitations (as is often the case with low-budget independent film), Niro successfully "owns" and incorporates the comedic potential of such restrictions into her film by making her audience smile while conveying her larger message at the same time. In doing so, she also evokes a unique Indigenous sense of humour around the condition of poverty in a way that makes her work resonate particularly well with Indigenous audiences.

The opening sequence of shots includes outdoor scenes of Shanna walking the banks of the Grand River in traditional clothes. These scenes are quite colourful, focussed, and lush, while the scenes in Toronto and Niagara Falls are grainy black and white, emphasizing the contrast between natural landscapes and urban spaces. The cities are also the places in which Shanna is most confused and upset. At the height of her distress she experiences a "vision" in which Elijah Harper suddenly appears in casual attire with a full feathered headdress. The entire scene is bathed in white, indicating that brightness and hope are being introduced to her mental state of sadness and despair. As part of their brief exchange, Elijah tells Shanna that "We must make a point of remembering those tribes [that are no longer with us]. We must keep them in our minds and our hearts.... Stop feeling guilty about your existence. You are here to live your life." With these words, she is visibly uplifted. The scene fades directly into the next, a dance number in which we see Shanna, now dressed in a brightly coloured gown similar to those of her aunts, frolicking with them around a honeymoon suite complete with heart-shaped bed. Their dance is choreographed to an original Niro song entitled "I'm Pretty," which begins "I'm pretty / I'm pretty / I'm pretty mad at you," but then goes on to include the lyrics: "I'm survivin' / I'm thrivin' / I'm doin' fine without you." Allowing herself to dance and laugh, Shanna is on her way to overcoming her anger and sadness by embracing her modern identity and seeing the joy in living her life on her own terms, learning an important lesson about resistance and decolonization in the process.

Although It Starts with a Whisper is a movie intended for all Native (and non-Native) audiences to share in "celebrating" our collective survival after 500 years of contact, it is also rife with specific Haudenosaunee references and meaning. From the movie's opening images of Iroquois beadwork based on the Tree of Peace and the "skydome" motif that symbolizes the natural world, accompanied by a voice-over and singing in Mohawk, to its final scene that includes a reading of Pauline Johnson's "The Song My Paddle Sings" and a fireworks display that eventually takes the form of the Tree of Peace on the back of a turtle, Niro brings a substantial Haudenosaunee aesthetic to the film. In addition to these visual/aural examples, Shanna's aunts are named Emily, Pauline, and Molly for three influential Six Nations women: Emily General was a highly respected teacher/educator at Grand River (and a close relative of Levi General, aka Deskaheh), Pauline Johnson was, of course, the famous poet/orator, and Molly Brant (1736–1796) was Joseph Brant's sister, wife of British colonial official Sir William Johnson, and later an influential figure in the Loyalist town of Kingston, Ontario, where she was a strong advocate for Six Nations rights. These references, together with the shots taken along the Grand River that are immediately recognizable to community members, make this a very Six Nations movie, even if most viewers may be largely unaware of their specific meaning. Finally, the river itself is an important metaphor in the film. Because it is a tributary that eventually contributes to the "natural wonder" that is Niagara Falls, it is no coincidence that the final scene takes place at the edge of the Falls, the site where the combined force of many streams and rivers eventually come together as a single, powerful one. This is Niro's comment on the many stories and experiences of Native people coming together after Oka and resulting in the great size and strength of their collective voices. But like Niagara Falls, which begins with many small streams far away, such a powerful, collective Indigenous voice first began with a whisper, a quiet expression of identity, self, and empowerment.

Following It Starts with a Whisper, Niro concentrated on her photography, installations, and paintings, which continued to draw on traditional themes in Haudenosaunee culture and history. She also produced a few short films, including the acclaimed Honey Moccasin, a thirty-five-minute film that was released in 1997. With the advent of home digital cameras and editing software, however, the costs of producing longer films decreased dramatically, and her first project to take advantage of this new technology was Suite: INDIAN, produced in 2005. The film is a series of seven vignettes, including a prelude which is a brief re-enactment of the story of Hiawatha, the cultural hero who figures prominently in the story of the Great Law. A female voice narrates how his despair led him to a great depression that was only lifted when the Peacemaker came upon him and used wampum beads to symbolically wipe away his sadness through a process known as the condolence, or "requickening," ceremony. After this, the narrator states, "Haudenosaunee life began and has remained alive through the need to express oneself and creativity." This is the prominent theme that also runs throughout It Starts with a Whisper, clearly an important one to Niro: an individual's emotional pain affects all those around them, and it is therefore the responsibility of those who are able to help lift this person's mind and spirit using their own "gifts" to do so. Niro, therefore, employs her skills as a Haudenosaunee artist to allow others to recognize our cultural stories and symbols as having relevance in the present, often combining this message with creative expressions of humour in the process.

Immediately following the prelude, we are shown the work of contemporary Six Nations members who are engaged in creating modern forms of traditional culture. In two-minute segments, the camera closely follows the hands and faces of three women and three men who continue the work of growing corn and cooking corn bread, as well as the arts of making wampum belts, cornhusk dolls, moccasins, carvings, and beadwork. Each person is shown informally in their home, and without any dialogue; the camera follows them as they produce a work from beginning to completed result. The musical accompaniment is piano and cello, which gives this segment a very dignified and stately feel. Viewers are being asked to understand such work as much more than simply Native "arts and crafts" that can be bought in a tourist shop; rather, such objects are physical evidence that contemporary Haudenosaunee artists continue to use both ancient and modern materials and tools to produce work that pays homage to our ancestors while at the same time being functional and aesthetically pleasing in the present. By not using the expected soundtrack of drums or flutes, which have come to be markers of Native "authenticity" in films and documentaries, Niro cleverly upsets the audience's perception of what modern Haudenosaunee culture is, and by juxtaposing classical music alongside of it, asks them to reflect upon it differently.

Another segment in Suite: INDIAN with strong Haudenosaunee content includes the two dance sequences "Living with Fire" and "From the Ashes," performed by Santee Smith with original music by Elizabeth Hill. Both women are Mohawks from Grand River. In the first piece, Smith (a member of the National Ballet of Canada from 1998 to 2002) appears distraught and alone in a buckskin outfit in the middle of a traditional Iroquoian-style longhouse. Her movements and the music reflect the emotions of a person who is both frightened and in much pain. At the end of the performance, she is prone on the floor, as if her situation is too much to bear, resembling the figure of Hiawatha in the Prelude. In the second number, "From the Ashes," she arises from this position and is joined by a young man in contemporary street clothes who initially mimics her movements from a close distance but eventually joins in her dance as a strong, confident, and supportive partner.

Visually, the two dancers form a link not just between man and woman, but also between the past and the present. Like Hiawatha, the young woman needs human contact to "raise her up" physically and emotionally so she can find balance and peace of mind, since human beings have great difficulty doing this on our own when we are suffering emotionally. Capturing the symbolism of dance on film, Smith and Niro use their own particular art forms to evoke this central idea found in Haudenosaunee oral tradition and philosophy, one which constantly appears in Niro's work.

The other short pieces that make up Suite: INDIAN form a diverse narrative about contemporary Native life in a general sense, from the young woman who immerses herself perhaps too much in "her Indian identity," to the young man who dreams of writing the "great North American Indian novel," to a middle-aged Native couple struggling to maintain their relationship in the city, and the young Native woman on the street who dreams of her "old life" among her family and children at home. There are also two more modern-dance numbers, choreographed by Smith, featuring a group of First Nations dancers who perform in gaudy, stereotypical "warpaint," feathers, and blue jeans, brandishing fake plastic tomahawks and accompanied by the theme song of the Russian Army. This piece, entitled "The Red Army is the Strongest," once again uses non-traditional music in a playful way that upsets expectations and also serves to satirize, and counter, the media image of the "Warrior" within First Nations communities. While these vignettes are not Six Nations specific in their theme and content, all of them are shot in and around Brantford, including Brant Park and along the Grand River, as Niro continues to find inspiration within the landscape—and the city—that is most closely associated with her community.

The themes of creative expression, movement, and human contact as a means to overcome loss and despair are once again a strong presence in Kissed by Lightning, Niro's most recent full-length feature film, which appeared in 2009. With her biggest budget yet and a cast and crew of professional film industry people, this is her most extensive undertaking, interweaving many familiar ideas from her previous works into a modern-day love story that touches on several elements of particular significance to contemporary Haudenosaunee communities. And, like her previous work, it is more evidence of Niro's great strength to be able to maintain a distinct

Haudenosaunee flavour in her projects while making them accessible to all Indigenous, and non-Indigenous, audiences.

The film follows the story of Mavis Dogblood (Kateri Walker), a Mohawk artist who lives in a rundown house trailer next door to her deceased husband's former wife and her teenaged son on an unspecified Haudenosaunee reserve. Through a series of flashbacks early in the film we learn that Jesse Lightning was a violin-playing musician of considerable talent who was also very passionate about Haudenosaunee history and the stories that resonate within the culture, going so far as to set them to classical music. His love affair with Mavis seems to have been brief but incredibly deep, and his death has had a devastating effect upon her, to the point where she appears in a constant state of mourning throughout much of the film. As the deadline to have her paintings delivered to a gallery in New York City fast approaches, Mavis must put her grief aside in order to produce her art. With the help of her friend Solomon King, a.k.a. Bug (Eric Schweig), who shows her unconditional love and support despite her indifference toward him, she is able to complete her work and drive to New York in time for her opening. It is while travelling through traditional Mohawk territory in upstate New York that Mavis begins to realize that the stories of her ancestors can assist her in learning how to let go of the past and move beyond loss. Significantly, on the road trip she connects the stories that Jesse had told her of the Peacemaker and Hiawatha, the very same stories she connects with her emotional state through her paintings, with physical places. By recreating these scenes on canvas, Mavis has therefore been able to express her own pain through her art and cultural connection to her ancestors, becoming healed in the process. Notably, Niro's own paintings are used in the film as modern renderings of ancient stories, demonstrating her talents as a multimedia artist and providing a compelling visual backdrop to the film.

In many ways, *Kissed by Lightning* is a considerable departure from Niro's earlier film projects, reflecting a bigger budget that allows for more fully developed characters and an evolved storyline. As a result, it is a mature, serious work that captures a realistic sense of contemporary life in a Haudenosaunee community. Although the quirky, offbeat humour of some of her previous characters and situations may be absent, Niro does not completely abandon comedy either, but allows the natural humour of the

Mavis Dogblood (Kateri Walker) and Bug (Eric Schweig) in her living room studio as she works on a painting of the Peacemaker and his stone canoe, an important image from the story of the Kaienerekowa/Great Law. (Photo by Calvin Thomas. Courtesy of Shelley Niro)

characters' personalities to bring a lightheartedness to the story that serves to balance Mavis's emotional state. This is most evident in the kind-hearted but bumbling character of Bug, who is there to assist Mavis overcome her depression over the loss of Jesse; also in Jenny, the gossipy and vain ex-wife of Jesse who seems the complete opposite to Mavis, but who shares her loss as she now has to raise their son, Mike, on her own. While their close proximity to Mavis may appear rather unrealistic to many viewers, on most reserves where land and housing options are very limited, such a situation can quite easily occur. Similarly, the border-crossing scene in which Mavis and Bug are discriminated against because they are Mohawk demonstrates the ongoing political battle of wills between Canadian/U.S. authorities and Haudenosaunee assertions of sovereignty. Subtle moments like these are what give *Kissed by Lightning* a unique Native sensibility that allows it to speak to Indigenous audiences on a particular level, while also providing a moment for observant non-Indigenous audiences to consider the political rights of First Nations, as well as conditions on reserves: of poverty, overcrowding, and the particular circumstances faced by single mothers. Like her photographs and paintings, Niro's film provide viewers with these images, but asks that they come to their own conclusions about what these issues mean for Indigenous people today by engaging with the stories that they tell.

As further evidence of the past always being present for the Haudenosaunee, Niro provides moments in the film in which our cultural ancestors appear in physical form, seen by both Mavis and Bug while driving to New York, and later only by the audience, as we see three men in traditional clothing observe and react to Mavis's paintings at the art gallery, alongside other patrons who are oblivious to them. It is to Niro's credit that their presence in the film is neither contrived nor unbelievable. Rather, we understand their appearance as the past literally "crossing paths" with the present, serving to remind Mavis, and the audience, that time is not as linear as Western society would like us to believe; that it too is a colonialist imposition seeking to separate us from our history. In her body of work, Niro achieves what Mohawk scholar Audra Simpson sees as a significant accomplishment, one that allows Haudenosaunee people to "start the process of 'writing' our pasts by entering into a conversation with it.... In doing so, we construct ourselves alongside each other, in laughter and dance that celebrates the many strata of our past and the glory, finally, of our present" (1998, 54). Via modern media, Shelley Niro's work ensures that Haudenosaunee culture maintains movement and achieves growth through imagination, creativity, and making traditional culture come alive, yet again, in the digital age and beyond. In this way, we "link arms" not only with each other in the present but with our ancestors from the past—and with those who are still to come.

The Intersections of History, Literature, Culture, and Politics at Six Nations of the Grand River

On 28 February 2006, a small group of Haudenosaunee people led by three young women entered a construction site on the housing development known as the Douglas Creek Estates near Caledonia, Ontario, and halted crews from continuing work on Six Nations land that has been under contention since 1839. A camp was quickly established on the development site, at which the Haudenosaunee and their supporters maintained a twenty-four-hour presence, and no further work was allowed to proceed. Talks between Six Nations and the provincial government began almost immediately but went nowhere for six weeks. At 4:45 a.m. on the morning of April 20, a task force of approximately 100 heavily armed Ontario Provincial Police forcefully removed sleeping men, women, and young people from the site with the use of billy clubs, Tasers, and pepper spray—four hours after assuring Haudenosaunee negotiators that no such action would occur without adequate warning to those who wished to leave. Fourteen people were arrested in the raid. Three hours later, approximately 100 Haudenosaunee pushed the police back off the site, hundreds more quickly arrived in a show of support, and blockades were erected across two provincial highways and a railway line as police helicopters circled overhead. The reclamation of 132 acres of land that soon became known as Kanonhstaton, or "the protected place," had officially begun.[1] Eight years later, this sometimes encouraging, often volatile, but always frustrating situation remains unresolved, costing the federal and provincial governments upwards of $80 million so far—with very little progress of any kind being made. Non-Native residents of Caledonia and Haldimand county have called for the resignation of the premier of Ontario and the commissioner of the Ontario Provincial Police due to their inability to uphold law and order, alongside of accusations of a two-tier justice system, complaints of falling property values, and exhortations to "Send in the Army!" Yet, the truly significant development in the midst of this crisis was the federal government's recognition of the Six Nations of the Grand River Confederacy Council's authority to negotiate land issues on a nation-to-nation basis for the first time since 1924, when this traditional, hereditary government was removed from power by force of arms under orders from Ottawa.

Although this series of events is certainly monumental for the Grand River Haudenosaunee and perhaps all Indigenous people struggling to assert nationhood, there are also some very serious issues that the Six Nations community has now been forced to address, issues that are shared by all First Nations struggling to decolonize their territories. They speak to many of the concerns discussed throughout this book, and force us to consider some vital questions about our ability to engage culture and nationhood in the present. How can ancient, traditional philosophies and oral traditions operate in the present-day context of land claims, legal processes, financial responsibility, justice, policing, and media relations, to name a few? How can traditional Indigenous governments maintain authority over community members who may not support, or respect, their cultural and political authority? What is the role and function of academic research and writing to support the causes of Indigenous land rights, traditional governments, and ultimately, decolonizing and re-establishing the sovereignty of Native communities? And how do we do this work in the face of often-distrustful community members, loss of cultural understanding, an uninformed media, and disinterested federal and provincial governments?

While these are by no means "new" questions, they have renewed importance to the Six Nations community as we sit at the negotiation table with representatives from Canada and Ontario, determined to resolve our outstanding land rights issues. The urgency of these matters, socially and politically, is dramatically apparent to us, as our Confederacy Chiefs, Clanmothers, and knowledge carriers are elderly, and many are not in the best of health. They know our history and grievances with Canada in regard to the erosion of our land base, but have been more concerned with keeping our ceremonies and languages alive than keeping current with modern land-claims negotiation procedures. No one was more surprised than they were when Canada agreed to recognize their ancient authority once again, after more than eighty years of ignoring their existence. But now that our traditional government has achieved this recognition, where do we go from here in terms of applying oral traditions to our present circumstances? How do we as contemporary Haudenosaunee understand the traditional protocols of dialogue and diplomacy in assuring a future for the "faces yet unborn," and what are our options and responsibilities if such peaceful negotiations fail? These very questions are the same ones that were faced, under different circumstances, by many of those I have discussed within this book, and they are indicative of the sustained nature of our grievances with the Crown, and Canada, since our arrival into the Grand River Valley in 1785.

As outlined earlier, the *Kaienerekowa*, or Great Law of Peace, is the social and political foundation of our collective ideology, the ancient, overarching structure that supports the metaphorical longhouse within which we all came to coexist as clans and nations—the Mohawk, Oneida, Onondaga, Cayuga, Seneca, and Tuscarora—after decades of warfare between us. It is this philosophy that gave us our name, Haudenosaunee, which means "We build the house (together)." It is the reason why we continue to see ourselves as a peaceful, free, and independent people. It is this belief system that was in place at the time of contact with Europeans, and that served as the guiding principle of the relationship between Haudenosaunee and European nations that now dates back four centuries. Our understanding of this political relationship is encoded in two wampum belts, the *Tehontatenentsonteronhtahkwa*, also known as the Silver Covenant Chain of Peace and Friendship, and the *Tekeni Teiohatatie Kahswentha*, or Two Row Wampum. These belts established and confirmed the relationship between our nations and the Europeans, and although they were concerned with trade and commerce, they also spoke more importantly to the ideas of coexistence, non-interference, and mutual responsibility—some of the same principles that are embedded in the *Kaienerekowa*, which had served our people well for centuries. We, in effect, were imposing our sociopolitical ideology onto the Europeans as a code of conduct for living upon our territories. As I have shown, the political philosophy behind these 400-year-old agreements have always been strongly upheld in writing and oratory produced by members of the Grand River Haudenosaunee. It is no surprise, then, that these two wampum belts were prominently displayed between federal and provincial representatives and our Chiefs and Clanmothers at the negotiation table around the Caledonia land reclamation, serving as constant visual reminders to Canada of their agreed-upon responsibility to honour the historical legacy of the British Crown.

Although the Haudenosaunee Confederacy is built upon the principles of peace and diplomacy, as are most Indigenous forms of government, over the past two centuries we have all been made extremely aware that Canada and the United States do not respect such political systems or the people that they represent. As a result, we as First Nations have come to realize that it is only through assertive action such as protests and blockades that disrupt the free movement of goods and the "average" Canadian or American citizen, or that prevent the ability of developers and corporate interests to make money, that the concerns of Native peoples are begrudgingly addressed by the state, and even then only superficially. Within this environment of dominant society's indifference and resentment, Indigenous leaders who try to adhere to more traditional approaches of careful consideration, dialogue, and consensus as the way to achieve positive results often become criticized for their inability to make progress, even by their own communities. Into this void, militant, "warrior" types often enter, convinced that violence is the most effective and expedient way to capture media attention and thereby force governments to pay attention to our grievances. Given our past experience with such protests, it is rather hard to argue against their effectiveness. But this is a dangerous path, for rarely are these kinds of actions accompanied by well-considered solutions to even the most basic questions such as "what will we do with the land once we get it back?" This is a fundamental concern that I have yet to hear discussed in any sustained and collaborative way in my Six Nations community, even as tensions continue to mount between Six Nations members and developers over other disputed tracts of land around Brantford, Ontario at the time of this writing. We have, unfortunately, become better equipped and more accustomed to conflict than to informed consensus and planning, largely due to the necessity of immediate action to counter the always-present threats to our land base.

As Mohawk scholar Taiaiake Alfred states,

> We must recognize the attraction of violence. It is a powerful strategic weapon. Violence gets attention, it consumes state resources, people have a morbid attraction to its effects, and it is perhaps the easiest means of resistance. But the drawbacks to violence are serious. Violence forces people to choose sides, and because it is repugnant to so many people, it causes them to disavow the cause; it limits potential allies; and it is addictive as a drug—its immediacy and paraphernalia are seductive and intoxicating in the short term; and in the long term, the inevitable cycle of repression creates a situation justifying further violence. (2005, 51–52)

As events at Kanonhstaton escalated a few years ago, we saw such activity take place first-hand; it not only affected non-Native perceptions of us and our historical rights to the land, but more importantly, it also had an impact on our own relationships to family, friends, and neighbours in negative and sometimes irreparable ways. We argued over the use and abuse of symbols such as "Warrior" flags, hats, and T-shirts; Confederacy flags; camouflage and bandanas; whether or not to dismantle the barricades; whether or not to support further violence; and even whether or not to support the Confederacy Council. The amount of gossip, rumours, and misinformation, and the ever-present threat of further confrontation between us, the police, and/or the non-Native residents of Caledonia, became almost overwhelming, sometimes to the point where our people lost sight of the real issue that we were faced with: the recognition of our rights to the lands through reparations of past injustice. And this internal division is seemingly what Canada wanted, and expected, to happen—for us to become so embroiled in the immediate after-shock of the police raid and clashes with townspeople that we would implode as a community, unsure of our leadership, critical of our spokespeople, and divided by radical versus traditional viewpoints on the issue.

But the Grand River community has been through such conflicts and affronts to its people many times before, and the police action at Kanonhstaton was merely the most recent in a long line of similar events that echoes back to the issues facing Joseph Brant, the creation of the Indian Act, and the divisions which Jake Thomas described during the Oka Crisis. Therefore, the people are able to look to the past, understand what sustained our ancestors, parents, and grandparents through turbulent times, and utilize those stories of courage, resilience, and unity to get us through this most recent crisis. The aforementioned overthrow of the Confederacy Council in 1924 was such an event, made more notable by the tactics that the Canadian government resorted to in order to impose a band-council system. At that time, Deskaheh went before a radio audience in Rochester, New York in March 1925 to present our claims against Canada. He addressed the collusion between Canada and the United States in a prophetic way: "The governments at Washington and Ottawa have a silent partnership of policy. It is aimed to break up every tribe of red men so as to dominate every acre of their territory.... Over in Ottawa, they call that policy 'Indian advancement.' Over in Washington, they call it 'assimilation'. We who would be the helpless victims say it is tyranny" ([1925] 2005, 49).

Since World War II, Canada has steadfastly maintained its independent status regarding political and military affairs, most recently in Iraq and Afghanistan, but the Canadian government appears less independent when it comes to its own backyard. This was made apparent in Caledonia in 2007, when U.S. federal undercover Alcohol Tobacco and Firearms (ATF) officers were discovered and confronted by Six Nations people at the reclamation site. Neither the provincial police, the federal government in Ottawa, nor the ATF itself was ever able to adequately explain their presence there, other than that they were "observing" the situation. While this unexplained presence seemed strange and somewhat ominous at the time, it began to make sense when Canada and the United States signed an agreement known as the "Civil Assistance Plan" on 14 February 2008. This agreement was not signed by the two governments, but by commanding officers of the military, and was given very little media attention in either Canada or the U.S. Air Force General Gene Renuart, commander of the U.S. Northern Command and signatory of the agreement, said, "This document is a unique, bilateral military plan to align our respective national military plans to respond quickly to the other nation's requests for military support of civil authorities.... Our commands were created by our respective governments to respond to the defense and security challenges of the twenty-first century, and we both realize that these and other challenges are best met through cooperation between friends" (quoted in Chossudovsky 2008). Such cooperation between Canada and the U.S. is of great concern to Indigenous people, to say the least, coming as it does in the wake of the two countries' refusal to sign the Declaration of Indigenous Rights in 2008. Both countries have much to lose by acknowledging their treaty agreements with Native people, after all, and appear very determined to protect their tenuous, if not fraudulent, ownership of lands and resources, so much so that they are prepared to cooperatively mobilize their militaries in order to quell large-scale protest or other potential forms of disruption to political authority.

Despite the tremendous amount of frustration we have felt over these past eight years of negotiations, the Grand River Haudenosaunee are determined to resolve our differences with Canada, using our traditional philosophies to demonstrate the continued legitimacy of our principles. In a statement released in 2007, the Six Nations/Grand River Confederacy Council called upon Canada to remember its responsibilities, as we continue to uphold ours: "We are not interested in selling land. We want the Crown to keep its obligations to treaties, and ensure all Crown governments—federal, provincial and municipal—are partners in those obligations.... We seek to renew the existing relationship that ... is symbolized by the Silver Covenant Chain of Peace and Friendship. Our ancestors met repeatedly to polish that chain, to renew its commitments, to reaffirm our friendship and to make sure that the future generations could live in peace, and allow the land to provide ... for the well being of the people." We believe that is not too much to ask, but we are now faced with the extremely difficult task of convincing those who continue to share our lands with us that they must realize their responsibilities to their ancestors and to the Six Nations, as we remember our responsibilities to ourselves and to the British Crown and, by extension, Canada.

The Grand River Haudenosaunee have employed many different methods to convey this essential information to settler society over the past two centuries in order to improve relations between us. This book has sought to demonstrate how our leaders, intellectuals, writers, and artists have consistently reiterated—in English—our ancient philosophies in the context of the political and social environment of their day to build upon the central belief structures of traditional thought in profound and creative ways. What Joseph Brant and Shelley Niro express in their work is little different than what Bernice Loft Winslow and Jake Thomas do in theirs. Respect for the land and what it provides for the people, and a belief in the stories of the Peacemaker and the ideology behind the formation of the Great Law and the Code of Handsome Lake are rather simple yet highly meaningful concepts that have sustained Haudenosaunee culture for centuries. One of the reasons for their longevity is the ability of the people to understand the strength and viability of these ancient narratives within their own social and historical realities, and to make use of them in empowering ways. The use of English to document important oral traditions does not compromise Indigenous sovereignty in any way, according to Acoma writer and scholar Simon Ortiz, who argues that Natives have used the colonizer's language under their own terms, and for their own purpose, for decades. "There is not a question of authenticity here;" he writes, "rather, it is the way that Indian people have creatively responded to forced colonization. And this response has been one of resistance; there is no clearer word for it than resistance. It has been this resistance—political, armed, spiritual—which has been carried out by the oral tradition. The continued use of the oral tradition today is evidence that the resistance is ongoing" ([1981] 2005, 257). Ironically, as our people's use of traditional languages fades, the English words spoken and written by our ancestors allow us to remain connected with these traditions in the present, however imperfect the best translations may still be.

Another issue to consider in the tensions between the oral and the written is raised by John Mohawk, who suggests that the collective "hearing" of cultural narratives is imperative to having people actively and deeply engage in "thinking" about their content—something that is often denied when such stories are committed to writing, and even more so when a colonized people no longer relies on traditional stories in their daily lives. This was a point that Jake Thomas often made to his critics when defending the importance of publicly reciting the Great Law in English. Mohawk states that it is an Iroquois way of doing things to tell a story and to refuse to tell the listener what he/she should have learned from the story. The Iroquois pattern would be to tell a story and to ask the listener to use his/her own mind to see what they think the story means.... Iroquois teachers of the tradition, in my experience, are willing to accept that different people at different stages of life are able to grasp and learn from different elements of a story at different moments. Their point might be only that the story should be told and discussed among the generations. (2005, xi–xii)

This proactive method of relaying and processing information has served Haudenosaunee culture well for several centuries, despite our communities being surrounded and affected by some of the most populated areas of North America.

Addressing the value of ancient narratives and the current state of Haudenosaunee culture, Mohawk suggests "that one of the most remarkable elements of Iroquois conservatism has been the retention and continual revitalization of the Iroquois ceremonial life. For more than 150 years both the U.S. and Canada have implemented policies designed to forcibly acculturate the people, including boarding schools, compulsory non-Iroquois education systems, forced replacement of traditional governments and every conceivable way of bringing the kinds of changes which would cause a people to abandon the belief systems which render them distinct peoples" (2005, x–xi). Mohawk asserts that the stories and ceremonies that have been passed on through oral tradition, both in the languages and in English, have allowed Haudenosaunee society to survive over the past century, and concludes that "[a] revitalization of Haudenosaunee cultural traditions seems far more likely than was thought in the recent past" (xi). For him, and for many other Indigenous thinkers, traditional stories, spirituality, and resistance are inextricably linked to Indigenous survival and the process of decolonization. Six Nations historian Rick Hill also argues that the rich symbolism and metaphor contained in Haudenosaunee culture allow and encourage us to ponder our lives and our children's future in meaningful ways despite widespread language loss. "In some ways this is the most natural affinity for Indigenous people who were raised to speak the language of their colonizers," he writes. "Our conscious mind is dazed and confused by the 'logic' of English; while our subconscious mind continues to seek the sanity and restfulness of Indigenous thought and philosophy. We seek to comprehend our place in the universe, learn to navigate that place, and then seek to excel in our navigation—be it as artisan, storyteller, speaker, or philosopher" (2011).

At Grand River, cultural narratives and traditional beliefs continue to play a prominent role within the community, most notably in the Cayuga and Mohawk Immersion schools that were established in 1991, where children are once again exposed to cultural knowledge in the language on a daily basis. While the number of fluent speakers still decreases with each passing year, the energy around the retention of our languages remains quite high and serves as evidence that more people are realizing the importance of teaching language within our community. In fact, education plays a significant role in the retention and perpetuation of Haudenosaunee knowledge and critical thinking at the post-secondary level as well, as demonstrated by Chief Jake Thomas's career as a professor with the Native Studies Department at Trent University from 1973 to 1990. More recently, others from Grand River have followed in his path, and important research regarding Six Nations culture and history has emerged in doctoral dissertations by Dawn Martin-Hill, Michael Doxtater, Susan Hill, Theresa McCarthy, Dan Longboat, and Bonnie Freeman. All of these Haudenosaunee scholars have made significant contributions to their respective fields and, more importantly, have imbued their scholarly work with an assured Haudenosaunee perspective and understanding, oftentimes directly countering the established, pre-existing narrative of Grand River history and tradition as written by non-Natives. Several others from Six Nations have also written and published books, M.A. theses, short stories, articles, and essays on a variety of issues pertaining to Grand River in recent years. These include George Beaver, Patricia Monture-Angus, Rick Hill, Wilma Green, Sandi Montour, Tom Hill, Pamela Johnson, Lynda Powless, Alex Jamieson Jr., John Moses, Bev Jacobs, Sara General, and members of the Six Nations Writers Group, to name just a few. Although space limitations have not allowed for a discussion of their work, each of these scholars and writers has contributed to a larger understanding of the unique nature of Haudenosaunee history, culture, and intellectual tradition, both within the Grand River community and beyond.

The recent establishment of the Deyohahá:ge: Indigenous Knowledge Centre and the creation of the Onkwehonwe Language Diploma Program at Six Nations Polytechnic is further evidence that fostering the relationship between modern scholarly research and traditional knowledge is important to the community and will ensure the preservation of Haudenosaunee culture into the future. In December 2008, a public ceremony was held at Six Nations to recognize traditional knowledge carriers who will be involved with these programs as Knowledge Guardians, with the rights and privileges accorded professors in other academic institutions. Ima Johnson, Lottie Keye, Hubert Skye, Jim Styres, Arnie General, Ariel Harris, Nora Carrier, Alfred Keye, and Tom Deer are all fluent speakers highly knowledgeable in Haudenosaunee traditions who will serve as advisors and core faculty to these new educational initiatives.

Despite divergent community interests throughout our history, assertions of Haudenosaunee sovereignty have persisted now for well over 200 years at Grand River, largely based upon a firm belief in our cultural narratives and sense of distinct, collective identity in the face of Canadian policies of assimilation aimed squarely at undermining Indigenous nationhood. Although the Six Nations community's understandings of traditional governance structures and its implications for land rights and economic development are often conflicting, we continue to remain united in our refusal to acquiesce to the federal and provincial governments' attempts to dictate the terms of our political existence. While community factionalism can be confusing to outside observers, a deeper understanding of Haudenosaunee history and cultural philosophy allows for a more nuanced interpretation of such internal debates existing alongside a unified belief system within Haudenosaunee communities. Addressing this particular feature of Haudenosaunee communities, Seneca legal scholar Robert Odawi Porter states, "What appears to the outside as chaos, makes us who we are" (quoted in Hauptman 2008, 203), meaning that openly challenging the direction of our leadership and each other's opinions allows for healthy debate and constant engagement with our cultural philosophies. This is important, for discussing the philosophy of the Great Law, the Two Row Wampum, and the Silver Covenant Chain in 2014 must seem rather frivolous to politicians who have little respect for First Nations history and cultural traditions; by doing so on a regular basis the Grand River community continually reaffirms the connection to our ancestors' political foresight and sharpens our ability to understand and articulate cultural beliefs in the present, whether it be in literature, film, photography, community meetings, classrooms, or the media.

Writing about the struggles of his own people, Palestinian scholar Edward Said describes the power and effect of repetition in the seemingly futile attempt to address injustice to an indifferent audience: "To outsiders this assertiveness is frustrating ... because it seems to renew itself ceaselessly, without ever producing anything new or anything outside it that might be illuminating.... [T]here is nevertheless something reassuring about ... repeating familiar patterns to the point where repetition itself becomes more important than what is being repeated. In the rigorous discipline of the repetition ... you cannot get out of it, cannot easily transform it into a symbol of something else ... It is as if the activity of repeating prevents us, and others, from skipping us or overlooking us entirely" (2000, 273–74). Such performative acts have this kind of resonance within Haudenosaunee communities as well. Not only do they constantly reinforce an understanding of culture, history, and identity within the community and younger generations in particular, they also serve to convey a consistent message of who we are to others.

Speaking at McMaster University in 1998, the late Cayuga Chief Harvey Longboat, who carried the Confederacy title of Deskaheh, addressed the concept of "development" from a Haudenosaunee perspective. He began with a brief account of our Creation story and explained how our ancestors understood themselves to be but a small part of the natural world, in which they as onkwehonwe, or "real human beings," were required to develop their intellect in order to always ensure the continued well-being of the earth. "In our culture our mind is a tremendous tool that was given to us," he stated, and it is therefore our ongoing responsibility to use our intellect and ability to communicate with others in order to "develop that [beneficial] relationship with our earth and everything that is on the earth ... so there is a relationship of respect." This is a philosophy considerably different than what development has come to mean for the Western world, where "progress" is viewed in materialistic measurements of time and money and most always results in environmental degradation. As a result, Chief Longboat cautioned that "development may have gone beyond the ability of the natural world to heal itself. The age of electronics and progress is pushing us into a world that is devoting less of its energy to feeding us naturally.... People of today are not only asking who they are but what they are ... and if we do not come to grips with who we are and our relationship with our surroundings we are assuredly headed for a catastrophe" (1998).

Such warnings are certainly not unique to the Haudenosaunee, but the fact that Indigenous cultures are built upon ancient, sacred relationships to the natural world would suggest that traditional knowledge has some insights into how to address the current environmental concerns that we all face as human beings on this planet. That we are still here to share our stories and knowledge at all is remarkable, a testimony to our resilience, strength, and courage in carrying out our sacred responsibilities by whatever means necessary, and to whoever will listen.

While the Grand River Haudenosaunee have undoubtedly changed in everyday culture, economies, and language, our understanding of ourselves as a Confederacy of nations with a distinct history and purpose has remained essentially the same since pre-contact times. As a result, our politics and cultural beliefs have been intertwined with our literature, art, and resistance. For despite centuries of sustained efforts by colonial governments we have persisted as a distinct people, and the 230-year-old struggle for justice along the Grand River continues—now aided by twenty-first-century technology, but more importantly, guided by our oral traditions and the words of Joseph Brant, Pauline Johnson, Deskaheh, and Jake Thomas, along with countless other Haudenosaunee who have not forgotten who we are, and who we will continue to be.

This is a book that will always be "in progress." For the Haudenosaunee, the world is continually unfolding, changing, and developing, while maintaining its perpetual cycle of seasons and constant motion across the universe. So too is the collective story of our traditions, history, and resistance to colonialism. This is but a very small contribution to the much greater, ongoing conversation.

Nia:wen to my many teachers at Six Nations who have patiently and unselfishly contributed to this work and to the continued existence of our cultural wellbeing. These include Arnie General, Tom Deer, Norma General, Pete Sky, Hubert Sky, Lottie Keye, Nora Carrier, Ima Johnson, Manuel Johnson, Jim Styres, Sadie Buck, Ron Thomas, Sr., Leroy "Jock" Hill, Alfred Keye, and Renee Thomas-Hill. Although Reg Henry, Marge Henry, Jake Thomas, Huron Miller, Oliver Jacobs, and Frances Froman have passed on, their words have also impacted on this book and upon our community. I would like to acknowledge and honour the late Harvey Longboat, Sr. who in many ways made this work possible at all. Nia:wen to those in other Haudenosaunee territories who have over the years taught me about our collective history and responsibilities. These people include Oren Lyons, Tom Porter, Katsi Cook, Richard Mitchell, and Bob Antone, as well as the late Leon Shenandoah. John Mohawk was, and is, an especially important influence on my thinking, and he is greatly missed by many. As John once wrote, "Somewhere in the dictionary is a definition of happiness which holds that happiness is a feeling of great good fortune. Our [Haudenosaunee] story holds that we have much that we should be happy about, and evidence of this great good fortune is the manifestation of the gifts of nature." I therefore feel quite fortunate to have the privilege to present some of that story here. If there are any mistakes or misinterpretations they are completely my own, and I take full responsibility for any inaccuracies presented herein.

I want to thank those who have travelled the academic path with me over many years, and who have all given me much guidance and encouragement, each in their own significant way. This book came into being through the many conversations, collaborations, disagreements, and achievements that were shared with Audra Simpson, Bonnie Freeman, Dawn Martin-Hill, Jasmin Habib, Jolene Rickard, Kevin White, Hayden King, Michael Doxtater, Rick Hill, Sara General, Scott Manning Stevens, Sean Teuton, Susan Hill, Taiaiake Alfred, Theresa McCarthy, and Vanessa Watts-Powless. Nia:wen akwe:kon.

For research and writing support, I would like to thank the Social Sciences and Humanities Research Council of Canada, the Ontario Graduate Scholarship program, the Canada-U.S. Fulbright Exchange Program, as well as the John and Helen Harvey Research Scholarship Award (McMaster University). The staff people at Mills Library, the Newberry Library, Woodland Cultural Centre, Deyohahá:ge: Indigenous Knowledge Centre (Six Nations), and the Smithsonian Institution were always extremely helpful during my visits. Portions of this work have also appeared in *Essays in Canadian Writing* 75 (Winter 2002).

Several people were involved with reading earlier versions of the manuscript in its various forms, and their comments have made it a much stronger study. For this, I thank Roger Hyman, Mary O'Connor, William Coleman, Robert Warrior, and David Newhouse, as well as the late Sylvia Bowerbank. I would like to give a special thanks to Daniel Coleman, who has been a consistent and much appreciated champion of this project from its earliest beginning. His editorial skills and thoughtful advice have been invaluable throughout. The Department of English and Cultural Studies at McMaster University has been a highly supportive place to be for many years now, and I am lucky to work alongside of excellent colleagues and friends. The good folks at the University of Manitoba Press have been tremendously patient and encouraging throughout the entire process of making this book happen. Glenn Bergen has been especially helpful right from our initial conversation to the present, and he, along with David Carr, have been avid supporters at every stage. Nia:wen to Shelley Niro, who gave me a photo a few years ago that has stayed in my head (and in my office) ever since, and which now serves as the cover image.

The staff, students, and instructors at the Indigenous Studies Program at McMaster have been like an extended family for over twenty years, and like any family they have provided much laughter and distraction, as well as support and encouragement. They have challenged, inspired, and motivated me to be a responsible teacher, a reluctant administrator, and a better person. Nia:wen. There are many, many others to thank and who have, quite simply, made this book possible. I am indebted to great friends who have contributed in ways that they are not even aware of. Thanks to you all. A special nia:wen goes out to the Fourth Line hro:non, who have taught me the importance of being a good neighbour and shown me what it means to be onkwehonwe. Nia:wen to Jennie Anderson for her friendship, laughter, and understanding.

Finally, and as always, I want to express my sincere gratitude and appreciation to the Frohman and Monture families—all of my grandparents, aunts, uncles, and cousins—who have through the generations experienced, endured, persevered, and celebrated each of the historical moments discussed in this book with great pride, character, and always with a sense of humour. To my late mother, Carole, and my father, Don, who have provided me with an understanding of who I am and given me a place to be from, I am forever thankful. Nia:wen akwe:kon.

Preface

1 J. Wesley Powell, founder of the Bureau of American Ethnology, famously referred to Lewis Henry Morgan's work as the "first scientific account of an Indian tribe" (Morgan [1851] 1993, v).

2 The "canon" of literature on the Iroquois includes: Morgan (1851), Hale ([1883] 1963), Hewitt (1904–1928), Goldenweiser (1914), Parker ([1916] 1968), Speck (1949), Fenton (1949, 1998), Shimony (1961), Wilson (1959), Wallace (1970), Graymont (1972).

3 Métis scholar Jo-Ann Episkenew sees colonial versions of history as constructing the "master narrative" that has perpetuated "the myth of the new Canadian nation-state, which valorizes the settlers but which sometimes misrepresents and more often excludes Indigenous peoples. Indigenous literature acknowledges and validates Indigenous peoples' experiences by filling in the gaps and correcting the falsehoods in this master narrative" (2009, 2).

4 See Donald Smith's *Sacred Feathers* for an overview of Mississauga land dealings with the British during this period (1987, 22–29).

5 This has long been a point of contention between anthropologists and Haudenosaunee sources. Historian Bruce Johansen (1995) cites Barbara Mann and Jerry Fields, who arrived at a date of August 31, 1142 for the formation of the Iroquois Confederacy, based on a combination of oral traditions, documentary history, and astronomical records (it is said that an eclipse took place during the final formation). Other dates have ranged from 1090 to the often-cited 1451, to as late as 1600 (Tooker 1994). Archeologist Dean Snow has recently suggested, rather vaguely, that the League was "probably complete by around 1525" (1994, 60). Today, Haudenosaunee knowledge holders simply contend that it "happened in very ancient times."

Introduction

1 Tuscarora ethnologist J.N.B. Hewitt recorded several versions of the Creation Story at Grand River and other Iroquoian communities beginning in the 1890s (1904–1928). More

recently published accounts include: Thomas (1993), Elm and Antone(2000), and Mohawk ([1978] 2005).

2 See Mitchell and Myers (1984) and Shimony ([1961] 1994) for further explanation of the Four Ceremonies.

3 For further discussion and analysis of the important role of women in Haudenosaunee social and political structures, see Spittal (1990) and Mann (2000).

4 For a fuller description of the Condolence Ceremony at Grand River in 1883, see Hale's *The Iroquois Book of Rites* ([1883] 1963). See also Fenton (1946, 1950) and Thomas (1996). For an account of an Iroquoian Condolence Ceremony in 1689, see Colden ([1727–1747] 1994, 101–107).

5 Seneca historian Barbara Mann's recent work ([2005] 2008) examines this often-overlooked event in American history and its profound impacts on Haudenosaunee society. See also Graymont (1972) and Taylor (2007) for extensive accounts of the Six Nations' involvement in the American Revolution and its aftermath.

6 Published versions of the Code of Handsome Lake (in English) include Parker ([1916] 1968), Mitchell and Myers (1984), and Thomas and Boyle (1994).

7 For an extensive discussion of the Haudenosaunee influence on the U.S. Constitution, see Johansen (1982), Grinde and Johansen (1991), Barreiro (1992), and Lyons and Mohawk (1996). Noted Iroquoianist Elizabeth Tooker argues against such claims of Iroquois influence in "The United States Constitution and the Iroquois League"(1988). In 2010, the United States minted a commemorative silver dollar in honour of the "accomplishments and contributions" of the Iroquois League of Peace.

8 Susan Hill (Grand River Mohawk) effectively argues that these "treaty relationships were informed and defined by the lessons of Haudenosaunee cultural history. They created a framework for respectful relations that both sides agreed would exist for perpetuity. The colonial period witnessed major offenses to the treaties, but the treaty relations still exist." (2008, 23)

9 For a substantial exploration of the deep connections between land, place, and Native intellectual and spiritual traditions, see Vine Deloria's *God is Red: A Native View of Religion* (1994) and *Red Earth, White Lies* (1997).

1 *"Sovereigns of the Soil"*

1 For a useful summary of this period in Haudenosaunee political and military history, see Dowd (2004). Fuller-length studies of the Six Nations' role in the formation of North America include: Jennings (1984), Richter (1992), Dennis (1993), and Anderson (2005).

2 Brant's conduct during these particular battles is examined in Bryant (1873, 23–25) and Graymont (1972, 190–92). For a first-hand account of Iroquois service and conduct in the Revolution, see Bloomfield (1996).

3 See also Johnston (1984).

4 Besides their great mistrust of the British, the Grand River Haudenosaunee were also reluctant to go to war with the United States because of the possibility of fighting against Seneca warriors who had joined with the Americans. See Carl Benn's *The Iroquois in the War of 1812* (1998) for a full historical account of Six Nations involvement in this conflict.

2 The Challenge to Haudenosaunee Nationhood

1 See Weaver (1972), Titley (1986), and Moses (2008) for fuller accounts of the "Dehorner" movement.

2 See Shimony ([1961] 1994) for an account of the White Dog Ceremony as practised at Grand River in the early twentieth century (185–87).

3 The history and legacy of the residential schools, which lasted roughly from 1879 to 1986, have been well documented in recent years. Two studies with Six Nations content are Graham (1997) and Milloy (1999).

3 "An Enemy's Foot is on our Country"

1 Six Nations lands (and trust monies) were expropriated for projects such as the Grand River Navigation Company, McGill University, and the Welland Canal, among others. See Titley (1986) and Susan M. Hill (2006).

2 For an in-depth historical study of Haudenosaunee participation in this conflict, see Barbara Graymont's *The Iroquois in the American Revolution* (1972). See also Taylor (2007) and Paxton (2008) for more recent analysis of Brant's influence and Haudenosaunee involvement in the Revolution.

3 Despite Scott's claims otherwise, the Confederacy Council was an often proactive government that attended to affairs on the Reserve quite effectively. For a fuller examination, see Noon (1949).

4 It is notable that Deskaheh travelled to Europe, via Switzerland, on a passport issued by the Six Nations Confederacy Council as a demonstration of Haudenosaunee sovereignty (Wright 1992, 322). Such passports were used again when a delegation of Haudenosaunee travelled to the League of Nations in 1977 (see Lyons 2005, 13–15). Six Nations members have continued this practice ever since, with limited degrees of success.

5 For an anthropological survey of the political and economic environment at Grand River during this era, see Shimony ([1961] 1994) and Meyers (2006). See also the highly interesting short film, *The Longhouse People* (Wargon 1951), a collaboration between traditionalists at Six Nations and the National Film Board during this period.

6 For first-hand accounts, see Dawn Martin-Hill's *Sewatokwa'tshera't: The Dish with One Spoon* (2007).

4 Displacement, Identity, and Resistance

1 See Hauptman (1986), Smith and Warrior (1996), and Josephy, Nagel, and Johnson (1999).

2 See Flanagan (1987).

3 For an extensive account and analysis of Six Nations' involvement in the First World War, see John Moses (2008).

5 "Linking Arms Together"

1 See, for example, Alanis Obomsawin's powerful documentaries *Kanehsatake: 270 Years of Resistance* (1993) and *Rocks at Whiskey Trench* (2000). See also *Acts of Defiance* (MacLeod 1993) and *Keepers of the Fire* (Welsh 1994).

2 At the time of this writing, our languages exist on the brink of extinction at Grand River. Recent studies have found that there are sixty-four fluent native Cayuga speakers, forty-two native Onondaga speakers, and one native Mohawk speaker.

3 See Michael Doxtater (1998, 5).

Conclusion

1 See Dawn Martin-Hill's documentary, *Sewatokwa'tshera't: The Dish With One Spoon* (2007).

Adams, Howard. 1975. *Prison of Grass: Canada from a Native Point of View*. Toronto: General Publishing.

Akwesasne Notes, ed. 2005. *Basic Call to Consciousness*. Revised edition. Summertown, TN: Native Voices.

Alfred, Taiaiake. 1999. *Peace, Power, Righteousness: An Indigenous Manifesto*. Don Mills, ON: Oxford University Press.

———. 2005. *Wasase: Indigenous Pathways of Action and Freedom*. Peterborough, ON: Broadview.

"An Account of John Norton's Mission to England in 1804." [1804?] In Johnston 1964, 270–71.

Anderson, Arthur. 1991. "Minute Book of the Six Nations Hereditary Council of Chiefs." In *The Constitution of the Five Nations or The Iroquois Book of the Great Law*. by A.C. Parker, edited by William Guy Spittal, 199–237. Reprint, Ohsweken, ON: Iroqrafts.

Anderson, Fred. 2005. *The War That Made America: A Short History of the French and Indian War*. New York: Viking.

Barreiro, Jose, ed. 1992. *Indian Roots of American Democracy*. Ithaca, NY: Akwe:kon.

Beaver, George. 1997. *Mohawk Reporter: The Six Nations Columns of George Beaver*. Ohsweken, ON: Iroqrafts.

Benn, Carl. 1998. *The Iroquois in the War of 1812*. Toronto: University of Toronto Press.

Bloomfield, Joseph. (1776) 1996. "Journal of Joseph Bloomfield." In *In Mohawk Country: Early Narratives about a Native People*, edited by Dean R. Snow, Charles T. Gehring, and Willam A. Starna, 274–91. Syracuse: Syracuse University Press.

Bowman, Rob. 2000. "Liner Notes." *Music From Big Pink*. Reissue, Los Angeles: Capitol.

———. 2005. *The Band: A Musical History*. Los Angeles: Capitol.

Brant, Beth. 1994. *Writing as Witness: Essay and Talk*. Toronto: Women's Press.

Brant, Joseph. (1791a) 1964. Joseph Brant to Dorchester. In Johnston 1964, 57–58.

———. (1791b) 1964. Joseph Brant to the Rev. Samuel Kirkland. In Johnston 1964, 269–70.

———. (1796a) 1964. "Brant's Address to William Claus on the Subject of the Indian Lands, November 24, 1796." In Johnston 1964, 81–84.

———. (1796b) 1964. Joseph Brant to Israel Chapin. In Johnston 1964, 78.

———. (1798) 1998. Joseph Brant to Captain Green. In *An Anthology of Canadian Native Literature in English*, edited by Daniel David Moses and Terry Goldie. 2nd edition, 14–15. Toronto: Oxford University Press.

———. (1801) 1998. "Condolence Speech." In *An Anthology of Canadian Native Literature in English*, edited by Daniel David Moses and Terry Goldie. 2nd edition, 16. Toronto: Oxford University Press.

———. 1872. *A Memoir of the Distinguished Mohawk Indian Chief, Sachem and Warrior, Capt. Joseph Brant*. Edited by William E. Palmer. Brantford, ON: C.E. Stewart and Co.

"Brant's Power of Attorney to Sell the Indian Lands, November 2, 1796." (1796) 1964. In Johnston 1964, 79–81.

Bryant, William C. 1873. *Joseph Brant, Thayendanegea, and His Posterity*. Philadelphia: American Historical Record.

Campbell, Maria. 1973. *Halfbreed*. Toronto: McClelland and Stewart.

Campbell, [Patrick]. (1792) 1964. "A Visit with Joseph Brant on the Grand River, 1792." In Johnston 1964, 59–65.

Campbell, William J. 2004. "Seth Newhouse, the Grand River Six Nations and the Writing of the Great Law." *Ontario History* 96 (2): 183–202.

Cardinal, Harold. 1969. *The Unjust Society*. Vancouver: Douglas and McIntyre.

Chalmers, Harvey, and Ethel Brant Monture. 1955. *Joseph Brant: Mohawk*. Toronto: The Ryerson Press.

Chossudovsky, Michel. 2008. "The Deployment of US Troops inside Canada." *Global Research*, March 13. http://www. globalresearch.ca/PrintArticle.php?articleId=8323.

Cocks, Jay. 1970. "Down to Old Dixie and Back." *Time*. January 12, 42–46.

Colden, Cadwallader. (1727–47) 1994. *The History of the Five Indian Nations, Depending on the Province of New-York in America*. Ithaca, NY: Cornell University Press.

Cook-Lynn, Elizabeth. 1998. "American Indian Intellectualism and the New Indian Story." In *Natives and Academics: Researching and Writing about American Indians*, edited by Devon Mihesuah, 111–38. Lincoln: University of Nebraska Press.

Deloria, Philip J. 2004. *Indians in Unexpected Places*. Lawrence, KS: University Press of Kansas.

Deloria, Vine, Jr. 1969. *Custer Died for Your Sins: An Indigenous Manifesto*. New York: Macmillan.

———. 1994. *God Is Red: A Native View of Religion*. Golden, CO: Fulcrum.

———. 1997. *Red Earth, White Lies: Native Americans and the Myth of Scientific Fact*. Golden, CO: Fulcrum.

———. 1999. *Spirit and Reason: A Vine Deloria Jr. Reader*. Edited by Barbara Deloria, Kristin Foehner, and Sam Scinta. Golden, CO: Fulcrum.

———. 2004. "Philosophy and the Tribal Peoples." In *American Indian Thought: Philosophical Essays*, edited by Anna Waters, 3–12. Malden, MA: Blackwell.

Dennis, Matthew. 1993. *Cultivating a Landscape of Peace: Iroquois-European Encounters in Seventeenth-Century America.* Ithaca: Cornell University Press.

Deskaheh. (1925) 2005. "The Last Speech of Deskaheh." In *Akwesasne Notes* 2005, 48–54.

Deskaheh (Levi General) and Six Nations Confederacy Council. 1924. *The Red Man's Appeal For Justice: The Position of the Six Nations that they Constitute an Independent State.* Brantford, ON: D. Wilson Moore, Ltd.

Dowd, Gregory Evans. 2004. "Wag the Imperial Dog: Indians and Overseas Empires in North America, 1650–1776." In *A Companion to American Indian History*, edited by Philip J. Deloria and Neal Salisbury, [46–67]. Malden, MA: Blackwell Publishing.

Doxtater, Michael G. 1998. "The Iroquoian Indigenous Knowledge Epistemology of Jacob Thomas." *Native Americas* 25 (4): 48–55.

———. 2001. "Indigenology: A Decolonizing Learning Method for Emancipating Iroquois and World Indigenous Knowledge." PhD diss., Cornell University.

Doxtator, Deborah. 1996. "What Happened to the Iroquois Clans?: A Study of Clans in Three Nineteenth Century Rotinonhsyonni Communities." PhD diss., University of Western Ontario.

Dragland, Stan. 1994. *Floating Voice: Duncan Campbell Scott and the Literature of Treaty 9.* Concord, ON: House of Anansi.

———. 2000. "Introduction." In Scott 2000, 1: xi–xl.

Elm, Demus, and Harvey Antone. 2000. *The Oneida Creation Story.* Translated and edited by Floyd G. Lounsbury and Bryan Gick. Lincoln: University of Nebraska Press.

Episkenew, Jo-Ann. 2009. *Taking Back Our Spirits: Indigenous Literature, Public Policy, and Healing.* Winnipeg: University of Manitoba Press.

Fenton, William. 1946. "An Iroquois Condolence Council for Installing Cayuga Chiefs in 1945." *Journal of the Washington Academy of Sciences* 36 (4): 110–27.

———. 1949. "Seth Newhouse's Traditional History and Constitution of the Iroquois Confederacy." *Proceedings of the American Philosophical Society* 93 (2): 141–58.

———. 1950. "The Roll Call of the Iroquois Chiefs: A Study of a Mnemonic Cane from the Six Nations Reserve." *Smithsonian Miscellaneous Collections* 111 (.15): 1–73.

———. 1998. *The Great Law and the Longhouse: A Political History of the Iroquois Confederacy.* Norman: University of Oklahoma Press.

Flanagan, Bill. 1987. "The Return of Robbie Robertson." *Musician*, September, 88–98, 113.

Francis, Daniel. 1993. *The Imaginary Indian: The Image of the Indian in Canadian Culture.* Vancouver: Arsenal Pulp.

Gibson, John Arthur. (1912) 1992. *Concerning the League: The Iroquois League Tradition as Dictated in Onondaga.* Edited and translated by Hanni Woodbury, Reg Henry, and Harry Webster. Winnipeg: Algonquian and Iroquoian Linguistics.

Goeman, Mishuana. 2013. *Mark My Words: Native Women Mapping Our Nations.* Minneapolis: University of Minnesota Press.

Goldie, Terry. 1989. *Fear and Temptation: The Image of the Indigene in Canadian, Australian, and New Zealand Literatures*. Kingston: McGill-Queen's University Press.

Graham, Elizabeth. 1997. *The Mush Hole: Life at Two Indian Residential Schools*. Waterloo, ON: Heffle.

Gray, Charlotte. 2002. *Flint and Feather: The Life and Times of E. Pauline Johnson, Tekahionwake*. Toronto: HarperFlamingoCanada.

Graymont, Barbara. 1972. *The Iroquois in the American Revolution*. Syracuse: Syracuse University Press.

Green, Richard G. 1994. *The Last Raven and Other Stories*. Ohsweken, ON: Ricara Features.

———. 1995. *Sing, Like a Hermit Thrush*. Ohsweken, ON: Ricara Features.

Greene, Alma (Gah-wonh-nos-doh). 1971. *Forbidden Voice: Reflections of a Mohawk Indian*. Toronto: Hamlyn.

Grinde, Donald A. and Bruce E. Johansen. 1991. *Exemplar of Liberty: Native America and the Evolution of Democracy*. Los Angeles: University of California.

Haldimand, [Frederick]. (1784a) 1964. "Haldimand's Proclamation of October 25, 1784." In Johnston 1964, 50–51.

———. (1784b) 1964. "Means Suggested as the Most Probable to Retain the Six Nations and Western Indians in the King's Interest." In Johnston 1964, 52–53.

Hale, Horatio. (1883) 1963. *The Iroquois Book of Rites*. Toronto: University of Toronto Press.

Hauptman, Laurence M. 1986. *The Iroquois Struggle for Survival*. Syracuse: Syracuse University Press.

———. 2008. *Seven Generations of Iroquois Leadership: The Six Nations Since 1800*. Syracuse: Syracuse University Press.

Hawkins, Ronnie, and Peter Goddard. 1989. *Ronnie Hawkins: Last of the Good ol' Boys*. Toronto: Stoddart.

Hewitt, J.N.B. 1904–1928. *Iroquoian Cosmology*. 2 vols. Washington: Government Printing Office.

Hill, Richard W. 2007. "Transitions in Haudenosaunee Realities: The Changing World of the Haudenosaunee as Seen in Historic Photographs." In *Sovereign Bones: New Native American Writing*, edited by Eric Gansworth, 203–17. New York: Nation.

———. 2011. "The Restorative Aesthetic of Greg Staats." In *Greg Staats: Liminal Disturbance*. Hamilton, ON: McMaster Museum of Art.

Hill, Susan M. 2006. "The Clay We Are Made Of: An Examination of Haudenosaunee Land Tenure on the Grand River Territory." PhD diss., Trent University.

———. 2008. "'Travelling Down the River of Life Together in Peace and Friendship, Forever': Haudenosaunee Land Ethics and Treaty Agreements as the Basis For Restructuring the Relationship with the British Crown." In *Lighting the Eighth Fire: The Liberation, Resurgence, and Protection of Indigenous Nations*, edited by Leanne Simpson, 23–45. Winnipeg: Arbeiter Ring.

"History of the Six Nations Indians Settlement on the Banks of the Grand River." n.d.

Hoskyns, Barney. 1993. *Across the Great Divide: The Band and America*. New York: Hyperion.

Howison, John. (1821) 1964. "A Critique of the Six Nations." In Johnston 1964, 290–91.

Jennings, Francis. 1984. *The Ambiguous Iroquois Empire: The Covenant Chain Confederation of Indian Tribes with the English Colonies*. New York: Norton.

Johansen, Bruce E. 1982. *Forgotten Founders: How the American Indian Helped Shape Democracy*. Boston: The Harvard Common Press, 1982.

———. 1995. "Dating the Iroquois Confederacy." *Akwesasne Notes* 1 (3–4): 62–63.

Johnson, E. Pauline. 2002. *E. Pauline Johnson, Tekahionwake: Collected Poems and Selected Prose*. Edited by Carole Gerson and Veronica Strong-Boag. Toronto: University of Toronto Press.

———. (1912) 1997. *Flint and Feather: The Complete Poems of E. Pauline Johnson*. Toronto: Guardian.

———. (1911) 1997. *Legends of Vancouver*. Vancouver: Douglas and MacIntyre.

Johnston, Charles M. ed. 1964. *The Valley of the Six Nations: A Collection of Documents on the Indian Lands of the Grand River*. Toronto: The Champlain Society for the Government of Ontario, University of Toronto Press.

———. 1984. "To the Mohawk Station: The Making of a New England Company Missionary—The Rev. Robert Lugger." In *Extending the Rafters: Interdisciplinary Approaches to Iroquoian Studies*, edited by Michael Foster, Jack Campisi, and Marianne Mithun, 65–80. Albany: State University of New York Press.

Josephy, Alvin M., Jr., Joane Nagel, and Troy Johnson, eds. 1999. *Red Power: The American Indians' Fight for Freedom*. 2nd edition. Lincoln: University of Nebraska Press.

Keller, Betty. 1981. *Pauline: A Biography of Pauline Johnson*. Toronto: Douglas Publishing.

Klinck, Carl F., and James J. Talman, eds. 1970. *The Journal of Major John Norton, 1816*. Toronto: The Champlain Society.

Konkle, Maureen. 2004. *Writing Indian Nations: Native Intellectuals and the Politics of Historiography, 1827–1863*. Chapel Hill, NC: University of North Carolina Press.

Lawson, Alan. 1995. "Postcolonial Theory and the 'Settler' Subject." *Essays on Canadian Writing* 56: 20–36.

"Letter." 1807. Ayers Collection. Newberry Library.

Liberty, Margot, ed. (1978) 2002. *American Indian Intellectuals of the Nineteenth and Early Twentieth Centuries*. Norman: University of Oklahoma Press.

Longboat, Harvey E. 1998. "Development: The Beginning to the End." Lecture at the In the Way of Development conference, McMaster University, Hamilton, 19 November.

———. 2004. "Development: The Beginning to the End." In *In the Way of Development: Indigenous Peoples, Life Projects and Globalization*, edited by Mario Blaser, Harvey A. Feit, and Glenn McRae, 351–53. New York: Zed.

Lynch, Gerald. 1982. "An Endless Flow: D.C. Scott's Indian Poems." *Studies in Canadian Literature* 7 (1): 27–54.

Lyon, George W. 1990. "Pauline Johnson: A Reconsideration." *Studies in Canadian Literature* 15 (2): 136–59.

Lyons, Oren. 2005. "Preamble." In *Basic Call to Consciousness*, Akwesasne Notes 2005, 13–25.

Lyons, Oren, and John Mohawk, eds. 1992. *Exiled in the Land of the Free: Democracy, Indian Nations and the U.S. Constitution*. Santa Fe: Clear Light.

MacLeod, Alec G. 1993. *Acts of Defiance*. National Film Board. DVD.

Mann, Barbara Alice. 2000. *Iroquoian Women: The Gantowisas*. New York: Peter Lang.

———. (2005) 2008. *George Washington's War on Native America*. Lincoln: University of Nebraska Press.

Maracle, Brian. 1996. *Back on the Rez: Finding the Way Home*. Toronto: Viking.

Marcus, Greil. (1975) 1997. *Mystery Train: Images of America in Rock 'n' Roll Music*. 4th edition. New York: Plume.

Martin-Hill, Dawn J. 1995. "Lubicon Lake Nation: Spirit of Resistance." PhD diss., McMaster University.

———. *Sewatokwa'tshera't: The Dish With One Spoon*. PixelDust Studios, 2007. DVD.

McCarthy, Theresa L. 2006. "'It Isn't Easy': The Politics of Representation, 'Factionalism,' and Anthropology in Promoting Haudenosaunee Traditionalism at Six Nations." PhD diss., McMaster University.

———. 2008. "Iroquoian and Iroquoianist: Anthropologists and the Haudenosaunee at Grand River." *Histories of Anthropology Annual*, Vol. 4: 135–171.

McLuhan, T.C. , ed. 1971. *Touch the Earth: A Self-Portrait of Indian Existence*. New York: Pocket Book.

Meyers, Merlin G. 2006. *Households and Families of the Longhouse Iroquois at Six Nations Reserve*. Lincoln: University of Nebraska Press.

Miller, Susan A. 2011. "Native America Writes Back: The Origin of the Indigenous Paradigm in Historiography." In *Native Historians Write Back: Decolonizing American Indian History*, edited by Miller and James Riding, 9–24. Lubbock, TX: Texas Tech University Press.

Milloy, John. 1999. *"A National Crime": The Canadian Government and the Residential School System, 1879–1986*. Winnipeg: University of Manitoba Press.

Mitchell, Michael Kanentakeron and Mike Myers. 1984. *Traditional Teachings*. Cornwall Island, ON: North American Indian Traveling College.

Mohawk, John. (1978) 2005. "Thoughts of Peace: The Great Law." In *Basic Call to Consciousness*, Akwesasne Notes, 2005, 31–40.

———. 1986. Prologue. In *The White Roots of Peace*, by Paul A.W. Wallace. Saranac Lake, NY: The Chauncy Press.

———. 2005. *Iroquois Creation Story: John Arthur Gibson and J.N.B. Hewitt's Myth of the Earth Grasper*. Buffalo, NY: Mohawk Publications.

Montour, Enos T. 1973. *The Feathered U.E.L.'s: An Account of the Life and Times of Certain Canadian Native Peoples*. Toronto: Division of Communications, United Church of Canada.

Monture, Ethel Brant. 1960. *Canadian Portraits: Brant, Crowfoot, Oronhyatekha—Famous Indians*. Toronto: Clarke, Irwin and Company.

Monture-Angus, Patricia. 1995. *Thunder in My Soul: A Mohawk Woman Speaks*. Halifax, NS: Fernwood.

———. 1999. *Journeying Forward: Dreaming First Nations Independence*. Halifax, NS: Fernwood.

Morgan, Cecilia. 2003. "Private Lives and Public Performances: Aboriginal Women in a Settler Society, Ontario, Canada, 1920s–1960s." *Journal of Colonialism and Colonial History* 4 (3): 1–16.

Morgan, Lewis Henry. 1851. *League of the Ho-De'-No-Sau-Nee, or Iroquois*. New York: Citadel.

Moses, Daniel David. 1980. *Delicate Bodies*. Vancouver: Blew Ointment Press.

———. 1990. *Coyote City, a Play in Two Acts*. Stratford, ON: Williams-Wallace.

———. 1992. *Almighty Voice and his Wife: a Play in Two Acts*. Stratford, ON: Williams-Wallace.

———. 2000. *Sixteen Jesuses*. Toronto: Exile.

———. 2005. *Pursued by a Bear: Talks, Monologues and Tales*. Toronto: Exile, 2005.

Moses, John. 2008. "The Return of the Native (Veteran): Six Nations Troops and Political Change at the Grand River Reserve, 1917–1924." MA thesis, Carleton University.

Newhouse, Seth. 1885. "Cosmogony of De-ka-na-wi-da's Government of the Iroquois Confederacy: The Original Literal Historical Narratives of the Iroquois Confederacy." National Archives of Canada, Ottawa. R7954-0-2-E.

Niro, Shelley. 1991. *Mohawks in Beehives*. Photographs.

———. 1998. *Honey Moccasin*. Turtle Night Productions.

———. 2005. *Suite: INDIAN*. Turtle Night Productions.

———. 2009. *Kissed by Lightning*. Kissed by Lightning Productions.

Niro, Shelley, and Anna Gronau. 1993. *It Starts with a Whisper*. Bay of Quinte Production.

Noon, John A. 1949. *Law and Government of the Grand River Iroquois*. New York: Viking Fund Publications in Anthropology, 1949.

Norton, John. (1804) 1964. "Memorial of the Six Nations, Presented by John Norton, 1804." In Johnston 1964, 272–73.

Obomsawin, Alanis. 1993. *Kanehsatake: 270 Years of Resistance*. National Film Board.

———. 2000. *Rocks at Whiskey Trench*. National Film Board.

Ortiz, Simon. (1981) 2005. "Towards a National Indian Literature: Cultural Authenticity in Nationalism." In *American Indian Literary Nationalism*, edited by Jace Weaver, Craig S. Womack, and Robert Warrior, 253–260. Albuquerque: University of New Mexico.

Palmer, William E. 1872. Introduction. In Brant 1872.

Parker, Arthur C. (1916) 1968. *Parker on the Iroquois*. Syracuse: Syracuse University Press.

"The Past and Present Condition of the Six Nations." (1842) 1964. In Johnston 1964, 305–11.

Paxton, James W. 2008. *Joseph Brant and his World:18th Century Mohawk Warrior and Statesman*. Toronto: James Lorimer.

Portland. (1797) 1964. "Portland's Instructions to Russell." In Johnston 1964, 84.

Red Jacket. 2006. *The Collected Speeches of Sagoyewatha, or Red Jacket*. Edited by Granville Ganter. Syracuse: Syracuse University Press.

Richter, Daniel K. 1992. *The Ordeal of the Longhouse: the Peoples of the Iroquois League in the Era of European Civilization*. Chapel Hill: University of North Carolina Press.

Robertson, Robbie. 1968a. "Caledonia Mission." *Music From Big Pink*. Capitol Records.

———. 1968b. "The Weight." *Music From Big Pink*. Capitol Records.

———. 1969. "The Night They Drove Old Dixie Down." *The Band*. Capitol Records.

————. 1972. "Caledonia Mission" (live). *Rock of Ages*. Capitol Records.

————. 1975. "Acadian Driftwood." *Northern Lights—Southern Cross*. Capitol Records.

Rogers, Edward S., and Donald B. Smith. 1994. *Aboriginal Ontario: Historical Perspectives on the First Nations*. Toronto: Dundurn.

Roppolo, Kimberly. 2001. "Toward a Tribal-Centered Reading of Native Literature: Using Indigenous Rhetoric(s) Instead of Literary Analysis." *Paradoxa: Studies in World Literary Genres* 6 (15): 263–74.

Said, Edward. 2000. *The Edward Said Reader*. Edited by Moustafa Bayoumi and Andrew Rubin. New York: Vintage.

Salem-Wiseman, Lisa. 1996. "'Verily, the White Man's Ways Were the Best': Duncan Campbell Scott, Native Culture, and Assimilation." *Studies in Canadian Literature* 21 (2): 120–42.

Scorsese, Martin. (1978) 2002. *The Last Waltz*. MGM Home Entertainment.

Scott, Duncan Campbell. 1912. "Traditional History of the Confederacy of the Six Nations." *Royal Society of Canada, Proceedings and Transactions*, 3rd set., 5 (1912): s. ii, 195–246.

————. 1926. *The Poems of Duncan Campbell Scott*. Toronto: McClelland and Stewart.

————. 2000. *Duncan Campbell Scott: Addresses, Essays and Reviews*. 2 vols. Edited by Leslie Ritchie. London, ON: Canadian Poetry.

Shanley, Kathryn W. 2001. "Born from the Need to Say: Boundaries and Sovereignties in Native American Literary and Cultural Studies." *Paradoxa: Studies in World Literary Genres*. 6 (15):3–10.

Shimony, Annemarie Anrod. [1961] 1994. *Conservatism among the Iroquois at the Six Nations Reserve*. Syracuse, NY: Syracuse University Press.

————. 1984. "Conflict and Continuity: An Analysis of an Iroquois Uprising." In *Extending the Rafters: Interdisciplinary Approaches to Iroquoian Studies*, edited by Michael Foster, Jack Campisi, and Marianne Mithun, 153–64. Albany: State University of New York Press.

Simpson, Audra. 1998. "The Empire Laughs Back: Tradition, Power, and Play in the Work of Shelley Niro and Ryan Rice." In *Iroquois Art: Visual Expressions of Contemporary Native American Artists*, edited by Doris Stambrau, et al., 48–54. Altenstadt, Germany: Christian F. Feest.

Six Nations/Grand River Confederacy Council. 2007. "Statement on the Douglas Creek Land Negotiations."

Six Nations' Council. [1806] 1964. "Proceedings of a Six Nations' Council at Onondaga, November 9, 1806." In Johnston 1964, 136–38.

Smith, Donald B. 1987. *Sacred Feathers: The Reverend Peter Jones (Kahkewaquonaby) and the Mississauga Indians*. Toronto: University of Toronto Press.

Smith, Paul Chaat. 1998. "Home Alone." In *Reservation X: The Power of Place in Aboriginal Contemporary Art*, edited by Gerald McMaster, 109–22. Hull, QC: Canadian Museum of Civilization.

Smith, Paul Chaat and Robert Allen Warrior. 1996. *Like a Hurricane: The Indian Movement from Alcatraz to Wounded Knee*. New York: The New Press.

Snow, Dean. 1994. *The Iroquois*. Cambridge, MA: Blackwell Publishers.

Speck, Frank. 1949. *Midwinter Rites of the Cayuga Longhouse.* Philadelphia: University of Pennsylvania Press.

Spittal, William G. 1990. *Iroquois Women: An Anthology.* Ohsweken, ON: Iroqrafts.

Stacey, Robert, Donald Smith, and Bryan Winslow Colwell. 1995. "Introduction." In *Iroquois Fires: The Six Nations Lyrics and Lore of Dawendine.* 11–21. Ottawa: Penumbra Press.

Stacey, Robert. 1995. "Afterword: How This Book Came to Be." In *Iroquois Fires: The Six Nations Lyrics and Lore of Dawendine."* 143–150. Ottawa: Penumbra Press.

Stone, William L. (1838) 1969. *Life of Joseph Brant—Thayendanegea: Including the Border Wars of the American Revolution, and Sketches of the Indian Campaigns of Generals Harmar, St. Clair, and Wayne.* 2 vols. New York: Kraus Reprint Co.

Strong-Boag, Veronica and Carole Gerson. 2000. *Paddling Her Own Canoe: The Times and Texts of E. Pauline Johnson (Tekahionwake).* Toronto: University of Toronto Press.

Taylor, Alan. 2007. *The Divided Ground: Indians, Settlers, and the Northern Borderland of the American Revolution.* New York: Vintage.

Thomas, Jacob. 1993. *Tshe Niyawe:oh Ne' One Tshaohweja:deh: Creation Story.* Wilsonville, ON: Sandpiper.

———. 1996. *Legend of the Peacemaker: The Great Law (John Arthur Gibson's Version).* Wilsonville, ON: The Jake Thomas Learning Centre.

Thomas, Jacob, and Terry Boyle. 1994. *Teachings from the Longhouse.* Toronto: Stoddart.

Titley, E. Brian. 1986. *A Narrow Vision: Duncan Campbell Scott and the Administration of Indian Affairs in Canada.* Vancouver: University of British Columbia Press.

Tooker, Elizabeth. 1988. "The United States Constitution and the Iroquois League." *Ethnohistory* 35 (4): 305–36.

———. 1994. "The Five (Later Six) Nations Confederacy, 1550–1784." In Rogers and Smith 1994, 79–91.

Vincent, John. (1813) 1964. "General John Vincent's Speech to the Six Nations, October 22, 1813." In Johnston 1964, 207.

Viney, Peter. 1997. "Caledonia Mission." The Band. http://theband.hiof.no/articles/caledonia_mission_viney.html.

Wallace, Anthony F.C. 1970. *The Death and Rebirth of the Seneca.* New York: Alfred A. Knopf.

Wargon, Allan. 1951. *The Longhouse People.* National Film Board of Canada.

Warrior, Robert. 2005. *The People and the Word: Reading Native Nonfiction.* Minneapolis: University of Minnesota Press.

Weaver, Jace, Craig S. Womack, Robert Warrior. 2005. *American Indian Literary Nationalism.* Albuquerque: University of New Mexico.

Weaver, Sally. 1972. *Medicine and Politics among the Grand River Iroquois: A Study of the Non-Conservatives.* Ottawa: National Museums of Canada.

————. 1984. "Seth Newhouse and the Grand River Confederacy at Mid-Nineteenth Century." In *Extending the Rafters: Interdisciplinary Approaches to Iroquoian Studies*, edited by Michael Foster, Jack Campisi, and Marianne Mithun, 165–82. Albany: State University of New York Press.

————. 1994. "The Iroquois: The Consolidation of the Grand River Reserve in the Mid-Nineteenth Century, 1847–1875." In Rogers and Smith 1994, 182–212.

————. "The Iroquois: The Grand River Reserve in the Late Nineteenth and Early Twentieth Centuries, 1875–1945." In Rogers and Smith 1994, 213–57.

Welsh, Christine. *Keepers of the Fire*. National Film Board, 1994.

Willcocks, Joseph. (1812) 1964. Joseph Willcocks to John Macdonell. In Johnston 1964, 196–97.

Wilson, Edmund. 1959. *Apologies to the Iroquois*. New York: Farrar, Straus, and Giroux.

Winslow, Bernice Loft (Dawendine). 1995. *Iroquois Fires: The Six Nations Lyrics and Lore of Dawendine (Bernice Loft Winslow)*. Ottawa: Penumbra.

Womack, Craig. 1999. *Red on Red: Native American Literary Separatism*. Minneapolis: University of Minnesota Press.

Wright, Ronald. 1992. *Stolen Continents: The "New World" Through Indian Eyes*. Toronto: Penguin.

Oakes, Richard, 142
Oka crisis, 179–80, 189, 191–92, 202
oral traditions: and beneficial help from
     outsiders, 56; and ceremonial life, 219–
     20; and dance, 205–6; J. Brant's lack of
     comfort with, 50–51, 52–53; J. Thomas'
     view of, 196; in negotiations with
     British, 48, 54–55; portrayed in Sing, Like
     a Hermit Thrush, 200; and repetition, 222;
     and resistance, 218; S. Newhouse study
     of, 69; as sustaining force, xiv–xv; and
     thinking about content, 218–19; use of
     English to document, 218
Ortiz, Simon, 218

Palmer, William E., 60
Paxton, James W., 30, 60–61
Peacemaker, 6–9, 20, 108, 128, 137, 204
political resistance, 18, 171–72, 214–15, 218

racism, 158, 160–61. See also colonialism
RCMP (Royal Canadian Mounted Police), 116,
     117, 118, 123, 139, 153
Red Jacket, 40, 78–81
Red Power activism, 141–42, 170, 189
Renuart, Gene, 216–17
residential school system, 99, 159–60
Rickard, Clinton, 163
Robertson, Robbie: early years, 142, 144;
     effect of Native culture on, 149; fame,
     142–43; musical education, 143–46;
     recognizes Mohawk identity, 143, 152;
     as songwriter for The Band, 146–52

Said, Edward, 222
Scorsese, Martin, 152
Scott, Duncan Campbell: and assimilation
     of Natives, 110–12, 113, 118;
     misrepresentations of history by, 112–
     13; and P. Johnson, 109; and Six Nations
     of Grand River, 107–9, 113–14, 117, 124,
     131; "The Onondaga Madonna," 110–11;
     "Watkwenies," 111–12
Seneca, 79–81
Shanley, Kathryn, 25, 28
Showdown at Big Sky (record), 152

Silver Covenant Chain, 14, 134–35
Simpson, Audra, 209
Six Nations of the Grand River: attempt to take
     Council House in 1959, 138–40, 153;
     and B. Loft poetry, 133–38; and Back on
     the Rez, 181–89; and Christianity, 58,
     65, 157–58; clash between traditional
     religion and Christianity, 39–41, 154,
     155, 169; Confederacy Council takes
     over leadership of land crisis, 50,
     53–54, 55–57, 60; and D. Campbell
     Scott, 107–9, 113–14, 117, 124, 131; and
     Deskaheh's campaign for sovereignty,
     116, 117, 118–24, 125–30, 216, 231n4;
     and Douglas Creek Estate dispute,
     211–12; educated v. illiterate view of,
     165; emigration off-reserve, 127; and
     European education, 58, 59, 157–60;
     and The Feathered U.E.L.'s, 154–65; fight
     against Bill 14, 114–17; as focus of
     sociologists/anthropologists, 153–54;
     and Forbidden Voice: Reflections of a Mohawk
     Indian, 165–71; and Haldimand Deed,
     37, 38, 168–69; J. Brant's advocacy
     for after American Revolution, xii,
     16–18, 35–38, 41–44, 45–48; and J.
     Brant's legacy, 29–30, 59, 60–61;
     makeup of reservation, 1–3; military
     contributions of, 57–58, 132–33,
     156–57; misappropriation of funds by
     Canadian government, 112, 124–25; and
     Oka crisis, 179–80; P. Johnson's view of,
     82, 83; political control in nineteenth
     century, 65–66, 69; portrayed in story
     and song, 147–48, 199, 204, 206;
     reaction to voting in Canadian elections,
     141; rejection of their sovereignty,
     17–18, 116, 123, 131; resilience of culture
     after dismantling of Confederacy in
     1924, 131–32; sovereignty campaign
     of 1930s, 130–31; and translations of
     Great Law, 71–78; view of Bread and
     Cheese Day, 164; view of elected council
     v. Confederacy Council, 184–87. See
     also Confederacy Council; Great Law of
     Peace; Haudenosaunee; oral traditions